Heterodox Economics

Hasan Gürak

Heterodox Economics

Foundations of Alternative Economics

PETER LANG
Frankfurt am Main · Berlin · Bern · Bruxelles · New York · Oxford · Wien

Bibliographic Information published by the Deutsche Nationalbibliothek
The Deutsche Nationalbibliothek lists this publication in the Deutsche Nationalbibliografie; detailed bibliographic data is available in the internet at http://dnb.d-nb.de.

Cover Design:
© Olaf Gloeckler, Atelier Platen, Friedberg

ISBN 978-3-631-63404-2

www.peterlang.de

Foreword

There are numerous 'toothless sorcerers, masquerading as economics experts'.
K. Velupillai

Orthodox economic textbooks propose a kind of economic world which can only exist in fictitious markets where producers and consumers interact like robots, relations are mechanical and assumptions utopian. Accordingly, all expositions related to output, price and demand are, in substance, nothing but sophistry.

Basic concepts like "equilibrium", or "given prices for producers" or "perfect competition" might seem logical and consistent for orthodox academicians who do not much care for the relevance of assumptions and/or transactions. Yet, many economists are becoming more and more discontent with the sophistries of orthodox, mainly neoclassical, doctrines. There is a globally growing interest and demand for more alternative economic ideas and analyses which should help to better understand the actual problems, help to make realistic analyses and offer implementable remedies or forecasts.

It is a fact that orthodox economists were not even aware of the presence and significance of "**technological developments**" until the "**rediscovery**" by Solow in 1950s. Who knows when they will "**rediscover**", among other things, the fact that **prices are not and have never been a "given"** for the producers in competitive markets? It will continue to be a great waste of the efforts of capable minds, if orthodox economists continue to defend this fictitious economic world and its relationships.

The purpose of this book is to present some realistic alternative approaches to the conventional unrealistic attitudes of orthodox economists. It is not claiming to present completely realistic alternatives to orthodox doctrines. Shortcomings and mistakes are inevitable and many ideas or models presented need deeper and more refined analysis. Therefore, I hope that the alternative approaches presented here will not be rejected on purely ideological grounds.

Acknowledgement

This book contains many original approaches and analyses differing from the perspectives of dominant "mainstream" theories concerning the well-known and common subjects of economics. I have presented many non-traditional, non-mainstream works before, which my Turkish colleagues, except for two or three of them, have to say the least, preferred to overlook and denied these works even a modicum of understanding which they generously provide for the fallacies of the mainstream economic theories.

A full downloadable copy of the book "Economics" has been available for about a year with the hope of provoking some response. Many academicians I know have been informed about its presence and content. Many of the approaches and analyses are so different from mainstream ideologies, that I was hoping, at least, that the proponents of these mainstream economic ideologies would rush to the defense of their ideologies, in the face of my challenging critique. However, my expectations were in vain; there was no response at all. I was disappointed to see that the prevailing attitude was one of total disregard.

While enduring and working in this unproductive and sterile atmosphere, there was one notable exception the well known academician, Prof. Dr. Cihan Dura, who not only cared enough to read the entire text with patience but also in order to improve my work shared his valuable criticism with me . I have benefitted to large extent from his views and proposals for which I am deeply grateful. I'm also grateful to John Lee from Bodrum who has not only improved the quality of the English translation of this manuscript but also offered valuable advice. And thanks are also due to Ute Winkelkötter of Peter Lang International Academic Publishers for her professional advice.

Hasan Gürak

November – 2011

Contents

Chapter 1: INTRODUCTION

"The neoclassical heritage still has a great influence, not only on the teaching of economics but in forming public opinion generally or at least in providing public opinion with its slogans. But when it comes to an actual issue, it has nothing concrete to say."

Joan Robinson
Economic Philosophy

Economic transactions are a popular subject for many people whether it is the academic or the man on the street. Economics is taught as a "social science" in universities. It is taught not only in economics departments but also in other faculties such as business, political sciences, and international relations. It is also taught in departments which at first sight appear to be rather irrelevant such as engineering and law. Therefore, it is a social science which attracts many students from many faculties and departments. In addition to academic interest, economics also attracts many professionals from other disciplines who like to discuss and make comments on transactions, outcomes and future developments. Actually there is nothing surprising about this wide interest, for economic subjects such as inflation, unemployment, income distribution, etc., have some influence on all of us, in one way or another.

However, there seems to be a rather large and serious difference between what is being taught at universities and what really happens in the world we live in. That is the important difference between "academic economics" and "actual economics". Many students of economics, especially those who take courses on introductory economics or micro-economics do not seem to enjoy what is being taught. The major reason for this is the inadequacies of academic text-books which do not adequately help students grasp actual economic transactions. For instance, according to the dominant neoclassical doctrine the main subject of study in economics is the efficient distribution of "scarce resources". If one wonders what these "scarce resources" are, textbooks claim that developed countries (**DCs**) have abundant capital (**K**) but scarce labor, i.e., laborers or workers (**L**), while less developed countries (**LDCs**) have an abundant labor force (**L**) but scarce capital (**K**). It is the goal of economic science to determine how to efficiently allocate these resources. If that were true, it would be rather easy to find a solution to the problem; transfer laborers from **LDCs** to **DCs** and capital from **DCs** to **LDCs**. However, in actuality we observe that though decision-makers, institutions and academicians are passionate supporters of capital transfer from **DCs** to **LDCs** they are more than reluctant to follow a similar policy regarding the transfer of laborers to **DCs**. Of course there is one exception; the transfer of the best trained brains to **DCs** which apparently is in the interests of **DCs** but clearly against the interests of **LDCs**.

The "efficient allocation" of scarce resources is not the only problem area for traditional economics. Another serious problem that one encounters is the definition of **"capital"**. What in fact is **"capital"**? Which one of the definitions below would be the most appropriate?

1- Capital (**K**) is money holdings?
2- Capital is tools and machinery employed during production?
3- Capital is property like buildings or factory sites?
4- Capital is the total sum of resources used for investment and production?
5- If capital is as described above in item-4, should it include payments for wages?
6- What should be the relationship of "human capital" which seems to have acquired a decisive role in economic theories to "capital" mentioned in the mainstream text-books?
7- What is "social capital" and its relation to the "capital" mentioned in the mainstream text-books?

It must be rather striking to observe that economists still do not have a unanimously acknowledged definition of "capital".

However, another serious problem that has gone unnoticed is that of the basic inputs of production, "labor" (**L**). The concept of "labor" in economic jargon is used to refer to the laborer or synonymously, the worker or the employee. However, literally "labor means "**the execution of work**" which quite distinct from the concept used in economic jargons. To put it differently, the word "labor" literally means; "**the result of the mental and/or physical efforts of laborer with given "inputs**". It refers to the exertion of mental and physical capabilities of a laborer to execute the labor, in other words, the task. In short, **labor is the result of work done by the laborer**. Given this fact, and the presence of three synonymous words like laborer-worker-employee, to describe the executor of labor, the logical question pops up; why do economists use a fourth and irrelevant word, "labor", to refer to the laborer, or worker or employee?

Another related problem with "labor", meaning laborer, is that the mainstream introductory textbooks usually assume that laborer is homogeneous and unqualified. That is to say that laborer is considered to use only his or her physical capabilities and the vital contribution of their mental input is overlooked. The latter concept is referred to in modern economic books as "human-capital" (**H**) and very few economists seem to question why such an important concept is related to the concept of "capital", not to the concept of "laborer"? **Could it be due to their ideological bias or their preconceptions**?

On the other hand, introductory text-books still seem to ignore the irreplaceable and vital input of "production" that is "technology", e.g., knowledge concerning production when referring to the allocation of “scarce” resources. Yet, the **imperfections in technology markets** are the real and major problem lying behind the inefficient allocation of resources around the world.

Proper realistic definitions of "labor" and "capital" are not the only problem areas in traditional doctrine. There are other and no less important issues that are subject to debate and criticism; e.g., the basic assumptions on "perfect competition conditions" which are analyzed below.

The "Given price assumption": According to the mainstream scientific (?) assumptions price is determined by supply and demand equality conditions. An enterprise has no choice but to accept the imposed price passively and behave as a price-taker in the market. Determining its own price for output is out of question. This assumption is probably the most striking fallacy of traditional scientific (?) theory. In the real world, every enterprise determines its own price with regard to specific production conditions. The enterprises are not "price-takers" but "price-makers". Inevitably, the "long term price" would be influenced by market conditions. However, they would never continue long term production when market price falls below production costs. This is a fact well known by all economic agents in society, except for the scientific (?) academicians and their scientific (?) academic models.

The "Perfect knowledge" assumption: By assumption, it is accepted that all economic agents have access to a "perfect knowledge" of the markets and their transactions, which is another fallacy of scientific (?) economics. No economic agent can have or ever has had access to this “perfect knowledge”. The imperfections in technology markets are an excellent proof of that.

The "Free entry into the market" assumption: This assumption is, unfortunately, yet another fallacy of the scientific (?) theories. No logical person would assume that any individual is capable of entering the market at any time and start to produce automobiles, airplanes, ships, or even bread or cookies, except for the faithful and loyal academicians of the “neoclassical heritage”. The free entry assumption for the producers of many advanced products especially in LDCs can only be a matter of scientific (?) gamesmanship.

The "Homogeneous product" assumption: The homogeneous product assumption implies there is only “one type of product” to be produced or consumed which is apparently another fallacy. If it were to be true, there would be no progress in technology and welfare. Nor would there be a long term dynamic growth process because the markets would gradually saturate as consumption increases and eventually demand would be for replacement purposes only. The neoclassical scholars cannot be unaware of this fact; yet they continue to make their "utopian" assumptions.

Another critical issue of traditional scientific (?) theory is the claim to be a "**positive science**" just like astronomy and physics. As is commonly known, positive sciences study subjects which are completely independent from our subjective values and evaluations. By assumption, economics is claimed to be as scientific as physics and astronomy which have independent laws of action. One of the most critical ingredients of scientific (?) economics is the concept of "value" which does not fit at all with the objective standards of the positive sciences. Given these facts, "perfect" market conditions can only refer to a market with ideal conditions which makes it more a "**normative**" social science rather than a natural science similar to astronomy or physics.

The shortcomings of scientific (?) economic theories are criticized not only by their opponents but also by their proponents some of whom I will quote below. Many of these proponents are the leading economists of the neoclassical heritage and a few of them are their more moderate critics. None of them is a hard-line opponent or a Marxist or a radical economist. Here are some of these criticisms without commentary.

On scientific (!) economics

After having criticized Walras' "general equilibrium" analysis, the well-known economic historian Blaug continues:

> "Here is a theory with absolutely no empirical content. Having "proved" the existence, uniqueness and local stability of multi-market general equilibrium, what have we learned about the economy? Absolutely nothing." (Blaug; in Skousen, 2001; p.217)

> "Tremendous ingenuity has been applied over several decades to the task of adapting general equilibrium theory to the needs of macroeconomic theory. This effort, I believe, must by now be judged a failure." (A.Leijonhufvud: in Zambelli, 2010; p.68)

> "A person is not likely to be a good economist who is nothing else." (J.S. Mill; in Marshall, 1990; p.636)

> "... economics cannot be compared with the exact physical sciences: for it deals with the ever changing and subtle forces of human nature." (Marshall, 1990; p.12)

> "The laws of economics are to be compared with the laws of the tides, rather than with the simple and exact law of gravitation. For the actions of men are so various and uncertain..." (Marshall, 1990; p.26)

"The part played by the net product at the margin of production...is apt to be misunderstood. In particular many able writers have supposed that it represents the marginal use of a thing as governing the value of the whole. It is not so; the doctrine says we must go to the margin to study the action of those forces which govern the value of the whole: and that is a very different affair. " (Marshall, 1990; p.339-340)

"Later in life, Marshall was to regret this attempt to scientize economics, suggesting that we are still greatly ignorant of economic behavior..." (Schumpeter; in Skousen, 2001; p.194)

"... economic science is a system of a priori truths, a product of pure reason, an exact science reaching laws as universal as those of mathematics, a purely axiomatic discipline, a system of pure deductions from a series of postulates, not open to any verification or regulation on the grounds of experience." (Machlup; in Caldwell, 1994; p.140)

"...the postulates of the classical theory are applicable to a special case only and not to a general case...... its teaching is misleading and disastrous if we attempt to apply it to the facts of experience." (Keynes, 1973; s.3)

"The fact that our knowledge of the future is fluctuating, vague and uncertain, renders wealth a peculiarly unsuitable subject for the methods of classical economic theory. . . . There is no scientific basis on which to form any calculable probability whatsoever. We simply do not know." (Keynes; in Skousen, 2001; p.339)

"... human decisions affecting the future ... cannot depend on strict mathematical expectation, since the basis for making such calculations does not exist." (Keynes; 1991; p.162-163)

"The neoclassical heritage still has a great influence, not only on the teaching of economics but in forming public opinion generally or at least in providing public opinion with its slogans. But when it comes to an actual issue, it has nothing concrete to say." (Robinson, 1962)

"Economics is a social study. It is concerned with the operations of human beings, who are not omniscient, and not wholly rational; who (perhaps because they are not wholly rational) have diverse, and not wholly consistent, ends. As such, it cannot be reduced to a pure technics." (Hicks, 1983; p.289)

By the way, according to one prominent economist, Harrod, *Keynes had no revolutionary contribution which substantially affected economic theory*. The main contribution of Keynes was the influence he had in readjusting the traditional theory and then pertinent issues (Harrod; 1937, p.85).

Now let us examine some recent criticisms and see what Hicks, Friedman, Leontief, Samuelson, et al., have to say:

"Pure economics has a remarkable way of producing rabbits out of hats -apparently a priori propositions which apparently refer to reality. It is fascinating to try to discover how they got in; for those of us who do not believe in magic must be convinced that they got in somehow." (Hicks, 1983; p.367)

"People, not mechanical "laws of the market," should be the focus of the discipline." (R.T. Ely, founder of AEA; in Skousen, 2001; p.235)

"... economics has become increasingly an arcane branch of mathematics rather than dealing with real economic problems." (Friedman; http-4)

"Page after page of professional economic journals are filled with mathematical formulas [...] Year after year economic theorists continue to produce scores of mathematical models and to explore in great detail their formal properties; and the econometricians fit algebraic functions of all possible shapes to essentially the same sets of data." (Leontief, http-4)

"Gunnar Myrdal, the Swedish economist, was able to convince the (Swedish) academy that economics, more than any other social science, had achieved such a high level of scientific inquiry that it deserved special honors (Nobel Prize) (although he later recanted and wished he had refused the prize because, he now argued, economics could not match the precision and value of the physical sciences)." (Skousen, 2001; s.394)

"There is really nothing more pathetic than to have an economist or a retired engineer try to force analogies between the concepts of physics and the concepts of economics." (Samuelson, Nobel Prize Lecture, 1970)

"... nothing is impossible in an inexact science like economics." (Samuelson, 1973; p.5)

"It has sometimes been suggested that our most advanced students know everything except common sense." (P. Samuelson, in Skousen, 2001, p.94)

"Samuelson's book is practically nothing but differential equations and assumptions far removed from reality." (Skousen, 2001; p.93)

"... the theory effectively denies the continuing and self-sustaining process of expansion of capital as an essential feature of the capitalist mode of production." (Harris, 1978; p.20)

"A 'crucial' assumption is one on which the conclusions do depend sensitively, and it is important that crucial assumptions be reasonably realistic. When the results of a theory seem to flow specifically from a special crucial assumption, then if the assumption is dubious, the results are suspect." (Solow, 1956; p.65)

Solow once confessed:

"I know the wheel is crooked, but it's the only game in town" (Solow; in Skousen, 2001; p.214)

"The markets for goods and for labor look to me like imperfect pieces of social machinery with important institutional peculiarities." (Solow, Dec. 1987)

" ... factor proportions might be variable only at the instant of gross investment and not after capital equipment had taken some particular form." (Solow, Dec. 1987)

“Today if you ask a mainstream economist a question about almost any aspect of economic life, the response will be: suppose we model that situation and see what happens…modern mainstream economics consists of little else but examples of this process.” (Solow, http-4)

“Mathematical economic theory has recently become more and more abstract, transparent and sterile.” (Morishima; in Skousen, 2001; p.359)

“The models were fundamentally wrong in that they assumed perfect information, perfect competition, and no technical change... Anybody looking at these models would say they can’t provide a good description of the modern world.” Stiglitz; in Cassidy, 1996; p.56)

“As questionable as those might be for an advanced industrial economy, they are clearly not appropriate for developing countries.” (Stiglitz, 1999; p.11,)

“[Economics as taught] in America's graduate schools... bears testimony to a triumph of ideology over science.” (Stiglitz, http-4)

“What is studied is a system which lives in the minds of economists but not on earth. I have called it ‘blackboard economics’.” (Coase, Dec. 1991)

"Existing economics is a theoretical [meaning mathematical] system which floats in the air and which bears little relation to what happens in the real world.” (Coase, http-4)

According to Lucas, “mechanics of development” refers to;

“… the construction of a mechanical, artificial world, populated by interacting robots that economics typically studies.” (Lucas,1988; p.5)

“Economics is a primitive science, and there is a lot we don’t know.” (Lucas; in Cassidy, 1996; p.52)

“I write down a bunch of equations, and I say this equation has to do with people’s preferences and this equation is a description of the technology... But that doesn’t make it so.” (Lucas; in Cassidy, 1996; p.55)

“One of the overriding problems of economics is that it is non-experimental science.” (Romer, 1994)

“We live in an uncertain and ever-changing world that is continually evolving in new and novel ways. Standard theories are of little help in this context. Attempting to understand economic, political and social change requires a fundamental recasting of the way we think.” (North, http-4)

“Modern economics is sick. Economics has increasingly become an intellectual game played for its own sake and not for its practical consequences for understanding the economic world. Economists have converted the subject into a sort of social mathematics in which analytical rigour is everything and practical relevance is nothing.” (Blaug; in Hodgson, 2004)

Now let us examine some recent criticisms, for instance those of the Head of The Association of National Business Economists and a senior economist of A.T & T, Mark Dadd:

> "Academic economics has taken a very bad turn in the road... It is very academic, very mathematical...it is nothing like as useful to the business community as it could be." (Cassidy, 1996, p.51)

According to Cassidy, some firms are closing down economics departments and will benefit from this action.

> "In recent years... some of the biggest companies in the country, including I.B.M., General Electric, and Kodak, have closed down their economics department. Meanwhile, many of the fastest-growing businesses in the economy... –have managed to prosper with the aid of hardly any economists at all." (Cassidy, 1996)

And finally what Roche has to say about economic education is highly likely to upset traditional economists of the neoclassical heritage.

> "We insist on at least three-to-four-year cleansing experience to neutralize the brainwashing that takes place in these graduate programs." (Cassidy, 1996; p.51-52)

In Pursuit of New Approaches

In last two to three decades the interest in and the search for alternative economic theories has increased sharply, due to the inadequacies of the traditional theories to understand and explain actual economic transactions. It appeared rather cumbersome to find a correlation between what really happens and what economic text-books teach or predict which seemed to have questioned the credibility of the traditional scientific (?) theories. Many students seem to have preferred to memorize the concepts like "capital" and "labor" and after a while they forgot what the key symbols **K** and **L** stood for, due to the inherent inadequacies of the traditional theories.

In contrast to students of economics, a large number of academicians continue to keep their initial positions, remaining loyal to the teachings of the traditional scientific (?) theories, in spite of their obvious inadequacies. However, there are a growing number of academicians, mostly known as the "heterodox economists", who are not really content with what they have at hand and search for alternative more realistic theories. Many departments at universities around the world offer courses in the so called "heterodox economics" and the number of heterodox academicians and their heterodox works is rising rapidly. In addition, the number of heterodox conferences, seminars and associations are constantly increasing. These developments clearly indicate a growing demand for more realistic approaches to the present economic situation as well as increasing attempts to satisfy these demands.

Given the conditions stated above, the main purpose of this work is to make a contribution to these growing demands for alternative approaches by presenting some "**different approaches**" to the mainstream economic thinking. By assumption, the only source which is capable of producing or adding "value" is the labor input of the labor force, given the gifts of nature which are continually being transformed by labor input for consumption. Technologies utilized for production are the products of the creative abilities of the labor, i.e., laborers. Efficient application of technology is also dependent on the quality of the labor which is the single most important factor of all "value" creation.

The Subject of Economics

The topics of economics have been the subject of lively debates for a long time amongst economists and as yet there seems to have been no globally acknowledged consensus. According to Adam Smith, one of the most prominent founders of economic science, the major subject of study should be the factors contributing to the wealth of nations. For Ricardo, subjects like the distribution of income among classes and foreign trade, appear as major concerns. Marshall was highly interested in how wealth was produced and how to calculate it. And traditional text-books teach us that the subject of economics is the "efficient allocation of resources".

According to the major principles on which this work has been constructed, economics can be defined briefly as "the analysis of all economic transactions, to propose solutions to problems, to increase welfare level and to predict future economic events." In a wider concept, economics can be defined as "the social study of production relationships, the exchange relationships of goods and services, income distribution, employment, inflation, etc., which interacts both at a local and at a global level interactively, and to make future projections. The main purpose of all transactions is to raise the individual-national welfare level and to satisfy demand.

It has been well known, since the 1870s, that the advocates of neoclassical doctrine have been attempting to make economics akin to physics and astronomy known as the positive sciences with accepted universally applicable laws; and they have come a long way. However, there is a significant difference between economics and the positive sciences; economics is constantly liable to the effects of external non-economic events which are beyond its control. For instance, political decisions, the sociological environment, psychology, international developments, etc., can directly influence economic issues and outcomes. In addition, economic agents known as "homo-economicus" behave completely rationally but without any emotion and resemble robots rather than human beings. This, in fact, has nothing to do with the reality of the situation. These two criticisms alone are sufficient to claim that economics cannot have the universally applicable laws and models which are able to explain social events like physics or astronomy do in explaining natural phenomena. Economics is in fact a "social science" more akin to sociology than physics. There are no "exact" mathematical relationships in social sciences; different places and times can produce different outcomes. There are certainly cause-effect relationships but definitely not identical to those found in the positive sciences. Therefore, it would not be an exaggeration to claim that the highly sophisticated mathematical models of traditional economics are incapable of thoroughly understanding and explaining social events. However, using mathematics as an aid to predict trends in economics is very likely to produce positive results.

In short; each economic event is unique and not testable under laboratory conditions with exactly repeatable results; one can only test "similar" events and "tendencies" at different times and places, not "the same ones".

As to the assumption of the universal applicability of economic laws, it is only valid in the "utopian" models of some economic researchers which help to produce nothing but "**utopian fallacies**".

Microeconomics vs. Macroeconomics

Economics is studied under two general headings in introductory text-books;

1- Microeconomics.
2- Macroeconomics.

Microeconomics

The main topics of microeconomics can be divided into three main headings.

1- Production (supply) conditions.
2- Price formation.
3- Demand and Consumer Behavior.

Actually, a closer inspection would see that the topic of microeconomics as taught in economics departments covers a similar range of subjects as are found in the syllabus of all business departments when dealing with such topics as the "Principles of Business" in regard to the market, price formation, demand, etc. To put it differently, the topics covered under the heading of microeconomics and those covered in business-principles courses are essentially the same. However, students of microeconomics and business-principles think that they belong to completely different disciplines.

If microeconomics and principles of business have a common basis, why are they regarded as two separate disciplines? In order to provide a sensible answer to this question we have go back to the 1870s when economics was referred to as "political economy", before becoming a "pure" science. Before the 1870s, Marxist winds were blowing rather strongly and the political messages were quite disturbing for capital-owners. The ideologists and proponents of the system were incapable of producing rational and logical counter-ideas to cope with Marxist political-economical thought. Then, thanks to the attempts of some prominent scholars like Jevons, Menger and Walras, the political economy began to change into a "pure" economic science free from values.

In the last 130 to 140 years, followers of the "pure" economic doctrine did, indeed, succeed in "inventing" universally applicable scientific laws and models, immune from historical, cultural, psychological influences, based on the mechanical behavior of economic robots which are fondly named as "homo-economicus". Nowadays, there are plenty of highly sophisticated and **universally applicable (?)** models with exact relations and equilibrium. However, the results of this development are frustrating. It appears that the more complex and sophisticated the models are, the less relevance they have to actual economics events. Many of the assumptions and analyses were only applicable to models, and of little use or value to real economic relationships. These sophisticated models seemed more and more like a science-fiction based text-book about alien economics. Under these conditions, it was inevitable that a new discipline called "Principles of Business" would arise to study the actual behaviors of enterprises and consumers.

Macroeconomics

Main topics of macroeconomics are:

1- Growth.
2- Global (international) economic relations.
3- Monetary policy and price stability.
4- Fiscal policies.
5- Economic crises.
6- Development economics.
7- Employment.

The criticisms addressed to Microeconomics are also applicable to the macroeconomic assumptions, concepts and models; because they are derived and nourished from the same ideological doctrine. Therefore, it is no surprise to see highly sophisticated models with dubious mathematical relationships, utopian assumptions and unrealistic economic transactions and behavior which seem to contribute more to a “do not to properly understand” point of view than to what is really taking place in the market place. For instance, traditional neoclassical growth models were either unaware or ignorant of the significant long term input of production which was called “**technological progress**” until the 1950s. Thanks to the contribution of Solow, neoclassical scientific (?) growth models “**re-discovered**” the critical role of technological progress which could be found A. Smith’s, Ricardo’s and Marx’ works which were written about 150 to 200 years ago. Nevertheless, this “**re-discovery**” of the importance of technological progress was an important contribution, except for one problem; according to the theory, the source of technological progress was unknown, and therefore was assumed to be an “**exogenous input**” of long term economic growth.

It would not be unfair to claim that the theory of value-price is the foundation of all other economic theories. However, in year 2010 the neoclassical scientific (?) theories were still incapable of providing a new value-price theory incorporating mental labor and technological progresses.

In short, the traditional microeconomic and macroeconomic theories seem to be inadequate in grasping, explaining and finding remedies for the actual events around the world. Starting with the value-price theory, economists have an obligation to review the "remedial" capabilities of traditional theories and put serious efforts to formulating new alternative theories with more realistic assumptions and insights.

A Science or an Ideology?

Science, or to put it other way, the Natural Sciences can be defined as "**the pool of knowledge** which relies on observation and experimentation and has been accumulated over thousands of years in order to improve the understanding of the environment in which we live. Its principle aim is to discover the unknown truths behind natural facts and phenomena such as whether there is life on other planets or the evolution of certain species. It is important to note that scientists aim "**to discover**", not "**to invent**", the facts behind natural phenomena. The outcome of scientific research gives rise to "**knowledge**" but not to "**absolute knowledge**”. In fact, there is no such a thing as “**absolute knowledge**” but only “**relative knowledge**” i.e., one cannot know everything about everything which is subject to how we perceive things with our level of knowledge over a given period of time.

In our age "science" has a wider meaning covering areas such as:

1- The Natural Sciences (astronomy, physics, geology, biology, etc.)
2- The Social Sciences (economics, sociology, psychology, etc.)
3- The Axiomatic Sciences (mathematics, logic)

Social Science vs. Natural Science

Natural Science

As described above, the Natural Sciences can be defined as "**the pool of knowledge**" with regard to the environment we live in. The most distinguished characteristic of natural scientific research is the attempts to explain natural phenomena based on human-value-free observations which can be repeated and tested. The laws that are discovered are universally applicable and objective but without precisely defined cause and effect relationships. Scientists always strive to "uncover" the unknown facts of life. For instance, what causes the seasons to change, why and how the sun is an uninterrupted source of energy, what conditions cause the universe to expand, how the universe and galaxies came into existence, are some of the subjects of scientific research. Natural science scholars have already provided some "objective" answers to these subjects. However, natural scientists never claim to have found the "absolute truth". As the accumulated knowledge and experience of scholars increases, we may in time discover "new truths" and also realize that an acknowledged "truth" is in fact incorrect.

Social Sciences

Economics as a social science, studies social facts, events and their interactions, just like the other social sciences, so by its inherent nature, it cannot be purely objective and entirely free from value or judgmental influences. This inherent unstable nature of social sciences is mostly due to the existence of too many uncontrollable and unstable variables. Therefore, it is illogical and unrealistic to claim to have universally, or even globally applicable laws for social sciences as one would claim for the natural sciences. The best a social scientist can do is to analyze and estimate tendencies and similarities between various social events which are influenced by subjective values. Economics is no exception.

Yet, the proponents of the neoclassical doctrine claim since the 1870s to have access to a science which has "**universally applicable laws**" with the logic and precision of the mathematical and natural sciences. Marshall was the principal economist who made the major contribution to the new and emerging economic ideology of his time.

> "By calling his textbook Principles of Economics, he altered the name of the discipline from "political economy" to "economics," sending a signal that economics was as much a formal science as physics, mathematics, or other precise body of knowledge. Moreover, it acknowledged that the economy is governed by natural law rather than by political policy." (Skousen, 2001, pp.193-194)

> "Later in life, Marshall was to regret this attempt to scientize economics, suggesting that we are still greatly ignorant of economic behavior, but the die was cast." (Schumpeter, in Skousen, 2001, p. 194)

What contemporary neoclassical economists whether consciously or unconsciously overlook or ignore is that natural sciences like physics and astronomy, have already developed significantly since the 1870s. Yet, the neoclassical economists still prefer to remain loyal to the principals of **some form of misinterpreted Newtonian mechanics derived from unrealistic assumptions.** Unrealistic assumptions and mechanical relationships in economics without an historical context do not seem to offer any realistic analyses or solutions to economic problems. Periodically, the utopian models may help to explain actual economic events properly but that appears to occur coincidentally rather than from the inherent strength of the conceptual models. As we well know, even a broken watch shows the time correctly twice a day. If it is sufficient to be scientific to propose logical theories to explain actual economic transactions, then it ought to be logical and consistent to propose that a fleet of flying dinosaurs will soon descend from the planet Neoclassicus (which is next to the Imperial star Oblivion in the Pseudoeconomica galaxy) and solve rising fuel costs in a trice.

Ideology vs. Objective facts

It is commonly acknowledged that the subjective ideological standpoints of social scientists exert a significant influence on the outcome of their research and propositions. No matter how hard social scientists try, they cannot have their research and analyses totally free from subjective values and judgments. To expect that, is beyond the realm of being human.

> "An ideology is a set of aims and ideas that directs one's goals, expectations, and actions… The main purpose behind an ideology is to offer change in society, and adherence to a set of ideals where conformity already exists, through a normative thought process." http://en.wikipedia.org/wiki/Ideology, 2010-03-02

If one accepts this definition, one can clearly observe that ideologies are an inseparable and unavoidable part of human life. Economics is no exception. In the past, at different periods of time rulers have always supported the emergence and application of goals which would serve their own interests best, depending on the developmental level of the societies, in which they lived. When economic power began to shift from rural landlords to the emerging capitalist classes, similar developments were observed because the new and powerful rising classes were in need of newer and in their interests more appropriate ideologies. A. Smith and many others of his time were the pioneering philosophical and intellectual leaders to whom they looked to, to develop new and more appropriate ideas in order to change society's values "in their favor". In the 1800s, the growing working class ideologists began to develop their own ideas to counteract the mindset of the capitalist class. Today the story is just the same. The ideologies of global economic powers are being promoted efficiently around the world.

Ideologies are a fact of life, just like the dynamic forces of societies specific to each country influenced and shaped by historical, cultural and political values. We cannot properly understand economic conditions today without paying attention to historical developments. Yet, the mainstream economic theories ignore historical facts and developments, treating producers and consumers as "rational" robots without feelings or values.

Given the critical role of an ideological standpoint, the purpose of this work will be to offer an analysis of the current situation as objectively as possible.

Skilled Labor(-er) & Technology

Looking at the present global situation developmentally, one can clearly see that some countries are relatively more developed than others. The gap between the developed and less-developed countries displays a tendency to widen, in contrast to the expectations and claims of the proponents for increased globalization. There are many reasons to account for this gap ranging from various social factors to historical-cultural background, environment, climate, natural riches, to name but a few.

10,000 years ago, the difference between the developments levels of countries were insignificant. As developmental progress continued in conjunction with technological progress, differences began to be more visible. Some countries and societies gradually became more prosperous than others. The determining force of prosperity or growth was technological progress, i.e., the knowledge of production that is a product of the creative mental abilities of the human brain. The gradually growing quality of the labor, i.e., the laborers, both in creating new technologies and efficiently utilizing them, contributed to the growing differences between developed and less developed regions. Rulers of societies like Ottoman Empire had failed to encourage secular education, while the Western European countries had done just the opposite. The outcome was obvious.

Yet, the Ottoman Empire's land known as The Fertile Crescent (Figure:1-1) is regarded as the genesis of all civilizations which is supported by Diamond's (2004) research. It would not be an exaggeration to claim that the pioneering revolutionary technological progress which is the product of mental capability, took place in this region.

> "The raw substance available to ancient peoples were natural materials such as stone, wood, bone, skins, fiber, clay, sand, limestone, and minerals, all existing in great variety. From those materials, people gradually learned to work particular types of stone, wood, and bone into tools; to convert particular clays into pottery and bricks; to convert certain mixtures of sand, limestone, and other "dirt" into glass; and to work available pure soft metals such as copper and gold, then to extract metals from ores, and finally to work hard metals such as bronze and iron." (Diamond, 2005; p.246)

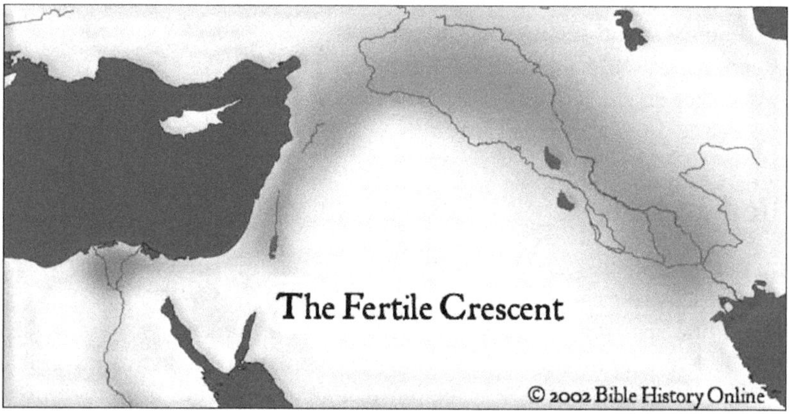

Figure: 1-1The Fertile Crescent,

The primitive tools that were invented and developed were the "capital-goods" or "means of production" at that time. In time, creative minds continued to invent and develop more and more sophisticated tools and machinery to change and control their environment which continuously helped to increase prosperity. To put it differently, developed countries owe much of their present prosperity level to technological progress which has its roots in The Fertile Crescent region which continued by successive technological and educational contributions until the present day. The raw materials existed in Nature and it was the human mind along with physical labor that managed to transform them successfully into useful inputs as well as the outputs of production.

Briefly, the differences in the development between countries and regions have their origin in the creative minds of humans and their successful utilization of their faculties. Economic historians emphasize that the Industrial Revolution which started in England around the 18th Century was "the true starting point of modern technological progress". However, the roots of this technological process go back much further. According to Diamond (2005; p. 260) technological progress began approximately 2.5 million years ago with the use of stones as tools. Data on Table:1-1 gives us reason to claim that a major "Industrial Revolution" actually started in The Fertile Crescent. For instance, metallic tools were widely used in The Fertile Crescent around 4,000 BC while they appeared in England around 2,000 BC that is approximately 2,000 years later.

Table:1-1 Historical trajectories of Eurasia and the Americas

	Fertile Crescent	China	England	Andes	Mesoamerica
Plant domestication	8500 BC	by 7500 BC	3500 BC	by 3000 BC	by 3000 BC
Animal domestication	8000 BC	by 7500 BC	3500 BC	3500 BC	500 BC
Widespread metal tools or artifacts (copper and/or bronze)	4000 BC	2000 BC	2000 BC	1000 AD	-
Writing	3200 BC	by 1300 BC	43 AD	-	600 BC
Widespread iron tools	900 BC	500 BC	650 BC	-	-

Source: J. Diamond, 2004, Tüfek, Mikrop ve Çelik (Rifle, Germs and Steel) p.482, redesigned data from Table:18-1

> "Nowadays, Islamic societies in he Middle East are relatively conservative and not at all at the forefront of technology. But medieval Islam in the same region was technologically advanced and open to innovation. It achieved far higher literacy rates than contemporary Europe; it assimilated the legacy of classical Greek civilization to such a degree that many classical Greek books are now known to us only through Arabic copies; it invented and elaborated windmills, tidal mills, trigonometry, and lateen sails; it made major advances in metallurgy, mechanical and chemical engineering, and irrigation methods; and it adopted paper and gun-powder from China and transmitted them into Europe. In the Middle Ages the flow of technology was overwhelmingly from Islam to Europe, rather than from Europe to Islam as it is today. Only after around A.D. 1500 did the net direction of flow begin to reverse." (Diamond, 2005; p.253)

At every stage of human existence the knowledge of production, i.e., technology has always played an indispensable role in the development process. All goods and services are originally a product of nature and are transformed by the laborers' inputs ranging from the most primitive products to the most advanced such as mobile-phones, TV-sets, computers, medical equipment, and so on. As Diamond put it quite correctly, technology has been an important moving force in the history of mankind (Diamond, 2004; p.323).

Basic Principles & the Study Plan

The analysis throughout the rest of book is based upon the principle that the source of all the inputs and outputs of production is the result of the efforts of a physically and mentally competent labor force, using the resources of Nature (Gürak, 2009). In other words, the original source of all the value added to products. Nature being a given, is the mental and physical inputs of labor which continuously create new technologies while at the same time making use of the available technologies. In other words, creative abilities of the laborers deserve special attention as being the source of all the technologies that have been created (Gürak, 2009).

The second section on "**Some Key Concepts, Definitions and Assumptions**" is concerned with making appropriate definitions in concurrence with the above principle.

The purpose of the third section on "**Production**" is to analyze the inherent features of production, related to technological developments and productivity growth in the long term.

Section four on "**Price**" deals with price formation and the effects of technological progress on prices which directly influences all related economic transactions.

The analysis of "**Demand**" and the impact of technological progress on demand will be the subject of fifth section.

The emphasis of the sixth section will be concerned with "**Functional Income Distribution**" and the impact of technological progress on income distribution.

Long term growth and the impact of technological progress on long term growth will be analyzed in section seven on "**Growth**".

Section eight on "**Global Trade**" contains the analysis of global economic relations such as global output, demand and distribution in a way somewhat different from the mainstream analysis.

"Global Technology Transfer", imperfections in technology markets and hidden costs will be the subject matter of section nine.

Section ten will focus on the impacts of "**Institutions**" on economic transactions and their related fields.

Finally, in section eleven, some proposals for the "**Future Economic Developments** will be presented.

Chapter 2: SOME CONCEPTS, DEFINITIONS & ASSUMPTIONS

Producing various goods and services for consumption in pursuit of profit is an economic event. Mostly, the goods and services supplied contain exchange-values while some of the supply is for personal or family consumption only containing use-value. For instance, some households grow their own tomatoes or potatoes on private land or in their garden for household consumption, while many buy them in markets in exchange of money. Some individuals are able to repair their own broken items while others buy a repair service on the open market for cash. Anything produced for private purposes is beyond the interest and scope of this book. Therefore, the analyses throughout the rest of the book will focus only on economic transactions for markets in pursuit of profit. Supply for personal use will be ignored. We shall start with the definition of the most frequently used concepts in economics some of which will be defined somewhat differently than in the teachings of the mainstream doctrines.

Some Key Concepts & Assumptions

In economic analysis, it is conventional as well as inevitable that some abstract and simplifying assumptions are made using the deductive method. The reason for this is that it is both impractical to and unreasonable to collect and evaluate all the ingredients by using the inductive method. To attempt to do this would be similar to attempting to measure the distance to the sun with a 5cm piece of wood: Possible but highly impractical and unreasonable. Thus, making abstract and simplifying assumptions is necessary in order to make economic analyses. However, in order to explain the actual transactions the assumptions made should conform to reality as closely as possible.

Extremely utopian assumptions of a given period's economic theories can be justified in the early stages of the development of theories at that particular time. One can even have an understanding of the attempts to construct models or theories that try to conform to the laws of a natural science such as physics. However, one should also comprehend that natural sciences and economics are two quite different disciplines sharing very few common features. In the natural sciences, scientists attempt to "discover" existing facts, while in economics there are no existing facts to be discovered or tested as in physics or astronomy. Economics is a social science and economists are obliged to grasp and interpret economic events with numerous variables which are subject to constant changes over time depending on a set of specific conditions. The present extremely high level of abstract thought in mainstream theories is considered to be a sign of inadequacy rather than a sign of merit.

There is no escape from abstract models and simplifying assumptions in this study, either. However, the utmost effort will be made to avoid the utopian assumptions of mainstream doctrines. Some conventional concepts will be redefined and new concepts introduced, while attempts will be made to make realistic assumptions with a closer relationship to reality. Let us begin with the definitions of some key concepts and introduce some more realistic but **simplifying** assumptions, before proceeding with further analyses.

The Enterprise, i.e. The Firm

The enterprise or the firm is an organization that is established by self-interested (i.e. profit driven) individual(s), i.e., the entrepreneur(s), in order to produce commodities and/or services. The enterprise is not a price-taker as the mainstream price theory claims; in fact, it is a price-maker for its own products that are supplied to competitive markets. Profit motive is the sole driving force behind investments in the long term, though the enterprise might have "other" motives in the short term. Profit, in general, is obtained after a transaction or an exchange of products for money.

The enterprise creates a "productive capacity" by bringing together the necessary inputs of production, e.g., machinery, tools, raw materials, and so on., and combines them with the services of labor-power, to supply products which are expected to meet the needs and wants of the consumers (end-users). Technology e.g. knowledge on production is used during the production process and is contained in the physical inputs of production such as machinery, tools, etc. The ultimate purpose of this process is to maximize the difference between the total costs of production and the total revenues, in other words, to maximize profits (π). However, the long term profit maximization objective of the enterprise can sometimes be pushed down to a lower order of priority in order to attain some other objectives in the short and/or medium term, such as keeping up with the competition, acquiring a targeted market share and so on.

During the process of production, the enterprise, by creating a productive capacity, makes various other contributions to the community ranging from the generation of employment opportunities, paying taxes, as well as meeting the needs and wants of the end-users. But, all these contributions are by-products of the self-motivated and profit-driven interests of individuals. No commercial enterprise is set up specifically to pursue such objectives. In this work, state enterprises and non-profit driven organizations will be ignored.

The **Giant Enterprises (GEs),** also referred to as the **Multinational Enterprises (MNEs)**, operating globally in the production and distribution of products, which shape the global structure of division of labor, the distribution of income and the rate of growth of nations, is one of the most important, if not THE most important, economic agent of our global socioeconomic order. Their intra-firm pricing and trading practices, especially their restrictive transfer-pricing practices and their global production-distribution policies, have always meant serious and significant implications for the global growth and distribution of income (see, Gürak, 2003). The practices of these Giant or Multinational Enterprises will be ignored until we arrive at Section 6 and 7, unless otherwise stated. By assumption, the Giant enterprises should not directly be influencing economic transactions in "competitive" markets.

Entrepreneur (owner of the capital)

The "Entrepreneur" is an individual or group of individuals who make investment decisions to produce goods and/or services with the ultimate purpose of making profits. It is the entrepreneur who decides where, how and what quantity to produce. Often an entrepreneur is both the owner and the manager of the enterprise, especially in small-sized enterprises. In large scale enterprises, ownership and management are not infrequently separated.

It is not rare to encounter managers with complete entrepreneurial authority in modern economic life, especially in globally operating Giant" Enterprises. The main reason for this is the impracticality for one person to assume full time managerial responsibilities in large- or global-enterprises. Thus, the capital-owners frequently prefer to delegate some or all of their responsibilities and authority to "professional managers" who, on behalf of the capital-owners, set the target policies and strategies for the enterprises and carry out them, both concerning their routine matters and their new investment decisions.

However, the interests of the capital-owners and their professional managers are not always fully compatible. The latter, i.e., the professional managers might pursue, from time to time, policies favoring or consolidating the professionals' interests in terms of salaries, fringe benefits, etc. Especially when an enterprise belongs to numerous small shareholders who have small voting rights and who are unable to alter the course of events individually. The professionals are now able to run the enterprise as they see fit.

Profit and Risk

Maximizing profits is the driving force of the capitalists' or "entrepreneurs' transactions. Depending on their specific duties, non-owner managers can also make long-term profit-maximizing decisions such as new investments. The success or failure of business transactions, however, is attributed to the entrepreneur who assumes all risks and bears the ultimate responsibility for the outcome of these economic transactions. The final goal for the enterprise is, as has always been and always will be the same; maximizing the **long-term** profits. Any professional management ignoring or undermining this fact would not survive.

Measuring the production costs is a relatively easy procedure which can be calculated in advance by adding all input costs. Under normal circumstances, each input cost adds to the total cost as much as the value it transfers, including the cost of wages for labor. The sale price of the final product which consists of various inputs, on the other hand, is always expected to be above the total input-costs, i.e., the value transmitted to the final product. The difference between the total input costs and the total revenue from sales represents the profit ($\boldsymbol{\pi}$) for the entrepreneur which is paid in relation to the risks undertaken.

Under fair competitive conditions there is always some risk involved for the entrepreneur because the outcome of the investment or transaction is uncertain. Uncertainty makes the outcome of an investment or a transaction risky. When the entrepreneur is successful, the reward will be in form of profits. Otherwise he/she would suffer losses which would imply the total or partial loss of capital at the end of a risky production or transaction process. If there were no expected increase in the capital used, i.e., profit, at the end of this risky production or transaction process the capitalist or entrepreneur would not have any incentive to invest.

The most common reasons for causing risks are the following:

1- Consumer response is unpredictable (insufficient demand problem).
2- "Unexpected" economic developments (such as tax-rate rise, slum, etc.).
3- "Unexpected" political developments (such as instability, war, etc.)
4- Response of the competitors (price-war, alternative products, etc.)
5- Management failures or mistakes.

As a result of the addition of profit margin to the costs of production, the final sale price of the product increases. However, this incremental increase in price is not the result of any value-addition to the product; the difference is due to the risks assumed. In other words, there is no specific added value to the product concerned. Profit plays the role of "reward" on the investment and risk undertaken; a process which fosters economic growth and individual- as well as national well-being. What the rate of the reward, i.e., profit, for risk assumed is dependent on the market conditions which are largely influenced by the supply and demand conditions. For instance, under a monopoly or oligopoly the rate of profit is likely to be much higher than under competitive conditions. Profit is an indispensable and inseparable part of the capitalistic economic system.

Science and Technology

To be able to make a proper and realistic analysis, the researcher should have access to the appropriate definitions of the concepts used in economic theories and other related areas. One of the most important and critical concepts is that of "technology". This may be defined as "a form of knowledge which is integrated into such physical outputs as machinery, tools, semi-finished goods, consumer goods, etc." The distinguishing features between science and technology should be robust and clear.

Knowledge

According to P. Drucker and many others, the most important input of production is "**knowledge**". But what kind of knowledge is implied? Does it imply "general knowledge" about history, geography, literature, etc., or some "specific" knowledge related to production, i.e., **technology**? Certainly Drucker refers to the latter (technology) though it is not stated explicitly. A more explicit account of what he meant would have avoided confusion and the correlation between this specific kind of knowledge and the growth of productivity which has been highly praised by A. Toffler, P. Drucker, R. Lucas, P. Romer and many others, would have been better evaluated.

"Knowledge" can be defined as a set of expressions based on the facts and understanding acquired through education, observation, experimentation and experience. In other words, knowledge is the intellectual product of a creative human brain which continuously adapts to changing conditions and experiences.

There is a distinction between "information" and "knowledge". Often people use information as if it were synonymous with knowledge. **Information** seeks answers to questions of a descriptive nature. For instance: "What color is the sky"? "Where does the President live?", or "What is on TV tonight?" It is normally acquired by means of the media or an acquaintance or from some form of awareness or association. Information as such does not directly contribute either to the explanation of facts or of incidents or to the increase of the prosperity of individuals or nations but might indirectly influence the receptive and creative capacity of human brain.

Knowledge can be divided into three categories;

1- General knowledge.
2- Scientific knowledge.
3- Productive knowledge (knowledge which has been internalized in the products and/or in the methods of production; i.e., **technology**).

General knowledge is beyond the scope of this section.

Science or Scientific Knowledge

Science can be defined as "the pool of explanatory knowledge" which can be used to better understand and control the environment we live in, and often provide commercial interests with the essential ingredients to invent or to develop new products and production processes. Science aims to discover the unknown truth behind facts and phenomena such as whether there is life on other planets or how certain species evolved.

There are some similarities but no clear distinctions between the concept of science and technology, except for the profit motive attribute to technology. In general, science seems to deal mainly with the acquisition of knowledge per se while technology is oriented towards the reshaping and the control of the environment in order to improve living standards. The contributions of science to technological developments and vice-versa, is indisputable. *"Science without the by-play of technology becomes sterile while technology without science becomes moribund."* (Jones,1971,p.6).

Productive Knowledge (Technology)

Technology will be defined as **"productive knowledge"**, that is "the set of specific knowledge to supply products or methods of production responding to the practical needs and wants of the community". A more concise definition would be: Technology is the "**knowledge applied to resources through human labor and internalized by the products**" which may range from consumable products to machinery, semi-finished goods, tools, etc. As an UNCTAD study postulates:

> "Technology is the key to the progress of mankind and that all peoples have the right to benefit from the advances and developments in science and technology." (UNCTAD, 1983,p.1).

Technology does not only assist us in satisfying our needs and desires but also increases our control over the environment in which we live. By combining the abilities of the labor services and nature's inputs, technology improves the qualitative and quantitative standard of living for human beings.

Technology is usually produced by people trained in disciplines that are oriented to the commercial exploitation of knowledge and sponsored by commercial interests. The most distinguishing feature between science and technology can be described as follows; science aims to "**discover**" facts while technologies are "**created**" by mental labor in pursuit of profits for the producers. Technological findings are most likely to be patented by either the researcher(s) or the sponsor(s) or both as both expect rewards from their application. However, technology is not always fully utilized for the benefit of mankind. In developing countries particularly, various factors are responsible for even the limited use of the available standard technologies (see, Gürak; 1990).

Technological changes are normally characterized by three phases all of each can be rather costly as well as resource and time consuming. These are:

1- The Research Stage.
2- The Invention Phase; and
3- The Innovation or Development Period.

The innovation or development of an invention is inherently a risky process. The innovation process is often a more time and resource consuming process than the initial research and invention phases. The longer the innovation process takes to develop, the higher the costs and risks will be. Technological and commercial circumstances are among the major determinants of the development process. The data on past technological expenditures indicate that all major breakthroughs have consumed enormous human and financial resources as well as time. Some important technological innovations appear to occur after a considerable period of time even several years after the invention of the said product. This time lag seems to be shorter for consumer goods than for other methods of production.

As "technology" (productive knowledge) is the "**key to the progress of mankind**", it is expected to pave the way for all economic development and to narrow the gap between the developed and the developing countries. It follows that not only in our present era, but also throughout the entire history of mankind "productive knowledge" has been the key to growth by increasing the productivity per employee. In other words, technology has always been the true source of improving standards of living even in pre-commercial societies where barter trade was the common means of exchange. Technology operated in exactly the same way in "hunter-gatherer" communities.

But there is something more important than the technology per se; that is its "source"; i.e., **the creative intellectual labor of human beings.** Human beings not only produce "productive knowledge (technology)", but also apply it to specific areas in order to supply various commodities and services. Let's assume that there is a grand pool of productive knowledge but no appropriate human resources to make use of it. Who would produce all the tangible as well as intangible output? And more importantly, who would continue to replenish this pool of existing knowledge? Therefore, it would be more appropriate to ask, given the physical labor inputs, institutional and cultural infrastructure and the level of natural resources, what has been the most important input of production throughout history? It has been the abilities and resources of human mind; i.e., **knowledgeable and creative human resources**, or in the neoclassical jargon, **"Human Capital".**

By the way, why is it called "Human Capital"? Why not **"Intellectual Labor"** or **"Mental Labor"?** Could it be because of some ideological clashes or, some cultural heritage that defines human beings who labor as "work horses[1]" and thus consequently as "insignificant"?

To summarize, the two most distinguishing features of labor force are;

1- The ability to create new technologies (productive knowledge); and

2- The ability to exploit existing technologies efficiently.

The Accumulation of Knowledge

Centuries and millenniums past by and the human brain continued to produce and accumulate more and more new knowledge, not only to enrich material living standards but also the standards of emotional life such as poetry, music, painting, etc. In time, human beings learned how to pass on the accumulated knowledge to the next generation in a written form, thus facilitating the faster advancement, accumulation and distribution of knowledge. Meanwhile, human beings had also learned to produce products in excess of their immediate needs so exchanged them with other goods, which helped to increase individual and society's prosperity. By the time of industrial revolution mankind had accumulated sufficient productive knowledge, experience and financial resources to start manufacturing commodities solely for exchange. Intellectual contributions accelerated the productivity growth and transition to a more advanced economy with enhanced property rights and appropriate institutions. In our era, not only tangible objects but also knowledge is subject to proprietary ownership.

---

1 In the medieval age, a human capital could be used and abused as the owner of the capital saw fit and so they were used "as work horses" as in the industrial revolution and since.

Nobody, no matter how brilliant his/her mind is, acquires knowledge as if it were "manna from heaven". The present pool of productive knowledge has been accumulated over thousands of years and is a common heritage. In the absence of successive advances and an accumulation of productive knowledge, there would be no products to exchange. In our era, creating the "productive knowledge" (technology) through schooling, training and research is very important to sustain as well as to improve the wealth of nations. There is a close correlation between a knowledgeable labor force and per capita productivity level, because better and longer education and training, generally improves the productivity of both the individual and nations.

If it were possible magically to move all the production facilities in Sweden over one night to Turkey, the total output would diminish both in terms of quality and quantity simply because the Turkish labor force is not as well educated or trained as the Swedish labor force. In other words, the quality of the labor force is a very important factor regarding the state of productivity and prosperity of a nation.

However, although it is necessary, it is not sufficient to have a well-educated labor force. Countries like Russia and Ukraine have a more educated labor force than their US counterparts in terms of hours invested in education (the so called human capital). Yet, per capita value added to the product per Russian worker is much lower than the US-worker. That is because the institutional and cultural settings in the sense of competitive firms, contemporary entrepreneurs or managers, the government's economic policies, the technological, financial and legal infrastructure, are all important factors for the efficient functioning and success of the system as a whole. The Education and training of an appropriate labor force is a long process, but the development of an appropriate institutional and or cultural environment might take even longer and be more troublesome.

The Importance of Technology

Technology, the product of creative mental labor, has been attracting growing attention from economists in last decades as the determinant input of continuous long term economic growth and prosperity. Without technology no supply would take place and without technological progress there would be no long-term dynamic growth in economies. Even the supply of the simplest products requires some sort of technology during the production process. For instance, even primitive hunter-gatherer societies used some tools regardless of how primitive they were. It is a well known fact that primitive tools have been employed for agricultural output or for household use for thousands of years.

Regardless of the development level of a country, all tools or means of production is the result of the combined utilization of both mental labor and physical labor which transforms nature's raw materials into the physical means of production. Given the natural products from which without the contribution of the labor-power services no output could be produced. On the other hand, no new technologies could have been placed at the service of physical labor without the contribution of the abilities of the human brain.

For long term sustained economic growth and to increase prosperity, new technologies are inevitable as inputs in the production process. New technologies may help to introduce new physical goods and/or new services into the markets. If there is sufficient demand for the new goods and/or services, employment, as well as the individual and the total welfare level is expected to grow. After a period of time, these "new" products become "standard products" as competition increases and markets mature. However, this is not the end of the dynamic process; the creative human mind incessantly produces "new productive knowledge", i.e., new technology, which introduces "new" goods and/or services, and so the process goes on.

If the "new" knowledge helps to reduce the production cost of a unit of a "given" product with a new production method, then the per unit profit rate is expected to increase with increasing added value, cet. par. Otherwise, the enterprise would have no incentives at all to utilize the new productive knowledge or technology.

Sometimes we observe that while the quality of a product improves due to new technology it's per unit production costs decline. We can see evidence of this in the computer or mobile phone markets. Such products are considered in this book as "new" products. Sometimes, new knowledge introduces entirely new products with new production methods and sometimes only the product is "new". Typical examples of "new" products are found, among others, in the communication or biology sectors which are products introduced in late 20th Century. Due to these new and continuing contributions by creative mental labor, neither do the markets fully saturate nor does the profit rate tend to fall towards zero.

Briefly, creative mental labor with the assistance of physical labor is the source of all "new productive knowledge", i.e., "new technology", "given the available natural resources.

The Importance of Knowledge

The role and importance of knowledge displays some different characteristics at the macro-economic level compared to the micro-economic level. With regard to macro-economic perspectives, three prominent factors draw one's attention.

1- General educational and training level.
2- The level of technological infrastructure.
3- The level of institutional infrastructure.

1- The quality of **general education and/or training** and its development level is essential both for national development and the efficient exploitation of resources at economic plant level. It appears to be the case that, the more advanced the educational level of a country, the higher the learning and efficient application capacity of present and future technologies would be. It is a well known and proven fact that the individuals who possess an appropriate general educational background display a better ability to absorb new learning and to better use new technologies compared to those individuals who are educationally less endowed. Therefore, beyond any doubt, the level of both general and specific education is an important factor for the efficient use of resources. In addition, having access to creative minds capable of creating new technologies is closely related with the qualitative level of general education and/or training.

2- The quality of the general **technological infrastructure** and its level of advancement are also of critical importance for the developmental level of both the country's prosperity and the efficiency of its enterprises. The inadequate quality and low level of technological infrastructure would inevitably lead to inefficient exploitation of resources and lead to weakness in the competitive markets.

3- Another important issue from the macro-economic point of view is the quality of the **institutional infrastructure**. Whenever the institutional infra-structure displays some inadequacies in relation to contemporary general development level, related economic efficiency problems seem to be inevitable. For instance, though the former Soviet Union and the East European countries had access to a highly educated labor force in terms of the number of scientists, engineers, etc., the countries failed to transform and adjust their societies successfully to Western conditions after the 1980s. The institutional infrastructure displayed all kinds of inadequacies that prevented a successful transformation of society for a long time.

The Contribution of Technology

The distinguishing feature of theories on natural sciences is that they can be categorized, tested, re-tested and measured, subject to certain universally applicable laws. Economists have been attempting, ever since the 1870s, to follow in the footsteps of sciences such as physics and astronomy and they claim to have succeeded to a large extent when referring to their highly complex models. However, regardless of the high expectations and aspirations of the scientific (?) economists, economics cannot be, nor has ever been, a natural science like physics and astronomy due to the inherent features of the social sciences. Whether they like it or not, economics is a typical social science with uncontrollable and highly flexible interdependent variables; thus it displays little resemblance to the natural sciences. Therefore, it is hardly feasible, if not impossible, to make accurate calculations in economic subjects using a set of universally applicable laws. Anyone who believes or claims to believe that there exists a set of universally applicable set of economic laws cannot be referring to actual economic events or transactions, but are referring to the "purely academic" economic models which exist only in the mind of some economists (see Gürak; 2007).

It would not be incorrect to claim that there are no measurements or tests that can be used in economics as there are in natural sciences. Certainly there are various methods to measure and test economic transactions and they could be useful as long as one recognizes that these methods can only reflect "tendencies" not the exact behavior or relationships of economic agents or universal truths.

Given the specific features of social sciences mentioned above, one can always attempt to estimate the contribution of technology and technological progress. For instance, the number of patent applications per 1,000 inhabitants could be used as a useful device for estimation and comparison purposes. However, such methods could never be a perfect method for reliable comparisons or estimation.

Products (Goods & Services)

Concepts like goods-commodities, service; output-supply and product will be used frequently throughout this work. In order to avoid misunderstanding or confusion, it is necessary to explain exactly what they mean in this work.

Commodities - Goods

A **commodity** or **goods** is a **processed** primary product, e.g., the gift of nature, in finished or semi-finished physical form, produced by the labor-power services often with the assistance of man-made tools and capital goods, in order to satisfy the needs and conveniences of consumers. For instance, while wheat is a primary product, a loaf of bread is a commodity or goods acquired after a production process; or, while iron-ore is a primary product, steel is a commodity or goods.

The production of a finished commodity (final goods) normally requires several complex production stages before reaching the final consumer (end-user). The higher the technological level, the more complex would be this process. After each stage, the laborers add more value to the previous existing **added value.** To put it differently, all commodities, before reaching the consumers, are processed by the laborers with the assistance of the physical implements of production and the final output can be considered to be a "physical unit". If the end-user of the commodity is a producer, the commodity continues to contribute to the supply of other products. If the end-user is the final consumer, it serves as an object of satisfaction.

Service

A "**service**" displays some distinctive properties that are distinct from physical commodities. In contrast to the commodities, a service is normally consumed, e.g. exhausted or vanishes as it is being produced, like a haircut or a concert or a taxi-ride. The distinctive feature is that it is a **none-tangible object** and **cannot be carried or stored**. To put it another way, in principle, all commodities are produced at an earlier period of time and consumed at a later stage while services are produced and consumed at the same time of the supply of service.

A service is not infrequently supplied with the assistance of tools or equipment like computers, musical instruments, vehicles, etc. However, tools or equipment are not always pre-requisites for the supply of services, for instance, a teacher or a consultant is always capable of transmitting his/her knowledge to others even without any tangible inputs.

The quality of a service supplied depends upon;

1- partly on the quality of physical inputs used;

2- mainly, on the quality of the laborer.

The lower the quality of the physical inputs, the lower the quality of the service provided is likely to be. For instance, the quality of the service supplied in tourism, banking, or health-care, normally reflects the development level of the firm as well as the community along with the infrastructure within which it is supplied. On the other hand, unless there is sufficient number of adequately "qualified" laborers, neither the desired quality nor the quantity of services can be supplied.

One of the frequently used concepts throughout this work is **product**, which is used to designate both the **services and commodities** supplied. In other words, all industrial goods and the services intended to meet the demands of end-users are simply referred to as products.

Inputs of Production

According to the conventional introductory economic textbooks, there are only two "**productive**" factors of production; capital (**K**) and labor(-er) (**L**), and the production function (**Q**) is defined as:

$$Q = f(K, L)$$

In fact, there are more production factors than **K** and **L**. Production factors are all the prerequisite inputs of production to produce anything with an exchange-value. Using an analogy, they are like the ingredients of a soup. Without the necessary inputs (ingredients) you cannot make the soup. Production factors, as distinct from "productive" factors, comprise of inputs ranging from raw materials to energy, semi-finished inputs, or plant site, etc., as well as labor services. For instance, thousands of inputs of varying qualities are required for the production of airplanes or computers. On the other hand, a teacher or a consultant in the service sector is able to perform their tasks with much less physical inputs. Accordingly, a house painter or a shoeshine boy requires considerably less inputs of production than the producers of computers or car producers.

The most frequently required inputs of production are:

- Mental and physical labor services.
- A production site (factory, workshop, etc.).
- Raw materials.
- Energy.
- Semi-finished inputs.
- Management services.
- Marketing and distribution services.

The related critical question that needs to be answered is: Which **production factors** are truly "**productive**" capable of generating value?

“Productive” Factor(s)

Throughout this book, we shall assume that there are only two “productive” factors capable of generating-creating value:

1- Nature (**N**), i.e., the origin of all use-values (utilities) in the shape of raw (unprocessed) inputs of production; and
2- Labor effort (**L**), i.e., which is the “only” factor capable of adding value to the original use-values supplied by nature.

Nature: as a “Productive” Factor

It is a commonly acknowledged fact that nature is capable of providing output, i.e., the raw materials, for any production even in the absence of any other assistance, including any intervention from the laborers. This feature makes nature, beyond any doubt, a “**productive**”, or synonymously, a “fertile” factor. There are thousands of kinds of life arising and surviving due to the fertility of nature. All kinds of species on earth, even human beings, the most advanced species of all creatures, take their nourishment from the gifts (products) of nature. There would be no form of life without the productivity (fertility) of nature. Thus, that nature is a “productive” factor is beyond any doubt or discussion in the sense that it provides the physical inputs with use-values (utilities) for the benefit of mankind.

The end-users, in our case human beings, consume the products of nature, not only to survive but also to produce various processed products. As long as the products of nature are used for personal or family consumption, they contain “use-value” only for the end-users. For instance, apples on a tree indicate **use-value** (**utility**) if used for personal consumption. But, if they are brought to the market by an effort of laborer such as collection and transportation, they contain an "exchange value".

For example, say that Deniz, the father of family which lived in ancient times, collects some fruits, the “free gifts of nature”, to feed his family. The fruits contain “use-value” (utility) for him and his family. Assume that Deniz possesses more apples than he requires and decides to exchange the surplus apples for oranges. The apples they consumed had a “use-value” for him and his family but the surplus apples which he exchanged for oranges had an “exchange-value”. These are the concepts and relationships often cited in the works of the Classical economists, which show us that “exchange-value” arises only when some labor-effort is expended on the product. Briefly, nature provides things with use-values, which are either consumed directly by end-users or used as exchange-values involving some use of labor time spent on the product.

In addition to being a productive factor, nature also provides all kinds of inputs required for output of all kind in the form of raw materials. Therefore, nature is not only a productive factor, but her products are the indispensable inputs of production in the form of raw materials. In the absence of the raw materials as the input factors of production, there would be no physical items re-shaped by labor for consumption, such as computers, cars, houses, TV-sets, etc.

Ecological Balance

The ever increasing number of advanced commodities offered to the end-users has their origins in nature in the form of raw materials. But, unfortunately, the generosity of the nature is not unlimited and unless the natural resources are used with caution, care and consideration, they can be exhausted completely or become unusable over time due to relentless usage and wastage. A polluted and eventually dying nature would mean an end of all civilizations and any technological advancement, regardless of any developmental level.

The extravagant and relentless exploitation of natural resources by humans has not yet reached the point of no return. However, the critical threshold does not seem to be too far away. The most important tool at hand to prevent the complete exhaustion of natural resources is the development of new technologies, or to be more specific, "**new environmental friendly technologies**" to recycle products and to preserve nature, before it is too late. In order to secure and sustain long term economic prosperity and growth, the utmost attention and care should be devoted to the saving of our "productive" nature which provides the irreplaceable inputs of production.

Laborer: a "Productive" Production Factor

Labor[2] or Laborer (L):

Given the human capital **(H)**, according to some economic textbooks and models, **L** refers to "i" number of laborers endowed only with eye-hand coordination. Although many analysts are well aware of the fact that **H** and **L** are actual-

2 Throughout this book the term "labor" is used primarily to refer to the "laborer", or "labor-power", or "worker", or "employee", and occasionally to refer to its original meaning, "the execution of work by a laborer".

ly two sides of the same coin and that no labor, especially in our time, is without some degree of formal or informal training and/or education, they continue to treat **H** and **L** as if they are two distinct factors of production. This “ideological” ignorance does not only confuse the mind but also leads to an incomplete and unsatisfactory economic analysis.

Yet, the word “labor”, literally, implies **the execution of work by a laborer**. It is the result of the mental and/or physical efforts of a laborer with given “inputs”. In other words, labor is the exertion of mental and/or physical capabilities of the labor to execute a task, i.e., to produce “use- and/or exchange- values”. In short, labor is the result of work by a laborer.

Labor (L) is, in fact, the able-bodied individual, who possesses some **mental as well as physical abilities**. He/she is the person who carries out the work or task by using his/her mental and/or physical faculties to generate use- and/or exchange- values. To put it differently, the labor is the human being who is hired by enterprises in exchange for a wage, i.e., he/she sell services in the market and “**earns**” wages in return. Wages are not paid for hiring the labor for his/her personality or body as such, but for the “services” to be obtained in order to realize the production.

Mental labor

Mental labor (L^m) refers to the faculties (abilities and skills) of the human mind developed through formal and/or informal training and/or education as well as experience gained, given the persons’ natural skills. Creative mental labor is the source of all present and future technology. As we have discussed elsewhere (Gürak, 2000-a; 2000-b; 2004-a; 2006), given nature’s supplies, mental labor-services are **the genesis and a continuous source** of all products and thus of economic growth and prosperity.

Physical Labor

Physical labor (L^P) is the simple eye and hand coordination of able-bodied man. The execution of physical labor requires, by definition, neither special training, education nor any mental capabilities. In reality, there is no such thing as “purely” physical labor; it exists only in theory. Every labor possesses some degree of mental capability. Even choosing the right electric button between, say red or white, requires some degree of mental ability.

The Labor Force

The term **Labor force (LF)** implies the total quantity of the labor (able-bodied men) willing to sell their labor services in return for wages. Economic models normally use **L** in the same sense as **LF** without making a distinction.

How to Estimate the Value of the Labor?

As we have already discussed, the genesis of all new technologies, e.g., knowledge about production is the mental capabilities of the labor and that there is no method to estimate the exact value of these technological contributions.

Estimating the value of physical labor by the "labor-time employed" criterion should not be any problem. However, what would be the meaningful use of such estimates to understand actual economic events? We all know very well that there exists no physical labor (**L**) which is absolutely unqualified, that is to say without any degree of human-labor (**H**), e.g., education, experience, or skill. On the contrary, every labor, in fact, possesses some degree of skill and/or education and/or experience which can be employed during a production process. On the other hand, there is no such thing as human-labor (**H**) independent or separate from physical labor(-er) (**L**). To put it another way, every labor-time employed in production consists of both physical labor and human capital (**H**) or the mental capabilities of a physical labor. These two concepts are not two independent variables, but two sides of **the same coin**.

Given the facts stated above with regard to labor, it would not be an exaggeration to claim that it is hardly feasible if not impossible to estimate the contributions of physical and mental labor. There exits, no method to exactly estimate the contributions of mental labor. However, making some rough estimates with regard to some tendencies can be considered as a logical effort. For instance, the average education years of a country's labor-force can be compared to another country's average education years. The credibility and use of the data which is collected and compared should not be exaggerated because;

1- The quality of education is not homogeneous;
2- The individual capabilities-abilities are not homogeneous; and
3- Experiences are not homogenous.

In short, the capabilities of the labor are not "homogeneous". Certainly, one can always make a simplifying assumption on the homogeneity of the labor to make estimates and comparisons. However, such utopian assumptions carry the risk of contributing more to a lack of understanding or a misinterpretation of actual economic events. In spite of all these aspirations, economics is still a social science with numerous independent and uncontrollable variables, unlike physic or astronomy.

Wages (W)

In our analysis the labor who sells their labor services to enterprises receive a predetermined wage for their efforts. What factors influence or determine the wage level is one of the topics that cause lively debates in economics. Once the wage level is determined, it would be easier for the entrepreneur to estimate or to determine the profit rate which in turn would determine the shape of functional income distribution as well. The functional income distribution will be analyzed in Chapter 8.

The concept of labor (L) - reconsidered

A proper definition of labor (**L**) is necessary for a sound analysis. In this work, **L** refers to laborers willing to work at the going market wage rate. **L** is not solely comprised of men endowed with only eye-hand coordination, for there is no such thing in reality. Each **L** embodies, in addition to physical abilities, some degree of mental ability which is acquired and developed through formal and/or informal training and/or education enriched by experience. As stated before, the term labor refers to the "laborer" or "worker" or "employee".

L is "not" a commodity like a TV-set or radio bought and/or sold in the markets. It is **the only source of any added value** and **the ultimate consumer** of the value produced, along with other income obtaining groups, of course. And these features make **L** a rather unique factor in production. Commodities belong to their owners, but **L** is only hired for labor services for a given period of time in return of wages. The ultimate control of labor services belongs to the labor. Otherwise, it would be slavery.

Since the labor is endowed with different skills, abilities and experiences, the wages paid by end-users in return for labor are not, and cannot be the same for all. In other words, the qualities of labor are heterogeneous, and so are the wages. As the terms "quality", "faculty", "education", "ability", "skill" and "experience" are all analytical concepts, a sound measurement and eventually any inter-firm or inter-country comparisons of labor services are cumbersome, if not downright impossible.

To summarize; taking into consideration other related discussions cited elsewhere (Gürak, 2000-a; 2000-b; 2004-a; 2006);

1- **L** is one of the indispensable and irreplaceable "factors of production" (**FoP**); and
2- **L** is also an indispensable and irreplaceable "productive factor" (**PF**).

Capital: a "Productive" Factor?

The first and major problem with the concept of capital arises with its definition. There seems to be no "globally" agreed definition of "**capital**". For some, it refers to "**capital goods**" implying machinery and perhaps tools. For others, it refers to all the inputs of production, ranging from buildings and energy to semi-finished inputs, except for labor services. For some, capital is the total value of assets used in the production process, including labor services.

Since the concept of capital is one of the key concepts of economic theories, it would be useful to take a look at it.

Capital in Retrospect

The concept capital has been one of the most frequently used and discussed concepts of economic theories. According to Hausman who made a comprehensive study of the subject: *"Economists possess no good theory of capital and interest."* (Hausman, 1981, Ch.10). The theories possess elegant models and theorems but they, he said; *"... do not enable one to explain real phenomena of capital and interest"* (Hausman, 1981, Ch.10) as they fail to grasp the essence of the issues.

For some "Classical" economists the concept of "capital" covers not only the "capital-goods" but also the laborer's wages as well as all the other inputs of production. Thus, according to Ricardo "capital" is;

> "... that part of the wealth of a country which is employed in production, and consists of food, clothing, tools, raw materials, machinery, etc., necessary to give effect to labour." (Ricardo, 1990: p.95)

For Marx whose views resemble Ricardo's, capital is the sum of money which contains some specific features.

> "... in itself this sum of money may only be DEFINED as capital if it is employed, spent, with the aim of INCREASING it, if it is spent expressly in order to increase it". (Marx, 1976: p.976).

Accordingly, the owner of the sum of money is called a "Capitalist". However, according to Marx' definition, the petty-bourgeois or owners of small-scale businesses would not qualify for the title "Capitalist" although the petty-bourgeois had the same goal as the true capitalist; that is increasing and/or maximizing the initial sum of money employed to produce commodities, i.e., making profits.

The well-known economist of the Classical period J.S. Mill had a similar definition of capital like his contemporaries.

> "What capital does for production is to afford the shelter, protection, tools and materials which the work requires, and to feed and otherwise maintain the labor during the process... Whatever things are destined for this use... are Capital." (In Schumpeter, 1954: p.634)

So called mainstream economists seem to prefer a somewhat different approach and assume that capital, as one of the main inputs of production, is a "scarce" input. According to this approach capital became another "productive" factor along with labor and thus was entitled to receive "a reward" called "profit". The competing Austrian School of economics objected to this "scarcity" approach claiming that capital cannot be a productive factor but mainstream economics overcame the challenge and it is nowadays common to encounter a "scarce factor" approach to capital in contemporary economic textbooks.

For Marshall, capital was an outcome of the productive employment of laborer and "waiting". Accordingly, capital should not be considered as a product of the labor only for it would lead to *"... by inexorable logic to admit that there is no justification for interest"* (Marshall, 1961: 687). Marshall had to introduce a new definition of capital which said: *"... a store of things, the result of human efforts and sacrifices, devoted mainly to securing benefits in the future rather than in the present"* (Marshall, 1961: p.787). Thus, the capital-goods produced by the laborer should be entitled to some profit, if they were not consumed immediately but employed in production for future benefits, i.e., to be rewarded for "**sacrifices**".

Is Capital a "Productive" Factor?

For the supply of goods and services with an exchange value, the entrepreneur has to combine certain production inputs such as labor, production plant, energy, raw materials, semi-finished inputs, tools and machinery. In order to combine these inputs, the entrepreneur has to have access to **assets for investment** which is "a prerequisite" of production. Throughout this work, all the assets required to enable the output of goods and/or services shall be called "**production capital**", or simply "**capital**", unless otherwise stated. In other words, with the employment of capital the entrepreneur creates a "**productive capacity**", which is not money, but is expressible in monetary terms. Capital invested endows the labor with production facilities and inputs with the goal of increasing the value of the original amount invested, and will be denoted by the letter "**K**". In the absence of capital, a combination of physical inputs together with the services of labor could not take place. In other words, production goals could not be realized.

To put it differently, **K** represents the stored-up values of the inputs of production including labor. As J.B. Clark pointed out, it is "expressible in money, but not embodied in money". When employed, it places the **factors of production** at the service of the labor, which is **the only value-adding productive factor.** According to this definition, neither "hoarded" money (savings) nor the "capital-goods", i.e., buildings or land fit our definition of **K**, which designates "**values**", not quantities. Given technology, **K**, consists of the following:

K = FC + VC + W

FC = plant + machinery + tools

VC = raw materials + semi-finished inputs + energy + etc.

LWC = labor wage costs (wages * quantity of labor)

Capital-goods

As shown elsewhere (Gürak, 2000-a, 2004-a, and 2006), given the output of nature, the labor is the generation of all the value added by virtue of its mental and physical abilities. The major role is played by the former, i.e., mental labor, which contributes to the growth of wealth by improving the productivity of present labor assisted by past-labor embodied in the implements of production, i.e., transformed natural products. Assume a barter-exchange economy consisting of two persons with no implements of production (no tools). And further assume that the mental labor of worker produces a new technology, which introduces a primitive tool which increases the productivity of the worker. That tool is a **capital-good**, a transformed, i.e., re-shaped, natural product. Accordingly, all the inputs of production, except for raw materials, are transformed natural products by the workers. The labor-time spent in the past in transforming the original natural outputs into physical inputs, are stored in the "**means of production**", i.e., "**capital goods and tools**", in order to assist the productivity level of "present" workers.

Let us attempt to find out the origin of capital-goods in a simple production equation:

$$Q_t = f(K_t, L_t)$$

L, denotes labor, **K**, capital-goods, **Q** output quantity and **t**, time. Let us take any capital-good, say a drill-machine and analyze its composition. The drill-machine is made of various physical components assembled by some for of labor. So, the capital-goods $\mathbf{K_t}$ embodies both $\mathbf{K_{t-1}}$ and, $\mathbf{L_{t-1}}$. Taking a closer look at $\mathbf{K_{t-1}}$ will show that it is not a pure physical input either, for it embodies some form of labor, as well.

$K_t = f(K_{t-1}, L_{t-1})$

As the backward composition analysis continues, labor services will appear at every stage of production.

$K_{t-1} = f(K_{t-2}, L_{t-2})$

$K_{t-2} = f(K_{t-3}, L_{t-3})$

At the end of backward process, there will be only two inputs left; natural input and labor-services. Adding new factors such as technological change (**T**) or human capital (**H**) to the production function would not affect the argument on capital. In short, capital is not a "productive" factor while the creative mental labor is the source of all **KGs**, given the natural products.

Is Capital a "Scarce" Factor of Production?

Given the amount of globally available financial resources, it would hardly be logical to argue in favor of the scarcity of capital in terms of financial assets. Financial assets can only be described as "abundant" rather than "scarce".

On the other hand, one can argue that the developing countries do not possess sufficient amounts of capital-goods and that is why capital-goods can be considered as scarce inputs in production. However, given the abundance of global financial funds, there should not be any problem in purchasing the capital-goods required for production, if funds are made available. In other words, if sufficient quantities of global financial assets are made available for production purposes wherever required, there would not be a scarcity problem regarding the acquisition of capital-goods.

Scarcity of human resources with the necessary qualifications to make the best use of capital-goods seems to be a greater problem; in fact, it is maybe the major impediment to economic growth. Imperfect global technology markets and the transactions taking place therein seem to be another major problem area with serious global implications. "Scarcity of technology", or rather global restrictions to accessing technologies, especially in developing countries, seem to be a major impediment.

Other "Factors of Production"

So far we have studied only three factors, nature (**N**), labor (**L**) and capital (**K**). Yet, as previously mentioned, there are many more factors (inputs) involved in production, especially in products with advanced technology such as airplanes and computers. The critical question is; are there other factors in production, which are, **productive** just like **N** and **L**, capable of producing and/or adding value?

The answer is a very short, clear and definitive: **NO!**

There are "no" other **productive factors** other than **N** and **L** capable of producing or adding value. All "other inputs" are the products of nature transformed (re-shaped) by the efforts of labor. The inputs of production **transmit value** to the product as much as the value exhausted during the process of production. If, say, 10 TL worth of steel is used, then the value transmitted to the new product is just 10 TL, nothing more and nothing less.

Human Capital: Labor or Capital?

According to the jargon used by many economists, like T. Schultz, G. Becker, R. Solow, R. Lucas, P. Romer, G. Mankiw and many others, there is, in addition to the factor "capital" in the conventional sense, there is another meaning of the capital concept which is vital and fundamental for production; "the human capital", designated by the letter **H**.

Lucas (1988), assigns **H** the role of "**the sole source of all economic growth**". For Romer (1990), it is the source of all technological innovations, thus of increasing returns and incessant long term growth. The so-called **K**-models refer to both, the "orthodox" meaning of the term "capital" as well as the "human capital".

What is "human-capital"? What is the difference between the conventional meaning of "capital" and "human capital"?

"Human capital" simply refers to the mental abilities and capabilities of the laborer acquired through education and experience. It comprises the skills, abilities and the learning-by-doing as well as experience of the laborer. In other words, it designates the quality of the mental abilities used in the labor-inputs provided, excluding simple eye-hand coordination. It does not make reference to the laborer itself but to the quality of the abilities demonstrated by the laborer. It is: "**The skills and abilities possessed by an individual, which enable him/her to earn an income.**"

The factors influencing the magnitude of **H** are:

1- Official school years attended; and
2- Learning-by-doing; or
3- Both.

However, there are two additional and extremely important factors influencing the emergence of human capital; these are;

1. Experience; and
2. Informal education gained from the socio-economic environment.

H is, normally, acquired and advanced through both formal and informal education and given the natural skills of an individual flavored by the experiences that they acquire over time.

Laborer without Human Capital

The concept "human capital" refers to the "mental abilities" of the laborer, or, alternatively, to the **skills of laborer**. The critical question is; is there any laborer without some degree of human capital? To put it differently, is there any laborer or part of any laborer, which employs eye-hand coordination, only?

The answer to this question was given above in the section on labor. The same answer is valid; NO! There is no known labor-force or part of a labor-force that relies solely on eye-hand coordination. That is to say that every laborer possesses some degree of mental ability along with simple eye-hand coordination. Because each movement of one's muscles receive an order directly from brain, the command center of all mental activities.

If human capital is the skill or the ability of a laborer, why, then, is the term associated with capital and not with the laborer and defined as **mental labor**? Is the choice of term, "capital", instead of, for instance "laborer", merely a coincidence?

The reason seems to be ideological rather than scientific. Any association with laborer could jeopardize the century long struggle of Marginalism to survive Marxist revolutionary ideological attacks on the capitalist system. Changing the expression from "human capital" to "mental labor" would produce different conclusions. As a result, the virtual world of the neoclassical parable may encounter serious questions which would lead to the shaking of its dubious and sandy foundations.

Competition

Enterprises operate in competitive markets, with various types of production methods i.e., technologies, producing heterogeneous products where future events are "uncertain", implying imperfect markets and imperfect information. There is "fair competition", suggesting that there are plenty of enterprises but none is big enough to influence the price and/or output in a market. The upper limit of supply for a firm is determined by the optimum plant capacity and, as we shall see below, output is subject to increasing returns. The market's upper limit of supply is determined by the maximum output capacity of all the involved enterprises.

In the short term, technology is a "given" for all firms, though it may vary in substance and quality from firm to firm. In the long term, due to the existing competition, dynamic firms may introduce either:

1- For the "given" product, cost-reducing technological innovations; or
2- "Entirely new" products" which often employ new production methods.

In the long term, technological innovations introducing cost-reducing processes or "new products" are of vital importance to the firms in a competitive environment. No competitive firm can afford to neglect technological innovations if it wants to survive in the long term. To secure long term growth and to overcome the unpleasant fact of falling profit rates, the firms have to introduce "new products", which are, in principle, the products of "creative mental labor". In the long term, not only technologies but also incomes, tastes and prices are variable.

Oligopoly & Imperfect Competition

The term "Oligopoly" or "cartel" implies an imperfect competition among a few producers, who can collectively determine the market price, the quantities supplied and/or the market-share. Oligopolies have a tendency, by their inherent characteristics, to raise the price above the average competitive level including the average profit rate. The expected outcome of this is extraordinary profits for the enterprise, which also implies higher prices for consumers, as well as an output and consumption lower than the optimum attainable levels.

Unfortunately, oligopolies are the unpleasant facts of life, but are avoidable if the decision-makers take the right steps in the right direction. Everybody agrees that increased competition is beneficial for producer efficiency, consumer utility and growth. However, there seems to be no intention or consensus on the means and measures to get results. Reassessment of the international "patent rights" system or of "restrictive clauses" of globally operating enterprises could be a good place to begin.

In spite of its immense importance from an economic efficiency point of view, market distortions allowing the rise of oligopolies or cartels are beyond the scope of this study.

Monopoly & Imperfect Competition

Literally, the concept of monopoly implies that there is only "one seller" of a product in the market. Excluding the sale of alcoholic drinks by only one authorized firm in some countries or the distribution of electricity-gas-water, it is rather difficult to encounter an enterprise in the modern economic world with a permanent monopolistic power. Nevertheless, there are "temporary" monopolistic practices leading to competitive distortions associated with the **patent rights** system. A right of patent whether on a new technology, a new product or a new process, implies monopolistic advantages of the "productive knowledge" for a given time span. Such monopolistic rights arising from the ownership of new technology may be acceptable for a given period.

There appears to be a serious problem in relation to monopolistic rights granted to the patent owner of a new technology. If the new technology is produced "solely" and "entirely" by contributions from the patent owner alone, there would be hardly any grounds for ethical challenges on the granted monopolistic right. However, we all know that the patent holder does not acquire the patented knowledge "from heaven", or develop it from scratch. The patented knowledge is, normally, only a marginal addition to the pool of past and present knowledge. In other words, the patented knowledge is culled from a pool of human knowledge accumulated over a period of thousands of years. Without access to such an accumulated pool of knowledge, no person, enterprise, or country would be able to further develop and obtain the "ownership rights" for any technology.

The patent owner also benefits heavily from the technological, institutional and financial infrastructure present in society. In addition, the creative minds developing the new technologies are raised and educated by others who are unconnected to the enterprise. In the absence of such fertile conditions, no enterprise would ever be able to develop the advanced technological products used in our societies. Therefore, it is rather difficult to morally justify the present patent rights system. It is, in fact, **unjust**, leading to a distributive injustice within as well as among the nations. It would not be unfair to claim that the present patent system is economically irrational for it restricts competition and is also morally unjustified.

Increasing Returns to Capacity

In the short term, there are many factors influencing the upper limit of the output that is supplied. In the absence of demand insufficiency and/or the scarcity of the inputs of production, "per unit" average cost of production will be minimized at the "optimum plant capacity" level. Because any utilization level less than optimum plant capacity level implies a higher fixed unit cost, than the optimum level which implies higher unit costs. The fact of fixed-costs and ever falling unit fixed-costs as output increases, imply increasing returns in relation to capacity utilization. Given the optimum plant capacity, the law of increasing returns to scale is applicable to all production in the industrial sector. In other words, given price, demand and process technology, the average unit cost would have a tendency to decrease while unit profits would have a tendency to increase, as output approaches the full plant capacity. At full plant-capacity utilization, both economic and technical efficiency level would be at the optimum level.

On Institutions

Institutions have always been a very important factor in all socioeconomic environments. Who can tell what the world economic order would look like in the absence of institutions, especially of any state organ? What would the global production and distribution look like, if the developed countries implemented the highly praised liberal economic policies in their domestic markets? There has never been full-fledged liberalism without a state intervention in order to protect the economic interests of their own nation. It is true that developed countries promote global competition to eliminate trade and investment restrictions, but only when and as they see it fit to their own interests. There are still many visible as well as invisible restrictions on imports from the less-developed countries. Though the analysis of protectionist interferences by the state is an extremely important factor, they will not be considered in this work.

In Summary

In this chapter, we discussed some concepts and assumptions in relation to the basic topics of economics. The reader may wonder about the reasons for this as there are countless and widely accepted books and articles on the previously discussed issues. The underlying reason is that in the following sections the major and basic aspects of economics shall be discussed and analyzed in a non-conventional manner for which we will need alternative concepts and assumptions instead of referring to traditional ones which do not have much practical relevance in actual relations. Accordingly, some basic concepts and assumptions are bound to be different when using these new approaches. Therefore, this chapter shall play a reference role for the reader in successive sections.

Chapter 3: PRODUCTION

In commercial societies, production is realized through the initiative of entrepreneurs who combine the various inputs of production along with the labor-power services who process all the inputs and turn them into products with exchange-values. The inputs of production vary from raw-materials to capital-goods, intermediaries, tools, energy which includes laborers. In the previous chapter, the laborer was determined as the only input of production capable of producing added value. It was also determined out that all input prices, including wages, i.e., production costs, are known in advance by the entrepreneurs. However, the market price (MP) is, in principle, always higher than the production cost (PC) due to the transforming process of any input by the labor force. This is called the end-product.

Technology is an indispensable during the process of production. Every production process benefits from "a technology" the level of which depends directly on the general technological development level of the country as well as the quality of the labor-force. The higher the general development level, the more advanced the technologies that are employed will be. Sometimes, a country might have access to both advanced technologies and an advanced labor-force in some specific areas, while remaining relatively less developed in others, depending on the specific conditions of the country.

Specific inputs with the exception of technology were analyzed in Part-2. Before proceeding further, it would be useful to consider the term "Technology", the indispensable input of production.

On Technology

Technology or **productive knowledge** can be defined as a set of specific knowledge required to produce commodities or to render services corresponding to practical needs and wants of the community. A more concise definition would be: it is the "**knowledge applied to the inputs of production through human labor"**. All the man-made physical inputs of production such as tools, capital-goods, intermediaries, etc., require a body of knowledge applied at previous stages of production. The origin of all man-made products is the benefits of nature which are processed and transformed by the services of mental and physical labor. As an UNCTAD study postulates:

"Technology is the key to the progress of mankind and that all peoples have the right to benefit from the advances and developments in science and technology." (UNCTAD,1983; p.1).

Technology does not only assist us to satisfy our needs and desires but also increases our control over our environment. Today, technology is usually produced by people trained in disciplines oriented to commercial exploitation driven by commercial interests of enterprises. The findings are most likely to be patented because the "technology owner" expects rewards from their application.

Technological changes which are aimed at either creating a **new product** or a **new production method** are normally introduced in the markets after three successive phases. Each one of them can be rather costly as well as resource and time consuming. These three phases are:

1- The Research phase.
2- The Invention phase; and
3- The Innovation (development) phase.

The innovation process is usually a more time and resource consuming process than the initial research and invention phases. The innovation (development) of an invention is inherently a risky process. The longer it takes for development, the higher the costs and risks will be. Commercial considerations are the major determinants of the development process. The most important innovations follow their invention after a period of time sometimes lasting for years. The time lag seems to be shorter for consumer goods than for production methods.

The **new product** could be a commodity or a service. If there is a sufficient demand for the new product, not only the options of end-users but also total output, employment and welfare level would increase. At the initial stage of a new product the patent owning producer would practically have a monopoly on the product and is expected to make "monopoly profits" due to the existing patent laws and certain features of the technology market. However, in time, the competitors are expected to develop similar or equally competitive products which would eventually make the "new" product a “standard product and reduce the profit rate of producer to the market average. It is highly likely that, enterprises would continue to develop and introduce new products and this process would go on "ad infinitum". If technological progress introduces a **new method of productio**n for the supply of a “**given**” product then it is expected to reduce unit production costs and to increase the profit rate cet. par.

Sometimes a new technology might have multiple impacts on a product. For instance, the market price might decrease while the quality improves due to the technological progress. Computers are a good example of this. Not infrequently, a new product is accompanied by a new production method; as in the automobile industry. It would not seem to be a mistake to classify products with new qualitative features as "new" products. Wireless home phones perform exactly the same functions as the traditional home phones, but, nevertheless, they are, in a way, "new" products.

Technological innovations are the result of a dynamic and unceasing progress. Due to this process, neither profit rates fall towards zero, nor do new investments come to an end.

Technology, Labor & Profit

The choice of technology is an extremely important factor as it directly influences the price, quality, quantity and competitive strength of an enterprise. An inappropriate choice is bound to produce serious shortcomings and even might cause the demise of an enterprise. The technology that is employed by the enterprise is normally considered as a "given" in the short term. On the other hand, in the long term, "**new products**" and/or **"methods of production"** are introduced unceasingly by competitive firms. Enterprises have no choice but follow new technological developments and make use of them, if they wish to survive the competition. Otherwise, they cannot avoid the demise of their enterprise.

The only input of any production **capable of value-creating** or **adding value** is the laborer. Therefore, the **quality of the laborer** is vitally important for production. Regardless of the quality and quantity of all other inputs, production cannot be realized at the required quality and quantity in the absence of a sufficiently qualified labor force. Therefore, access to qualified labor capable of efficiently **using a given technology** is extremely important.

The rational expectation of an enterprise, which invests capital and brings together the inputs of production, is to make profits, in other words, obtain revenue in excess of the total costs or the capital employed. In absence of profits, there would be no incentives to invest capital. The profit motive in free market economies, or synonymously, in capitalist economies, is and has always been the driving force to initiate and to extend production.

Under fair competitive conditions, given the technology, short term full production capacity is also a "given". On Figure:3-1:a, straight line MP indicates the market sale price while the q^*q^* line shows the short term maximum output level with a given technology. The price of each product is determined by the enterprise with regard to production costs, the competitors' prices and the strength of the expected demand. Once the price is determined, all output subject to the limits of plant-capacity is expected to be sold at that price in short term. In other words, once determined, the price is constant, cet. par.

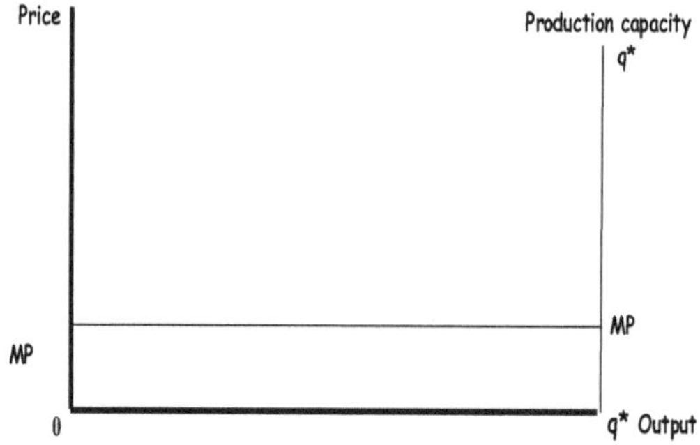

Figure: 3-1:a Average market price and total production capacity

It is very easy to test the validity of constant price in short term in competitive markets. All we have to is to observe the prices of objects in markets around us. Whatever the price of a refrigerator or an automobile on January 5, it is most likely to be the same on January 15 or 29, cet. par., except for the additional use of specific advertising campaigns. Unless there are extraordinary shifts in demand, the market price is highly unlikely to display a trend as predicted by the traditional doctrines as demonstrated by Figure: 3-1:b.

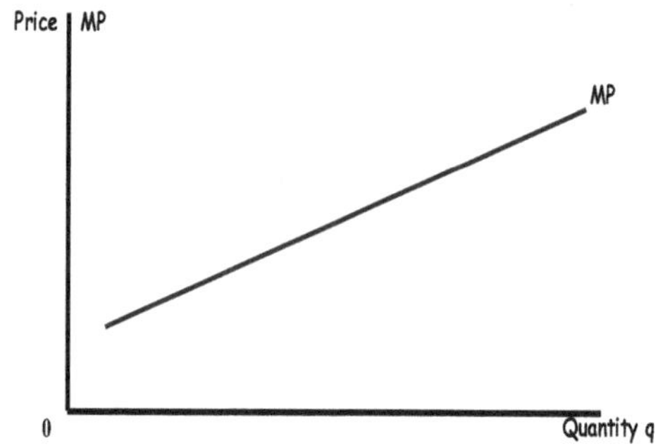

Figure: 3-1:b Supply-price relation according to traditional doctrines

The rule of a constant price level for the enterprise in the short term, cet. per., is also valid for the average prices of other enterprises in the market (Figure: 3-1:a). In other words, the short term market price for a sector is also given, cet. par.

The Profit–Cost Relation with "Given" Plant Capacity

There are several factors influencing the quantity supplied, which also affect the cost and profit rate. Assuming that there no quantitative restrictions regarding the supply of inputs, the unit costs would be minimized while expected profit rate would be maximized at the optimum plant capacity utilization. In the case of below optimum level capacity production, the average unit cost would be higher when compared to the optimum capacity unit cost and lesser profit rate. To put it differently, the closer the output to optimum plant capacity, the less the average unit cost, thus the higher average unit profit will be and vice versa.

Scale Economies & the Production Capacity

Economists, especially those trained in a Neoclassical fashion refer to the "variable unit cost" as the "average unit cost" whilst ignoring fixed cost and the effect of plant capacity utilization level on cost and price. For instance, if quantity supplied is doubled from 100 to 200 units, the average unit cost is expected to decline, while the profit rate increases. Though the claim seems to be rational, there is a serious inadequacy which has been overlooked. The costs, profits and quantities that are supplied are all directly related to the plant output capacity which is not unlimited. In theory, one might expect the average unit cost to decline and the profit rate to rise as output increases from 100 to 200 units which is the maximum output level. Therefore, any analysis of an output growth above 100, say to 200 units, disregarding capacity limit or fixed cost is not only irrational but also unrealistic. In conjunction with this, given technology, fixed cost and the output capacity in the short term, every unit output growth is subject to the **law of increasing profitability for scale.**

On Figure: 3-2, q* designates maximum plant capacity, **ATC** the average unit cost, **MP** the market sale price of product, **q'** the break-even point of output supplied where cost is exactly equal to income. When output supplied is less than **Oq'** quantity, average unit cost is greater than average unit income indicating a loss. When quantity supplied is between **q'q*** income exceeds costs which implies that the enterprise is making profits. Beyond **q'** as the output approaches **q*** each additional unit supplied means less unit cost and a higher profit rate. At optimum or maximum output level, average unit cost is expected to be at the lowest and profit rate at the highest, cet. par.

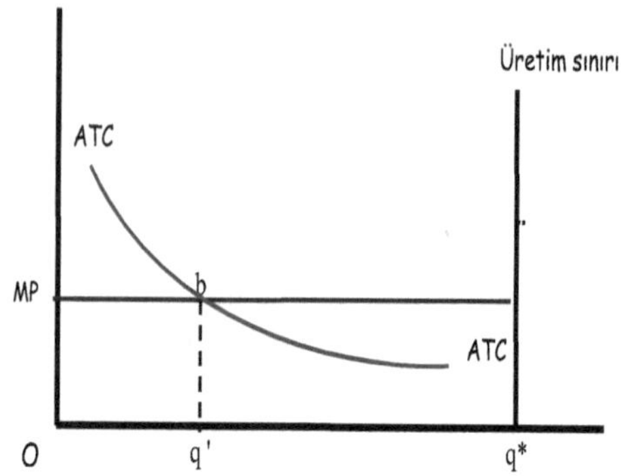

Figure: 3-2 Economies of scale – plant capacity and cost relation

Transactions of a Hypothetical Firm- "Technology "given"

Assume that an enterprise called Atlas produces 100 units of product-X. And further assume that the output capacity is 100 units. Total cost (TC), fixed-cost (FC), average total cost (ATC) and variable cost (VC) curves would look like Figure: 3-3. Total fixed cost is 100 TL while variable cost of each additional unit is 2 TL.

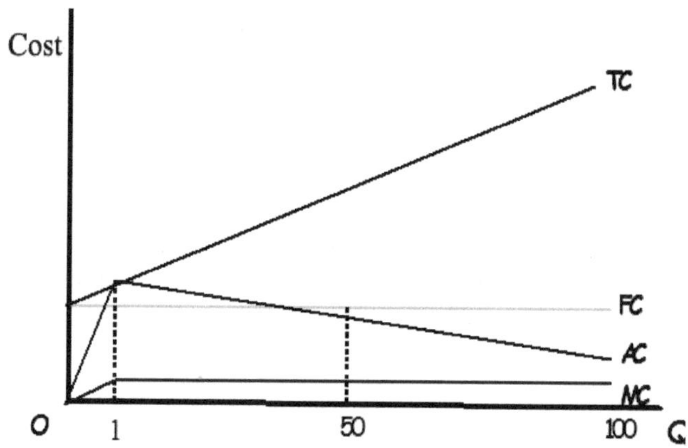

Figure: 3-3 Short term Cost Curves (given technology)

The Average unit cost (AC_1) as well as the Marginal cost (MC_1) of the first unit produced would be the same; 102 TL. (100+2). Each additional unit produced would alter the average unit cost structure considerably. For instance, the average unit cost and the marginal cost of the second unit produced would be (AC_2) 52 TL [(100+2*2):2], and (MC_2) 2 TL, respectively. The reason for the high AC of the first unit is the high unit fixed cost, 100 TL. Average cost of 10 unit would be (AC_{10}) 12 TL [(100+10*2):10] while marginal cost remain unchanged (MC_{10}) 2 TL.

In order to undertake production, the "expected" revenue of the enterprise has to exceed the costs of production. At point **B** as shown in Figure:3-4, the break-even point, when costs equal revenue is the quantity **qb**. Any quantity below this point implies loss and above this point profits for the enterprise. When output is 100 units, the maximum quantity to be produced, unit costs would be minimized while profit reaches peak level.

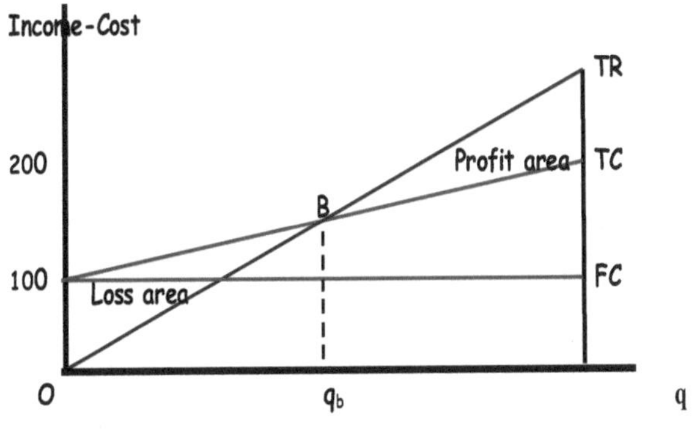

Figure: 3-4 Revenue, Cost and Output

Fixed-cost investments are important for the break-even point, or rather for the level of profits. If the enterprise employs a process technology with relatively high fixed-costs, the break-even point is likely to be reached at a higher quantity of output, cet. par. (Figure: 3-5a). In an opposite case regarding relatively lower fixed-costs, break-even point is likely to be reached at lower quantity of output, (Figure: 3-5b).

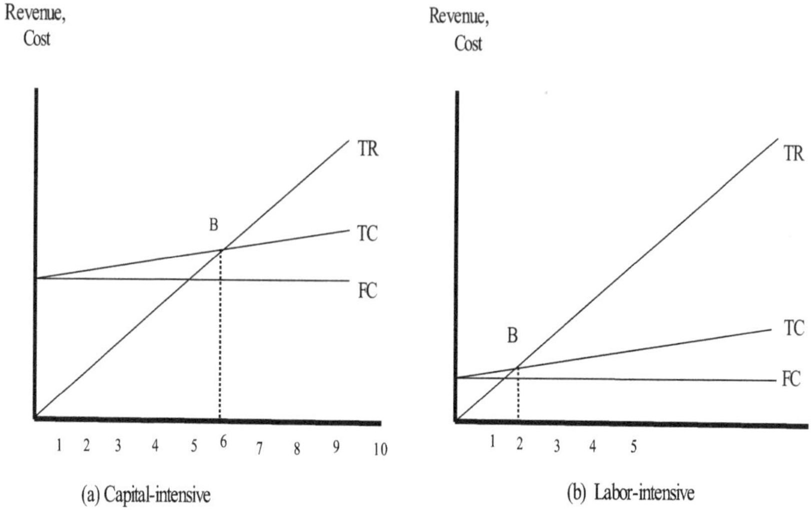

Figure: 3-5 Different fixed-investment levels and break-even points

Now, alternatively, let us study the same case with the assistance of Table: 3-1. Excluding the fixed costs, marginal cost (**MC**) is constant at 20 TL per unit. However, when fixed-costs are included in the cost analysis, the first unit output would have the highest cost per unit, because it would include both **FC** plus **MC**, that is 100+2=102 TL. However, with each additional unit output, **AC** would display a continuous decline, until reaching the full capacity at 100 units (**AC_{100}=3 TL**).

So far, the emphasis has been on the constant marginal cost, i.e., marginal cost fluctuating in constant amounts. In practice, marginal costs (**MC**) might show a tendency to change progressively or regressively, as in the Figure: 3-6, as the quantity supplied changes. When **TC** increases faster than the marginal cost this is called the "progressive cost" (Figure:3-6:a). When **TC** increases at a slower pace than the marginal cost this is called "regressive cost" (Figure: 3-6:b).

Table: 3-1: Decreasing average costs-increasing marginal revenue–constant price (MP=5 TL) a: Hypothetical figures for two shift work

Quantity q	Fixed Cost	Operating Cost	Marginal Cost	Average Unit Cost	Total Cost	Revenue
0	100	0	0	0	100	0
10	100	20	20	12:00	120	50
20	100	40	20	7:00	140	100
30	100	60	20	5:33	160	450
40	100	80	20	4:50	180	200
50	100	100	20	4:00	200	250
60	100	120	20	3:66	220	300
70	100	140	20	3:42	240	350
80	100	160	20	3:25	260	400
90	100	180	20	3:11	280	450
100	100	200	20	3:00	300	500
200[a]	100[a]	400[a]	70[a]	2:50[a]	500[a]	1,000[a]

Technological Progress & Output

Technologies employed during the production process as well as the production capacities of plants are subject to change. Some technological developments may have a cost-reducing impact while others may increase output with "given" inputs or introduce entirely new products and/or production methods. In order to survive long term competition and counteract their rivals' moves, enterprises incessantly have to strive to develop more sophisticated production methods and introduce new products with more sophisticated features. Otherwise, they would not be able to cope with their competitors in the long term and would in time be eliminated from the market.

From the point of view of national economies at a macro level, new technologies are of vital importance with regard to the total added value. However, since the focus is on micro-level production in this chapter, we shall concentrate on the impact of technological innovations on the output supplied and the profit rate.

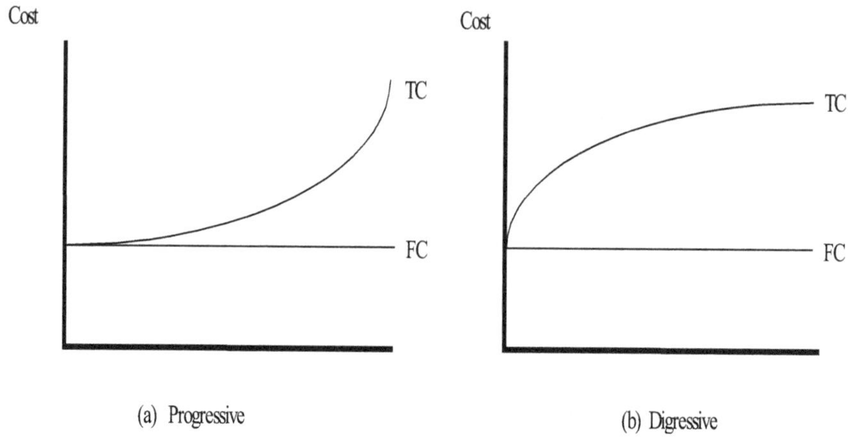

Figure: 3-6 Progressively or Regressively Changing Costs

Technological Productivity Growth

It would be useful to analyze technological productivity under two subcategories:

1- The Given product – with a new production method.

2- The New product – with a new production method.

1-) "Given" product–"New" process

One of the rational undertakings of competitive enterprises when producing a "given" product to improve their profit rate would be to introduce a new production method which would reduce production costs. To serve this goal and given constant prices and wages, new technology has to either;

1- produce the same quantity of output with less quantity of inputs, including labor; or

2- produce greater quantities with the given quantities of inputs; or

3- increase the quantity supplied faster than the growth of the input quantities; or

4- reduce the quantity supplied more slowly than the fall of the input quantities.

A new production method may cause a growth in the quantities supplied of a given product or in the rate of profit, in the short term. However, encountering a serious problem with regard to demand would soon become inevitable. Since the product supplied is a "given", demand for it would tend to decline as the market saturates which would lead to declining product utility and falling profit rates. The only way to overcome this "falling profit rate" syndrome is by introducing new technologies which lead to "new products" in long term.

2-) "New" product - "New" process

The only reasons of long term dynamic growth processes are technological innovations which introduce entirely new products often accompanied by new production methods. It is absolutely essential for enterprises that want long term survival in competitive markets to closely watch all technological innovations. If the long term profit rates do not seem to decline, the reason for this is the constant introduction of new products, particularly in dynamic sectors like biochemistry, semi-conductors, communication, etc.

Due to unceasing technological progress, new demands for new products are being created which motivates new investment which is expected to lead to higher profit rates, especially in the early phase of a new technology which facilitates monopoly profits. If the expected profit rate after the introduction of a new technology was not above the prevailing market rate, there would be no incentive to develop or to employ them. As a result of this inherent feature of the system, individuals too enjoy a constantly improving material welfare.

There are three major reasons for enterprises to search for and employ technological innovations which introduce "new products" and "new production methods":

1- To gain competitive advantage; "given" product.
2- To maximize long term profits; "new" products.
3- To counter attack their competitors technological attacks; "defensive strategy".

1-Competitive lead: Assuming constant short term wages and other input prices, every cost saving technological development, e.g., "new production method" would cause the profit rate as well as total profits to increase. If the new technology, e.g., the new production method, helps to produce a "given" product at a lesser cost, then the enterprise would have the option to reduce its price and gain a competitive advantage against its rivals in the market.

2-Monopoly advantage: Assume that a new technology introduces a "new product" probably accompanied by a "new production method". The technology owner would be highly likely to acquire a patent which would provide monopoly rights in the market, at least in the short term. Until the rivals catch up, the monopoly position is expected to last which would lead to monopolistic profits which are likely to be above the average market profit rate. Otherwise, the enterprises would have little incentive to develop and introduce new technologies.

3- Defensive strategy: Assume that a competitive enterprise introduces a new technology with monopolistic patent rights; a cost-saving technological method for a given product. This development would enhance its competitive position while increasing its profit rate, if the market price remains unchanged, cet. par. The other option is to reduce the market price in order to gain a competitive advantage. Under these circumstances, to survive in the market, other enterprises which technologically are lagging behind would feel obliged to follow suit and strive to acquire a new and a more competitive technology whether by inventing it or transferring it. This defensive counter attack is of vital importance to survive the competition in long term.

With respect to the relationship between technological progress and competitive market conditions, every enterprise has to strive, in order to survive in the long term, to keep abreast of contemporary technological development. To achieve this goal, the enterprise should pay close attention to conditions listed below:

1- Have access to a qualified labor force equipped with creative abilities and opportunities and a technologically appropriate infrastructure in order to be able to create "new technologies".
2- If the new technology is to be transferred, access to a sufficiently qualified labor force in order to successively adapt and eventually to further develop transferred technology as well as its infrastructure.
3- The labor force, as the productive force has to be subject to continuous up to date education and/or training in order to not lag behind. In other words, the enterprise should adopt a policy of being a "continuous-learning organization, which is open to participation in decisions and to constructive criticism at every stage of production.
4- Organizational and economic efficiency should always be among the top priorities for an enterprise.
5- Expectations should be realistic and rational and in harmony with economic realities.
6- Always be aware of the risks and challenges involved and be ready to undertake risks when necessary.

Briefly, the only reason for the profit rate not to fall towards zero in the long term is technological innovation, especially those innovations which lead to "**new products**" which in return create more demand and investment opportunities. New technologies are also of vital importance for enterprises to survive the long term competition. Due to the technological innovations, not only the average profit rate do not fall towards zero, but the total added value increases which implies a greater pie, and as a result bigger slices for everyone.

In Conclusion

For instance, it was shown that while new production methods with a "**given**" product increases productivity in the short and medium term only, long-term productivity growth requires "**new products and new production methods**". In addition, it was shown that the source of all technological innovations was the intellectual contribution of labor force that is the "mental labor".

In this chapter, we discussed not only the significance of technological innovations on production but also their impact and outcome. It was shown that while new production methods with a "**given**" product increases productivity in the short and medium term only, long term productivity growth, e.g., economic growth, requires "**new products and new production methods**". In addition, it was shown that the source of all technological innovations was the creative intellectual contribution of laborer that is "**creative mental labor**" of the laborer.

Chapter 4: PRICE

Price Theory holds a very crucial position in economics since it is the **fundamental basis of all other economic theories** ranging from production- consumption theories to international trade and income distribution. For instance both producers as well as consumers adjust their market behavior according to the price signals from markets. Price signals are also capable of causing serious fluctuations in the magnitude of crucial variables like growth, inflation and unemployment. If there is no "realistic, sound and reliable" price theory at hand, then it is highly unlikely to have a "realistic, sound and reliable" theory for growth, foreign trade, inflation, or any other area of economics. Therefore, it is imperative to have access to a realistic and competent price theory, which is logically, consistent as well as practically relevant.

A price theory should not only be able to explain exchange ratios, e.g., the relative prices between two commodities, but also actual market prices. In addition, price theory should also be able to explain price formation in the **service sector**, which accounts for a greater part of the **GDP** of all countries than the manufacturing sector, both in terms of output and employment. This important issue, however, seems to be completely ignored in traditional price theories. Moreover, a price theory should also be able to account for the sources of and the further generation of exchange-values in the long term. Only then, could we get a more realistic insight into economic transactions, how to design realistic policies, and also to pave the way for the further development of both logical and relevant theories in related fields such as growth, distribution, etc. Since the traditional neoclassical price theory fails to satisfy these expectations, there appears to be an urgent need for an alternative price theory.

In the fictitious world of the Neoclassicists relative values and prices are perfectly capable of being precisely studied mathematically as "imaginary" exchange-relations and thus they enrich our purely academic thinking. However, these fictitious exchange relations fall short in explaining actual economic transactions. Thus, a need arises to account for actual market prices in an economy where products are exchanged for money, instead of imaginary markets with fictitious transactions. The main objective of this study is to attempt to fill in this void.

In the following sections two new approaches to the study of price analysis will be introduced. These are:

1- A market price (**MP**) analysis separated from production cost (**PC**) and production price (**PP**).
2- A separate price formation analysis in the **service sector** as distinct from the commodity producing sectors.

Short Term Price: technology as a "given"

The basic **short term** assumptions, unless otherwise stated, are:

- Profit driven rational economic agents:
- Single-product enterprise:
- Competitive conditions (no monopoly-cartel-oligopoly):
- A "given" wage-level:
- A "given" technology:
- No scarcity of any kind of the inputs of production:
- A "given" optimum plant capacity:
- Operating costs, including wages, fluctuate proportionately with output:
- Profit rate fluctuates with capacity utilization:
- No market distortions or restrictive practices:
- No inflation:
- No state intervention (no taxes, subsidies, or regulations):
- No shift work or overtime.

Production Price vs. Market Price

In order to make a realistic price analysis, it is necessary to separate production cost (**PC**) from the production price (**PP**). The **PC** will only refer to the "realized" or "actual" costs of production, excluding profits and the imaginary "forgone incomes" of the entrepreneur as presented by traditional theories.

The distinctive and unconventional feature of the analysis in this work is the separation of price formation analysis into three distinct sectors, which are;

1- the manufacturing sector;
2- the service sector; and
3- the primary sector

The **PP** in the industrial (manufacturing and primary) sectors includes ex-factory profits (**PC**+π). The reason for this is that in commodity-producing industrial sectors, production process and complementary marketing-sale-distribution activities are often carried out by separate and independent enterprises though the owner might be the same. Therefore, it would be more rational and appropriate to make a separate analysis of such complementary services. Due to the inherent differences of production in the service supplying sector, a separate price formation analysis will be made below.

We shall begin the analysis below with a commodity-producing industrial sector price analysis and continue with the service and primary sector analyses. Price formation in the agricultural sector will be ignored on the grounds that this output depends heavily on natural conditions such as weather or climate condition. These factors are still, to large extent, beyond the control of human beings and as a result it is rather cumbersome to make a proper price analysis in this particular sector.

1- Ex-factory Production Price (PP)

A manufacturing enterprise combines the inputs of production ranging from raw materials to energy, intermediary goods, capital goods, etc., with the hired services of labor-power to produce commodities, which satisfy the needs and wants of end-users. During the production process, the enterprise incurs some fixed and variable costs called "production cost" (**PC**), e.g., payments for labor-power services and all the other inputs of production, all of which are paid from the capital. Since entrepreneurs are driven by the profit motive, the per unit market sale price is, naturally, expected to exceed per unit cost of production in order to compensate for the **risks** incurred by **productive employment of savings,** that is employing **capital**. Therefore, the ex-factory sale price of manufactured commodities ($\mathbf{PP^m}$) including the profit is expected to be higher than the $\mathbf{PC^m}$.

$\mathbf{PC^m}$ = Fixed costs ($\mathbf{FC^m}$) + Operating costs ($\mathbf{OC^m}$)
$\mathbf{OC^m}$ = Variable costs ($\mathbf{VC^m}$) + Wages ($\mathbf{LWC^m}$)
Unit $\mathbf{PP^m = PC^m + \pi^m : Q}$

Thus, the manufacturing sector's per unit ex-factory sale price ($\mathbf{PP^m}$) is equal to the total production cost ($\mathbf{PC^m}$) plus total profit ($\boldsymbol{\pi}^\mathbf{m}$), divided by the quantity supplied (**Q**), excluding the post-production "service" costs such as transportation, marketing, selling, etc. By assumption, an independent and separate trading company provides the complementary services such as transportation, marketing, etc. $\mathbf{FC^m}$ denotes fixed costs such as plant site, tools, and capital-goods; $\mathbf{VC^m}$ refers to all variable costs ranging from raw materials and energy to intermediary components, which fluctuate with the quantity of output; $\mathbf{LWC^m}$ refers to the earnings of blue and white-collar employees; and $\boldsymbol{\pi}^\mathbf{m}$ refers to the size of profits. $\mathbf{VC^m}$ and $\mathbf{LWC^m}$ together comprise the "**Operating Costs**" ($\mathbf{OC^m}$) of the manufacturing enterprise and, by assumption, $\mathbf{VC^m}$ changes at a constant rate in relation to the quantity supplied.

As discussed elsewhere (Gürak, 2004), profit, π, is defined as the surplus value or the additional income in excess of the initial production capital advanced to start the production process. The rate of profit is defined as $\mathbf{r^m}$.

$r^m = \pi^m : PC^m$

Or equivalently;

$r^m = \pi^m : TC^m$

A Hypothetical Price Analysis

If one assumes an optimum productive capacity utilization and no demand shortage, then what would be the $\mathbf{PP^m}$ and rate of profit ($\mathbf{r^m}$), assuming the following hypothetical production figures?

$\mathbf{PC^m} = 50{,}000$ TL
$\mathbf{FC^m} = 25{,}000$ TL
$\mathbf{VC^m} = 15{,}000$ TL
$\mathbf{LWC^m} = 10{,}000$ TL
$\mathbf{Q^m} = 1{,}000$ units
$PC^m = FC^m + VC^m + LWC^m = 25{,}000 + 15{,}000 + 10{,}000 = 50{,}000$ TL

The enterprise's income must exceed the initial costs of production ($\mathbf{PC^m}$) in order to generate profits for the entrepreneur. If one assumes that the average profit rate is 20 percent, total revenue including the profits would be:

$\mathbf{TR^m} = \mathbf{PC^m * (1+r^m)} = 50{,}000 * (1.2) = \mathbf{60{,}000\ TL}$

Where the $\mathbf{PP^m}$ per unit is:

$\mathbf{PP^m} = \mathbf{TR^m : Q} = 60{,}000 : 1{,}000 = \mathbf{60\ TL}$

And, the size of profit:

$\boldsymbol{\pi^m} = \mathbf{TR^m - TC^m} = 60{,}000 - 50{,}000 = \mathbf{10{,}000\ TL}$

When production capacity and input costs are known as set out in the example above, cet. par., then calculating unit costs should be an easy process. Unit market price, on the other hand, should be a function of "expected" profits, competitors' prices and strength of demand, cet. par. Assuming no demand shortage, then the enterprise should be in a position to determine price and profit at any desired rate.

The Market Price (MP) in Manufacturing

That the service sector has become the largest sector in terms of both employment and value of output, in the developed as well as in the less-developed countries, is common knowledge. What is astonishing, however, is the neglect of the service-sector price formation analysis in contrast to that of industrial sectors. This is not only a serious shortcoming but also a major impediment in making a "proper and realistic analysis" with "proper and realistic predictions" and to formulate proper policies.

The effect of using one's own capital versus using loan capital with regards to profitability

In the estimation of the profit rate (r) in the real world, a serious problem pops up; should one take into consideration the "actual" amount of the capital advanced by the capitalist or the "total" capital supplied, including loans? The choice of one of these criteria affects the outcome considerably.

Assume that **Enterprise-X** aims to produce 1,000 chairs and has to invest 50,000 TL to establish the necessary productive capacity. Further assume that the Enterprise has two alternative sources to acquire the required amount of production capital, i.e., 50,000 TL. Does it:

a-) use its own resources only; or

b-) borrow some of the amount, say 20,000 TL, from financial institutions and supply the rest, 30,000 TL, from own resources.

The expected total revenue is 60,000 TL, meaning 10,000 TL profits. The profit rate will be quite different in different cases:

Case-1: The rate of profit on its "own" capital that is worth 50,000 TL

$\mathbf{r^m_1 = \pi^m_1 : K^m_1}$ = 10,000 : 50,000 = **20 percent**

Case-2: The rate of profit on its "own" capital that is worth 30,000 TL

$\mathbf{r^m_2 = \pi^m_2 : K^m_2}$ = 10,000 : 30,000 = **33 percent**

In Case-1, where a higher amount of one's "own" capital is provided, profit rate is lower than in the Case-2 where the owner-supplied capital is only 30,000 TL. Certainly, there are interest costs on the loan, which adds to the production costs. However, taxation-systems, generally, provide generous deduction clauses and/or subsidies, in order to relieve most of the burden of such costs, in favor of the investor.

In contrast to conventional theories, in real business transactions, the separation of the "complementary" service sector costs or incomes from the commodity production sector costs or incomes is a common practice. There are numerous wholesale as well as retail enterprises operating either as independent profit-making entities or as a profit-making extension of the manufacturing unit, constituting vital and indispensable intermediary chains of economic relations between the producers and end-users. Their activities display a wide range of different services that are required before commodities reach the end-users.

In the following section, an independent and separate price formation analysis will be presented focusing on service-sector transactions only. Below, however, we shall focus first on some "complementary" service sector transactions such as marketing-distribution as an extension of manufacturing transactions in the formation of **MP** of commodities.

$\mathbf{MP^m}$ including Marketing & Distribution Costs

The purpose of complementary services provided by an enterprise after the production of the industrial goods is to convey commodities from the factory to the consumer i.e. the end-user. These activities involve some costs, which raise the $\mathbf{PP^m}$, before commodities reach the consumer. The final unit $\mathbf{MP^m}$ of a commodity consists of the following components:

$MP^m = PC^m + FC^s + VC^s + LWC^s + \pi^s : Q$

$\mathbf{MP^m}$ covers, in addition to the ex-factory cost ($\mathbf{PC^m}$), fixed costs ($\mathbf{FC^s}$), variable costs ($\mathbf{VC^s}$) and wage cost ($\mathbf{LWC^s}$) for the supply of the complementary services as well as the profits of the trading enterprise ($\boldsymbol{\pi^s}$). The quality of the complementary services supplied depend mainly on the skill level of the labor force, partly on the quality of the material inputs of production and partly on the quality of the technological or institutional infrastructure in the complementary service sector.

Now, let us see what the ultimate unit $\mathbf{MP^m}$ will be after the manufacture of 1,000 chairs at the total cost of 50,000 TL, which are sold with a 20 percent service sector profit rate. In other words, what would be the ultimate unit $\mathbf{MP^m}$ price including the complementary service costs? First, let us consider the initial position with no complementary costs:

Case-1: Assume that the sale to the ultimate consumer takes place at the gate of the manufacturing unit and the firm provides no complementary services, nor incur any additional costs. Production price ($\mathbf{PP^m}$) would equal market end-user sale price ($\mathbf{MP^m}$).

$MP^m_1 = PP^m = 60$ TL

Case-2: The manufacturing enterprise undertakes the complementary service costs as an extension to its manufacturing costs which adds, say 5,000 TL to the previous total cost. Profit rate is still 20 percent on the total capital invested.

$\mathbf{MP^m_2} = \mathbf{[(PC^m + PC^s)*(1+r)]:Q} = [(50{,}000+5{,}000)*1.2]:1{,}000$

$MP^m_2 = 66$ TL

$MP^m_2 > MP^m_1$

$\mathbf{PC^s}$ denotes the complementary service costs. The sale price including service costs and profit is 66 TL per unit output.

Case-3: Assume that an independent profit driven trading enterprise takes on board the complementary services and its related costs. The total cost of services supplied is 5,000 TL and the enterprise adds a 20 percent profit on top of the total costs incurred.

$\mathbf{MP^m_3} = \mathbf{[(TR^m + PC^s) * (1+r)] : Q} = [(60{,}000+5{,}000) * 1.2] : 1{,}000$

$\mathbf{MP^m_3} = 78$ TL

$MP^m_3 > MP^m_2$

As we see in Case-3, the undertaking of complementary service activities by an independent profit driven enterprise causes $\mathbf{MP^m}$ to rise from the 60 TL ex-factory price to 78 TL per unit, a difference of 30 percent (78-60:60). When the manufacturing enterprise undertook the trading activities as in Case-2, the **MP** had already jumped from 60 TL to 66 TL per unit. But it was still about 18 percent cheaper than in the third case, where manufacturing and the complementary service supplied were carried out by independently profit driven entities at an assumed 20 percent profit rate. This outcome clearly indicates that there is a considerable difference between the ex-factory $\mathbf{MP}^{m}$ without complementary service costs and $\mathbf{MP}^{m}$ with complementary costs.

2- Price in the Service Sector

In the previous section, price-formation in the commodity producing manufacturing sector was discussed, which is the accepted focus of study of the neoclassical doctrines. Now, in this section, it is time to focus on an analysis of price-formation in the service sector, which comprises the largest share of GDP in terms of added value and employment. As discussed in the previous section, the concept service has the same meaning as "manufacturing sector complementary service" implying that it is always consumed at the site of the production. The only difference between a “complementary” service and the "service" discussed in this section is that the latter is not an extension of commodity production but of independent service supply. For example, the supply of services such as education, health-care, entertainment benefit from the use of physical products but are "independent" in the sense that they are supplied by totally separate enterprises from those producing physical goods.

The share of service sector output and employment in contemporary economies is continuously growing both in size and significance. The sector’s share in the GDP, in terms of both, value of output and employment, has already exceeded that of the manufacturing sector both in the developed as well as in the less developed countries. The supply of services covers a wide range of services from trading activities, as observed in the previous section with regards to the manufacturing sector’s complementary services even including services such as consulting services, hair-care, education, banking, tourism, health-care, sanitation services, etc., with which we are all very familiar. New kinds of services such as space tourism and personal image communication are constantly being added to the list.

During the process of supplying a service, the employment of some equipment or tools may be required. For instance, to supply a "flight" service one needs an airplane, or for an operation a doctor needs some medical instruments. However, there are some services which in order to supply them, would not require any physical tools. For instance, a teacher or a tour guide can be productive even without the assistance of any physical devices.

Service sector transactions display different distinctive features than the commodity producing sector. One of the most distinctive features is that the services supplied by the service sector are exhausted at the time they are supplied. For instance, a haircut, transport or a massage service is consumed during the process of supply. To put it differently, in the service sector, there is **no tangible and storable output** and, accordingly, as distinct from the industrial sectors, there can be **no inventories of services**. Since the output cannot be stored, there cannot be successive stages of production where at each stage value can be added to total exchange value. Another interesting feature of the service sector is that the quality of the output is dependent upon the level of the labor-skill employed and the quantity produced depends on labor-time employed.

Price formation in the service sector is, in general, subject to the same short term conditions as in the manufacturing sector, that is, decreasing costs and increasing returns as output increases (economies of scale), cet. par.

Components of price in service sector:

$$MP^s = FC^s + \underbrace{VC^s + LWC^s}_{} + \pi^s \quad \overline{}^{\;\mathbf{OC^s}}$$

A Case for Consideration

Assume a hotel with 100 guest rooms and 100 beds. Assume that in order to reach the break-even point, (B), where total income covers the total costs at zero profit rate, say, 50 rooms must be hired during a given time-span. Furthermore, assume that, even in the absence of any hotel guest, there is an operating cost (**OC^s**) of 300 TL for the basic services required for maintenance of all the rooms. There is an additional cost (**OC^s**) of 4 TL for each room hired.

The management of hotel, as maximum profit driven rational individuals would naturally not be content with the performance at break-even point and make efforts to increase the number of rooms hired above 50 units to reduce the per hotel room costs, in order to secure some additional profits. More than 50 rooms hired, means the fixed costs would be lower and the total income and profits greater. The profits would continue to increase as capacity utilization approaches the optimum level of 100 rooms, because of the decreasing average of fixed costs per room hired. The total fixed cost is assumed to be 500 TL while operating cost which increases with each room hired is 4 TL (see Table: 4-1).

Let us study the case with the help of Figure:4-1. Assume that only 75 rooms are rented, which means less than optimum capacity utilization. Profits would be the area "Bcd", while the maximum attainable profit area is "Bef". The total number of rooms hired determines the size and the rate of profits, given the room prices, the number of rooms available and the production costs of the services provided. When all 100 rooms are hired, the cost will be minimized and profits maximized, as denoted by the area of Bef.

Table:4-1 Capacity Utilization and Costs in Service Sector (in TL)

Rooms hired	Revenue (p*q)	Operating costs	Fixed costs	Total costs	Average cost Per room
0	0	300	500	800	800:00
25	500	400	500	900	36:00
50	1,000	500	500	1,000	20:00
75	1,500	600	500	1,100	14:66
100	2,000	700	500	1,200	12:00

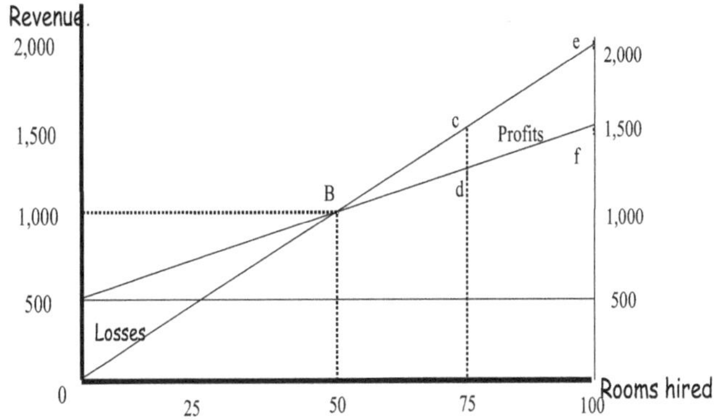

Figure:4-1 Capacity Utilization, Costs & Profits

3- Price Formation in the Primary Sector

This example of primary sector transactions covers mining only, where output mainly depends on the generosity of nature and the ecological conditions. For instance, if a country does not possess natural copper or borax mines, they cannot be produced artificially. The share of the primary sector transactions in the GDP tends to decline as the countries climb up the developmental ladder. However, the decline in the share of GDP does not imply a decline in the importance of the primary sector inputs because every commodity has its genesis in the inputs of Nature. By providing the basic inputs of production, e.g., raw-materials, nature always plays a vital and indispensable role in determining future living conditions. Without the gifts of Nature, it would be not be possible to supply the products some people so lavishly enjoy. Nature is the mother of our material well-being.

Price formation in the primary sector resembles that in the manufacturing sector. For instance in the mining sector production price (**PP**) ex-factory is:

$$PP^p = FC^p + \overbrace{VC^p + LWC^p}^{OC^p} + \pi^p$$

The market price (**MP**) including complementary services in relation to physical supply costs would be:

$MP^p = PP^p + PC^s + \pi^s$

Inferior Land, Rising Costs, Price and Profit

Assume that the best mine from which to dig out lead has reached its limits, but demand is still growing at a given price. There is, by assumption, more mines to be exploited but of a lesser fertility, which implies higher production costs for an additional per unit output. The only way to keep pace with growing demand is to increase the price of lead in order to provide "incentives" for the producer to increase output. In other words, unless the price increases enough to compensate for the increasing average and marginal costs and to provide a sufficient profit rate, supply would not increase.

Decreasing Returns & Rent

Assume the following values for a hypothetical enterprise in the mining sector, the mine used had the highest grade productivity, but it has now reached its limits.

Q = 1,000 kilos
MP = 5 TL: kilos
TR = 5,000 TL (MP * Q)
TC = 4,500 TL (FC+VC+LWC)
π = 500 TL (TR-TC)
r = ~ 11 percent (π : TC)

Assume that demand grows from 1,000 tons to 1,100 tons, with a “given” technology, human skills and profit rate in the short term. Increasing output under these conditions is subject to increasing costs and falling rate of profit, due to use of a less fertile mine. Assume that the cost of each additional ton is 4.9 TL; that is 0.4 TL higher than per ton output (4.5 TL) in a more fertile mine, cet. par. Given the market price (MP=5 TL), the size and the rate of the profit on an "additional" 100 tons would be as follows:

π = 1 TL (50 TL - 49 TL) and,
r = ~ 2 percent (π : TC) = (1 TL : 49 TL)

Since the average rate of profit for the initial 1,000 tons is greater (~11 %), there will be no incentive at all for the primary sector enterprise to increase its output beyond the initial 1,000 tons, unless **MP** increases. In order to secure additional output at an 11 percent profit rate, the price for the "additional" output must increase to about 5:45 TL/ ton.

If the new price applies for the initial output of 1,000 tons as well, the new average rate of profit would rise to ca. 21 percent.

r_1 = (5,450 - 4,500) : 4,500 = ~ 21 percent for the initial 1,000 tons,
While profit rate for additional output is ca. 11 percent,
r_2 = (5,450 - 490) : 490 = ~ 11 percent for additional 100 tons,
indicating an average profit rate about **15 percent for the "total output"** of 1,100 tons.

Impact of Technological Changes on Price

So far, we assumed that technology was a "given", that is;

1- no new production processes; and
2- no new products;

It is time to let go of this assumption and include advances in technology. Demand continues to adjust itself to the variations in supply, thus maintaining supply-demand stability.

The **long term** assumptions:

1- New products as well as new production methods.
2- Prices, incomes, plant capacities and tastes are variable.
3- Fixed costs do include R & D expenditure.
4- Increasing returns.

A "Given" Product & a "New" Production Process

According to mainstream economics textbooks, we are accustomed to classify new process technologies as being:

1- Capital-saving,
2- Labor saving, and
3- Neutral.

However, this classification seems to be short on explaining actual economic relationships. First of all, a technological innovation does not introduce "only" a capital-saving or a labor-saving process. Generally, it introduces both of them at different rates depending on the specific features of the new technology. As to the "neutral" impact of new technological processes; this occurs only in the minds of mainstream economists or in miracles. Therefore, **new process technologies to reduce the production costs of a "given" product** will be studied under four different sub-categories:

1- **Fixed-"capital saving" technology**, given **VC** and **LWC**, while **FC** per unit output decreases.
2- Operating-"capital saving" technology, given FC, while OC (=VC+LWC) decreases the per unit output.
3- a **(Total) "capital saving" technology**, given inputs (**FC and OC**), while output increases which causes per unit costs to decline.
3- b **(Total) "capital saving" technology**, given total output (**Q**), while the inputs required decreases which causes per unit costs to decline.

Let us study each case more closely.

Cost-saving technological progress in all the cases above causes per unit costs to decline. As a consequence of **cost-saving** technology per unit output, the enterprise would be in a more advantageous competitive position compared to its competitors. As a result, the enterprise is now in a position to lower its price and eventually drive its competitors out of the market, unless, of course, the competitors catch up with its technological progress.

An Initial Case

Before the introduction of new production process let us assume that the following prices and quantities reflect the initial production conditions for a given **Commodity-X**, where the rate of return (r) is 10 percent. The price, which is ex-factory, does not include complementary service costs like marketing, distribution, etc.

FC = 6,000 TL
VC = 4,000 TL
w = 20 TL
L = 100 number of employees.
LWC = 2,000 TL total wage bill
TC = FC + VC + LWC = 12,000 TL
Q = 1,000

PP (production price) per unit output is:

PP = [FC+VC+LWC)]* r : Q = (TC*r):Q

= [12,000] * 1.1 : 1,000 = 12,000*1.1 : 1,000 =**13.20 TL**

Average total cost:

ATC = TC:Q = 12,000 : 1,000 = **12.00 TL**

Size and rate of profit per unit output:

π^* = pp-ATC = 13.20 – 12.00 = **1,20 TL**

r = π : ATC = 1.20 : 12.00 = **10 percent**

Case-1: FC-saving technology

Assume that the same productions conditions found in the initial case prevail, except this time FC is saved by 20 percent and the cost reduced from 6,000 to 4,800, after the introduction of a new production method, which is in fact a FC-saving technology. The costs of production and profits will change as follows, cet. par.:

TC = [4,800 +4000+2000) = 10,800 TL

ATC = 10,800 : 1,000 = 10.80 TL per unit

π^* = 13.20 – 10.80 = 2.40 TL per unit profit

While,

r = 2.40 : 10.80 = ~ **22 percent**

The new **FC-saving** production method increases the profit rate from 10 percent to about 22 percent, cet. par.

However, there is also another option for the enterprise using cost-saving technology apart from increasing profits. For instance the producer can reduce the market price of product and obtain a competitive advantage over his rivals. Assume that the producer is content with the initial 10 percent profit rate and wishes to maintain it at that level. Now, the new technology owner can reduce the market price from its initial level of 13.20 TL to 11.88 TL (ATC*1.10=10.80*1.10=11.88 TL) and still continue to make a 10 percent profit. Any price level above 11.88 TL and below 13.20 TL implies a higher profit rate and a lower price compared to the initial position (Figure:4-2:a).

Case-2: OC-saving technology

Once again, assume that the same initial production conditions prevail, but this time an operating-capital saving new technology is introduced which reduces the number of employees from 100 to 80. The new values, given the same price and quantity, would be, cet. par.:

TC = [10,000 + (20 * 80)] = 11,600 TL

ATC = 11,600 : 1000 = 11.60 TL per unit

π = 13.20 – 11.60 = 1.60 TL per unit

While,

r = 1.60 : 11.60 = ~ **14 percent**

The new **OC-saving** or **LWC-saving** technology increases the profit rate from 10 percent to about 14 percent.

However, once again, as in Case-1, there is yet another option available for the cost-saving technology user. The producer who employs the new technology can reduce the market price of the product and obtain a competitive advantage against his rivals. Assume once again that the producer is content with the initial 10 percent profit rate. Now, the new technology using enterprise can reduce the market price from its initial level of 13.20 TL to 11.88 TL (ATC*1.10=11.60*1.10= 11.88 TL) and still continue to make a 10 percent profit, assuming there are no restrictions on the production capacity or shortage of demand. Any price level above 11.88 TL and below 13.20 TL leads to a higher profit rate and a lower price compared to the initial position. (Figure:4-2:b).

Case-3:a Capital-saving - (output increasing) Technology

Assume that the new method of production increases total output by 20 percent from 1,000 to 1,200 units, while sustaining the same "total" costs of production. In other words, the amount of capital required to produce the same quantity of output and the quantity of the inputs of production remain unchanged while the output increases by 20 percent, cet. par. The total production cost is still 12,000 TL as in the initial case, but **ATC** falls considerably. Assuming a constant price, the profit rate would rise to 32 percent.

ATC = 12,000 : 1,200 = 10.00 TL per unit.

Given demand and **pp**:

π = pp - ATC = 13.20 – 10.00 = 3.20 TL per unit

And

r = 3.20 : 10.00 = **32 percent**

However, once again, as in Cases 1 and 2, there is another option for the cost-saving technology user. Once again, the producer can reduce the market price of a product and obtain a competitive advantage against his rivals. Assume once again that the producer is content with the initial 10 percent profit rate. Now, new technology using enterprise can reduce the market price to from its initial level of 13.20 TL to 11.00 TL (ATC*1.10=10.00*1.10=11.00 TL) and still continue to make 10 percent profits, assuming there are no restrictions on productive capacity or shortage of demand. Any price level above 11.00 TL and below 13.20 TL implies higher profit rate and lower price compared to the initial position (Figure:4-2:c).

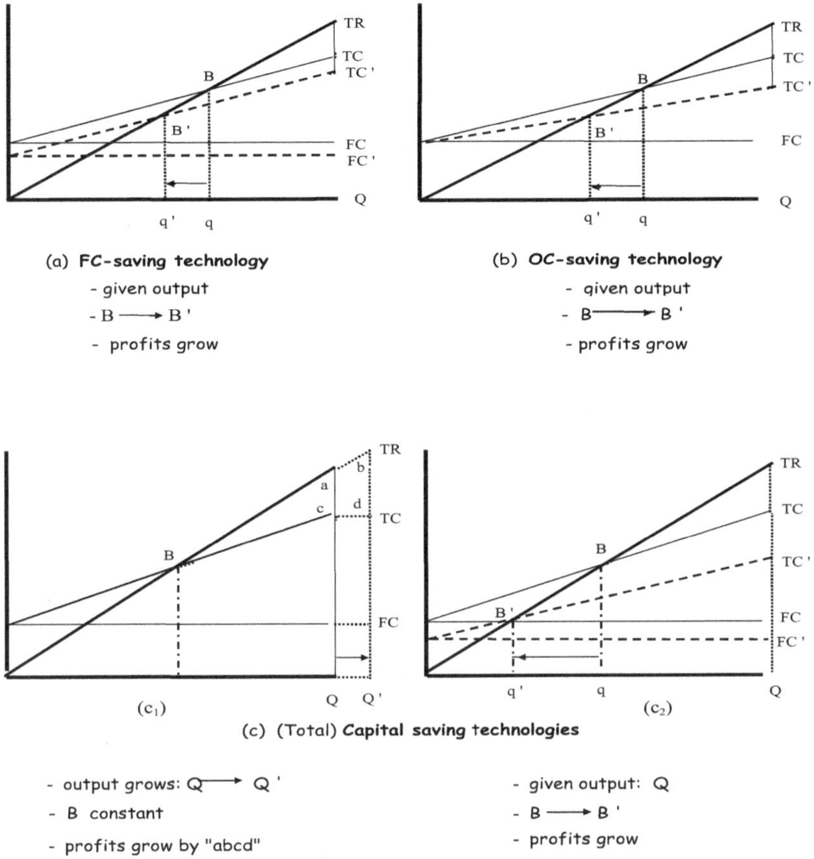

Figure:4-2 Types of Technological Changes

Case-3:b Capital-Saving Technology with a "given" output but "less" inputs.

Once again assume the initial conditions prevail and as a result of technological innovation in the production process, production cost is reduced by 10 percent or by 1,200 TL. As a result, the average unit production cost will fall, while profit will increase, with a "given" price, cet. par".

ATC = 10,800 : 1,000 = 10.80 TL

π = PP - ATC = 13.20 – 10.80 =2.40 TL per unit and;

r = 2.40 : 10.80 = ~ **22 percent**

However, once again, as in Cases 1, 2 and 3a, there is another option available for the cost-saving technology using enterprise. Once again, the producer can reduce the market price of the product and obtain a competitive advantage over his rivals. Assume again that the producer is content with the initial 10 percent profit rate. Now, the new technology user can reduce the market price from its initial level of 13.20 TL to 11.88 TL (ATC*1.10=10.80*1.10=11.88 TL) and continue to make a 10 percent profit. Any price level above 11.88 TL and below 13.20 TL gives rise to a higher profit rate and a lower price compared to the initial position (Figure:4-2:c).

All the technological progresses discussed so far were "per unit cost-reducing". Unless the competitors keep up with cost-saving technological changes, they would eventually be eliminated from the competitive market.

"New" Production Process in Service Sector & their Effect on Price

Although there is a clear distinction between the supply and consumption of tangible and storable physical goods and the intangible and non-storable services, the impact of cost-reducing new processes (technology) is, in practice, similar in terms of competitive conditions and price formation. However, there appears to be a different situation in the case of a new process, which increases output with certain given inputs.

Case-1: FC-saving Technology

Assume that a service supplying enterprise introduces a FC-saving process as in Figure:7-a, cet. par. Just as in a cost-saving new process introduced into the industrial sector, the service supplier, e.g. a hospital, would gain a competitive advantage. Given the price, it can now either supply the services at lower cost while increasing profits or reduce the service supply price and expand its service output, cet. par. There is also the option to combine price reduction with service output growth, as in the commodity-producing sector studied above.

Case-2: OC-saving Technology

Assume that the service supplier, the hospital in our case, introduces a new OC-saving new process (technology) as in Figure:4-2:b. In regard to price and competition, the options would be the same as in Case-1.

Case-3:a Capital-saving (output increasing) technology

The vital question is whether it is possible to increase the supply of a service with a given amount of inputs. Since the output in the commodity producing sector is tangible and storable, measuring the increased supply would be relatively easy (see Figure:4-2:c_1). Yet, the output in the service sector is neither tangible nor storable; thus it is hardly possible to attempt to calculate any differences in service output in terms of the quantity supplied. This problem can be overcome, however, if the increase in output is measured in terms of added value.

Case-3:b Capital-saving Technology- (a "given" output produced with fewer inputs)

Given the price and competitive conditions, the outcome is expected be the same as in Cases 1 and 2. Such a cost-saving new process in the service supplying enterprise would help to increase the size and rate of profit, cet. par. In addition, the cost-saving enterprise can gain a price-competitive advantage over its competitors by reducing the supply-price of a service. Another option is a combination of price reduction and an increase in the quantity supplied of a service which would help to increase total profit, assuming there are no restrictions on production capacity or shortage of demand. An important assumption is that the quality of service remains unchanged.

New Products & Long Term Price

Since the products are **new**; there would be no preceding prices on which to make a comparative analysis. In other words, a study of the price effect of a **new technology** would give us information only on a "new set" of prices. It can be claimed; however, that the **expected** profit rate would likely be higher than the prevailing average market rate, until the competitors catch up. Because the owner of a new technology would enjoy a monopolistic power in the market, until the competition catches up.

In the absence of technological progress, products and methods of production supplied would remain unchanged, i.e., in the jargon of mainstream economics "homogeneous", in the long term. Markets would gradually saturate as demand declines. Eventually, enterprises would only produce to replace the worn-out products and profit rate would decline towards zero. There is only one remedy to overcome this problem in the long term that is: **"to develop new**

technologies which in turn will introduce new products and/or production processes". Only in this way can the economic system sustain a long term growth and prevent profit rates declining towards zero.

Patent Rights & Temporary Monopoly Price

Patent rights grant the enterprise a monopolistic right over the markets. Assume that Enterprise-X possesses the "only" patent for a product in demand, e.g. a medicine against cancer. There would be a huge demand for such a medicine and the enterprise would enjoy a monopoly position due to its patent ownership. It can set the sale price at a level that leads to a greater profit margin than the market average, say, a 50 percent profit rate, while the average profit rate in the competitive markets is by assumption only 10 percent.

Given time, other enterprises in the same sector will eventually catch up and develop similar products with the same effect. Due to growing competition, Enterprise-X will soon be no longer in a position to dictate the market price as a monopolist. Consequently, as price falls, the rate of profit would fall, cet. par. Due to the fall in price and profit rate, the revenue curve per unit of output will display a declining slope over time (see Figure:4-3).

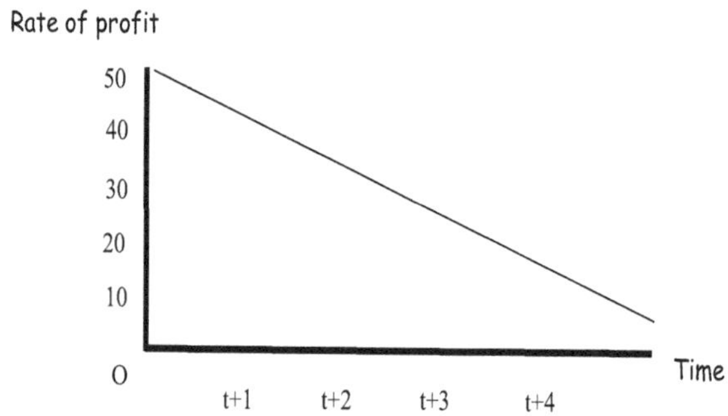

Figure:4-3 Competition and diminishing returns

Concluding Remarks

As stated at the beginning of this chapter, the theory of price is the basis of all other related economic theories which makes it special and crucial. All producers and consumers base their decisions on the price signals coming from the market. The most distinctive difference of this chapter from the mainstream doctrines is the introduction of the impact of technological innovation on price. Certainly the analyses here are not claimed to be perfect in reflecting market conditions as they actually are, however, it wouldn't be unfair to state that they are much more realistic and comprehensive than those presented by the mainstream doctrines.

Chapter 5: DEMAND

So far, we have assumed that "demand" created its own "demand" that is to say the shift in demanded quantities was in the same direction and in equal proportion to quantity supplied. In other words, demand followed supply. However, in fact the quantity supplied is determined by the fluctuations in **demand** rather than the productive plant capacity or the technology employed. In addition, fluctuations in demand also affect both the market price of a product and the profits, in the short as well as the long term. Supply adjusts to demand rather than vice versa. If demand is low, supply will be slow; if there is no demand, there will be no supply. Since demand is shaped by the end-users (consumers), we should first analyze the end-user as well as the nature of the demand.

The Consumer (The End-user)

The consumers or end-users consist of all the buyers of a supplied output ranging from individuals or households to all enterprises using raw materials, intermediary inputs or final products. According to this definition, an end-user is a consumer not only of items for personal use but also entrepreneurs who purchase the products of other producers in order to maintain the supply of goods and services for other end-users. In other words, it is not only the person who buys an automobile but also the automobile producer who buys, tires, is also an end-user or consumer.

In contrast the utopian doctrines in traditional economic textbooks, end-users are not mechanically interacting robots, but individuals, households and economic units with an historical past and a cultural legacy accumulation. All end-users, e.g., individuals, households, enterprises and non-commercial institutions, are generally assumed to make rational choices in competitive markets in their demand decisions. Otherwise, the end-users might not get the "expected" benefits from products which in turn could lead to reduced demand for the products supplied which, eventually might lead to the elimination of the less competitive firms from the market. Yet, however, it is common knowledge that, in contrast to propositions of the traditional doctrines, end-users, especially the individuals, households and enterprises often make irrational choices or decisions. This is because decision-making human beings are not purely rational mechanical robots without emotions.

End-user, e.g., consumer demand plays a significant role in the formation of market price, but demand alone does not determine the market price. However, given the productive capacity in the short term; the strength of demand certainly determines the size and rate of profit. The rate of profit is again directly affected by the utilization of plant capacity.

Demand (Needs and Desires)

Demand can be described as the desire of the end-user (consumer) to buy commodities or services from the markets to satisfy his/her needs or wants. In the absence of end-user demand, there would be no need for a supply of products. The needs of individual can be described as basic items like food, shelter, clothing, etc., which are required for survival. The needs of any enterprise cover all the inputs required for the supply of a commodity or service. No economic units i.e., enterprises and institutions can survive when there is no demand for their goods and services.

Individually desired products (wants), unlike needs, emerge and increase with the level of development. For instance, demand for telephones, automobiles, TV sets, etc., are directly influenced by economic level of a society and the purchasing-power of individuals. It is an important fact that human beings can continue to survive even if desires are not met. Because desires are, in a way, artificially created demands. Once upon a time, needs were met by the domestic production of households. As societies climbed up the ladder of development, the individuals and/or households began to exchange products with each other. Technological innovation and the related division of labor made for productivity growth and increased prosperity, which continues as an unending process.

Utility

Utility indicates the level of satisfaction acquired from the consumed items. Production of a commodity and/or service would never be undertaken unless there was a sufficient demand in order for it to set up a plant and hire employees. Therefore the concept and degree of utility is important for the production process. The quantity demanded is shaped by both the level of income (purchasing-power) and the utility obtained from the product. It is the "assumed" rational behavior of all end-users to maximize the utility from the products purchased.

From the point of view of economic units, the utility of a product used as an input of supply, is the satisfaction the commodity-service producer obtained from the realization of supply for the final consumer. In other words, the utility obtained from the input is directly related with the utility obtained by the end-users of the commodities or services supplied.

The Short Term Demand

Individual consumers

As stated above, products satisfy the needs and wants of the end-users. However, in regard to the consumption of the individual or household, the marginal utility obtained tends to diminish with each successive product consumed. In other words, the marginal utility diminishes as the quantity of product consumed rises. For instance, the utility obtained from the second slice of a loaf is expected to be less than the first one. To put it differently, as the quantity consumed increases the marginal use-value (utility) along with strength of demand for the product decreases for the individual (Figure: 5-1).

The degree of total and marginal utility of products depends on the specific conditions in regard to individuals and societies. For instance, while the utility of any kind of wine is zero for dedicated Muslims in Islamic countries, demand for it is widespread in other countries due to their cultural differences.

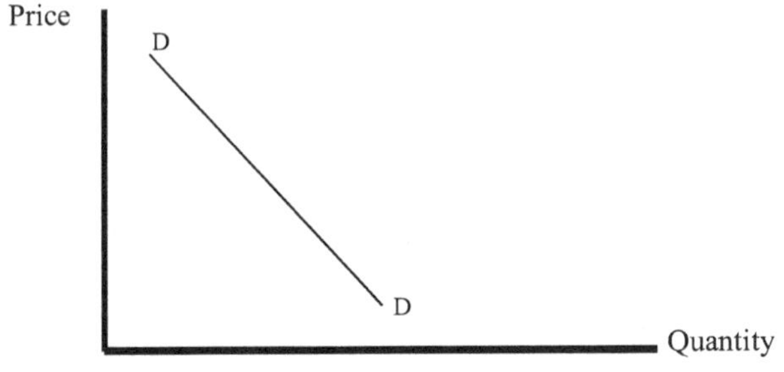

Figure: 5-1 Diminishing demand schedule for individual consumption

While demand falls rapidly for some products used for individual consumption in certain cases, it falls less rapidly in other circumstances. For instance, the human consumption capacity of food or drinks is limited in a given time period and demand for such products is described as an "**inelastic demand**". The reason for this is that, individual end-users can only consume a certain amount of the product, regardless of the price and quality. On the other hand, there are products like shirts, shoes, watches, etc., where strength of demand depends, to large extent, on income, price and tastes. The demand on such products is called an "**elastic demand**". In Figure: 5-2, elastic demand is designated by D_2D_2, while D_1D_1 designates the inelastic demand.

When demand schedule is like D_1D_1, that is inelastic, "one" unit price fall is expected to be accompanied by a less than one unit increase in demand and vice versa. On the other hand, when D_2D_2 schedule is valid, "one" unit price fall is expected to be accompanied by a more than one unit increase in demand and vice versa.

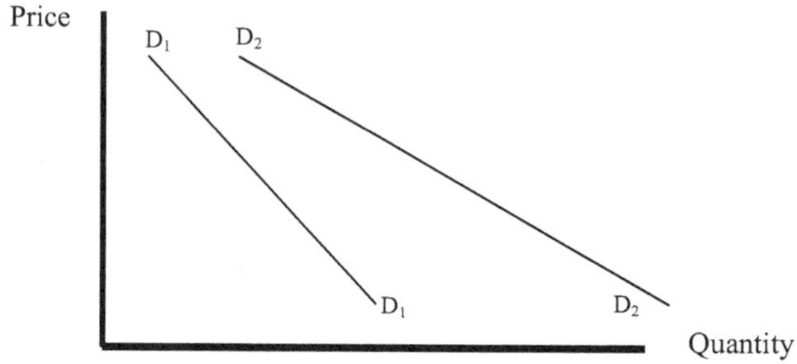

Figure: 5-2 Elastic and inelastic demand schedules for individuals

The demand schedule in economic sectors

In the section above, the focus was on the features of a demand schedule for individual consumption, which was subject to the law of decreasing marginal utility. As the law predicted, the marginal utility was decreasing as the quantity consumed increased, which eventually affected the effective demand. However, the consumers of the final products are not only individuals but also the many economic units which purchase the various inputs to realize their supply of commodities or services for individual consumption. For instance, an automobile is the final product for an individual consumer; but the automobile producer is also a final product consumer of some inputs such as engines, tires, etc., which are required for the realization of the supply of automobiles. Although many parts of finished automobiles are produced within an enterprise, it is a common knowledge that tens or sometimes hundreds of various inputs are purchased from other enterprises. Therefore, the producers of commodities and services are at the same time consumers of many other inputs.

However, there is a very important difference between the demand schedule for individuals and the demand schedule for economic units in the purchasing of inputs for the supply of commodities and services; inputs for economic units are not subject to the law of diminishing utility. Given a sustained demand for the final product and a sufficient supply of the inputs of production, the economic unit would naturally aim output at an optimum supply capacity level which would imply constant marginal utility for all the inputs of the required output. At optimum supply capacity, unit total costs will be minimized and profit rate will be maximized for profit-driven enterprises, cet. par. Thus, the demand schedule **DD** is expected to look like Figure: 5-3.

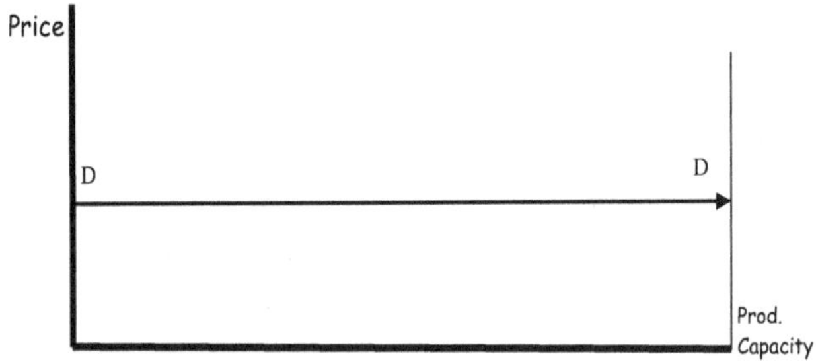

Figure: 5-3 Demand schedule for final-product producing enterprises

Basic Factors Determining Individual Demand

Given the quality, the price of a product is probably the most important factor determining the strength of demand for that particular product; but there also other factors which may affect the quantity demanded. The main factors influencing the strength of individual demand for the final products can be summarized as follows, cet. par.:

1- The price of the product.
2- The prices of competing products.
3- The income level of consumers.
4- Consumer tastes and preferences.
5- Official regulations and interventions.

1-) The critical importance of price on the quantity demanded was analyzed in the chapter on "Price". To repeat this briefly, both the quantities produced as well as the quantities demanded were heavily influenced by price level. As shown in Figure:5-1, the quantity demanded increases with falling price level and vice versa, cet. par. The price-demand relationship can be estimated as outlined below with "price elasticity" concept. "i" stands for the individual.

$$\text{Price elasticity } (e^i) = \frac{\text{Proportional change in quantity demanded}}{\text{Proportional change in price}} \qquad \text{eq.5-1}$$

Equation (eq. 5-1) indicates how a change in price affects the change in demand, while e^i designates the elasticity rate. To set an example, assume that the price of the final product X declines by 10 percent, while demand for it increases by 20 percent. The price elasticity (e^i) of X would be 2, (see eq. 5-2). If the demanded quantity at the initial price level was 100 units of X, now since price is 10 percent lower, demanded quantity would rise to 120, cet. par. Whenever the elasticity for a product is greater than one, it is called an "elastic demand" as shown by D_2D_2 line in Figure: 5-2. If elasticity is smaller than one, it would be called an "inelastic demand" as indicated by D_1D_1 line on Figure: 5-2.

$$e = \frac{(\Delta X:X)}{(\Delta P_x:P_x)} = \frac{\%\ 20}{-\ \%\ 10} = 2 \qquad \text{eq. 5-2}$$

An important note: if one assumes that the price elasticity for a product is greater than one meaning "elastic demand", the producer of the final product may be reluctant to reduce the price. The main reason for this is because it is more important for a profit driven enterprise to maximize profit rather than to increase sales. In Table: 5-1a and Table: 5-1b below, we observe the impact of a 10 percent price reduction and a 10 percent price increase, respectively, on the total revenue of the enterprise.

Initial price:	p= 5 TL
Initial quantity demanded:	Q= 100 units
Initial total income:	TR= 500 TL

Assume, as before, the price drops by 10 percent from 5 TL to 4.5 TL and the quantity demanded increases by 10 units displayed as the first option on Table: 5-1:a. As a result, total revenue declines by an amount of 5 TL to a total sum of 495 TL. Since the positive impact of price decline is also insignificant, the enterprise might be reluctant to reduce the price, as this would also reduce the profit rate.

If a 10 percent price reduction is accompanied by a 20 unit increase in demand as displayed on Table: 5-1:a as the second option, the total revenue of the enterprise would rise by 40 TL to a total sum of 540 TL. In this case, there would be more incentives for the enterprise to reduce its price compared to the first option. The final decision would be influenced by the change in profit rate of the enterprise.

Table:5-1:a Impact of 10 percent price reduction on total revenue

	New P (P * -1.10)	Extra demand ΔQ	New TR	ΔTR
Option-1	4.5	10	(110*4.5) 495	- 5
Option-2	4.5	20	(120*4.5) 540	+ 40

Now, let us look at the impact of a 10 percent rise in price on the total revenue of an enterprise. As a result of this increase, the price would rise from 5 TL to 5.5 TL. The quantity demanded is assumed to drop by 10 units as on Table: 5-1b as the first option and the total revenue of the enterprise drops by 5 TL to a sum of 495 TL. Depending on the revenue policy, the enterprise might be reluctant to reduce its price. However, the final decision would depend on the rate of profits which in all likelihood would tend to increase.

Assume that the quantity demanded declines by 20 units as a result of the price rise, as indicated in Table: 5-1:b, as the second option. The total revenue of the enterprise would drop by 60 TL to 440 TL. From the point of view of revenue, there is no incentive to reduce the price, but the final decision would again depend on the rate of profit.

Table:5-1:b Impact of 10 percent price rise on total revenue

	New Price (P* +1.10)	Extra demand ΔQ	New TR	ΔTR
Option-1	5.5	- 10	(90*5.5) 495	- 5
Option-2	5.5	- 20	(80*5.5) 440	- 60

2-) The prices of competing products are important factors in determining the demand curve, because end-users would tend to demand more of the lower price products, cet. par. Another related and important issue shaping the demand curve is the prices of the complementary products. For instance, as the gasoline price rise, demand for gasoline driven cars is expected to fall while that of diesel or hybrid cars is expected to increase. The price elasticity of competing and complementary products can be estimated as indicated below. It shows us how much demand for Y would be affected as a result of a price change of product X.

$$e_r = \frac{(\Delta Y:Y)}{(\Delta P_x:P_x)} = \frac{\Delta Y}{\Delta P_x} \frac{P_x}{Y} \qquad \text{eq. 5-3}$$

If $e_r > 0$; than X and Y are competitive products.
If $e_r < 0$; than X and Y are complementary products.

3-) The income level of individuals or households directly influences the shape of the "effective" demand. Regardless of the strength of the "potential" demand, it is the real purchasing-power of the consumers that determines the actual demand for products. Therefore, per consumer effective demand is greater in developed countries compared to the less developed ones. The elasticity of demand differs with the different income levels of individuals involved and this relation can be shown as in the equation below:

$$\text{Income elasticity } (e_g) = \frac{\text{Proportional change in quantity demanded}}{\text{Proportional change in income}} \qquad \text{eq. 5-4}$$

Or;

$$e_g = \frac{\Delta X:X}{\Delta G:G} = \frac{\Delta X}{\Delta G} \frac{G}{X} \qquad \text{eq. 5-5}$$

Assume that there is only one product in the market the consumption of which increases by 10 percent due to a 5 percent rise in income (purchasing-power). Income elasticity would be 2.

$$e_g = \frac{10\ \%}{5\ \%} = 2 \qquad \text{eq. 5-6}$$

4-) Individual consumer taste and preference is another factor influencing the shape of demand. For instance, even if they are of the same quality, a consumer, regardless of income level, may prefer shirts, shoes, phones, etc. with a well-known trade-mark over others although their price might be much lower. This behavior of the consumer might seem irrational, at first glance, especially if their income level is comparatively lower. Nevertheless, this is a fact of life.

The use of various types of commercials is another important factor in as far as it influences individual tastes and preferences, thus influencing effective demand and paving the way for "irrational" market behavior. It is common knowledge that many consumers under the influence of commercials quite often prefer to own products which are of minor importance in the utility ranking, undermining their income level, thus leading to irrational behavior. Especially the demand for items such as cars and mobile phones are typical examples of the irrational behavior of consumers. It is a frequently observed fact that such “unnecessary” luxury expenditures are met by cutting down on necessary items.

5-) Market regulations are also capable of affecting the individual demand for consumable items. For instance, environmental regulations often influence the consumer behavior in one way or another. A typical example of this is a governments’ price policy on cigarettes and its restrictions on smoking in specific areas.

Basic Factors Determining Enterprise Demand

Just as for individual or household consumers, the price of an input is probably the single most important factor determining the shape of the demand for it; there are others. Given the quality, the main factors influencing the shape of the demand for the inputs of production can be stated as follows, cet. par.:

1- The strength of the demand for the output of an enterprise.
2- The price of the input.
3- Regulations and interventions.

1) The single most important factor influencing the strength of a demand for the inputs of production is the strength of the demand for the final products of an enterprise. The strength of demand for the inputs of production would be in the same direction as the strength of demand for the final products shaped by both the actual and the expected demand. If the actual demand or expected demand is increasing, then, accordingly, the enterprise would be expected to increase its demand for inputs.

2) Given the quality, prices of the inputs are important from the profit point of view. The lower the input prices, the higher the expected profit rate would be, cet. par. Thus, enterprises would always attempt to find the lowest priced cost inputs.

3) Regulations play a significant role in determining the direction of investments, as well as of the demand for inputs. Regulations related to environmental conditions are typical examples which shift the direction of investments, and consequently the supply of inputs.

Basic Factors Determining Institutional Demand

It is always possible to compare the institutional demand to the enterprise demand for the inputs in order to supply the planned services or commodities. However, in general, there is, a significant difference between institutional behavior and purely profit driven enterprise behavior. The expenditure of governmental institutions are generally, and to a large extent, financed by taxes and to some extent by payment in return of the services provided. The expenditure of non-government institutions, on the other hand, is often financed by donations. Some institutional supplies are occasionally free of charge. However, even if the beneficiaries have to pay for some supplied services, the price is, normally, not influenced by the profit motive. For instance, patients in Turkey have to pay a small fee to benefit from the health service of state hospitals, while it is completely free in some other countries and extremely expensive in the USA. On the other hand, institutional services such as the fire brigade or public parks or public security are provided without direct charges. In a similar fashion, non-governmental institutions often provide services free of charge or in return for a small fee.

In regard to the institutional services supplied, it is always possible to compare the institutional demand for inputs to an enterprise demand for inputs. However, no other factors can be compared to the behavior of a profit driven enterprise. Therefore, this analysis will suffice in regard to institutional demand and no further analyses will be undertaken in the following sections.

Short Term Demand, Production & Profits: Technology a "given"

Let us consider a case where technology and plant-capacity are a "given", while demand is flexible and see how fluctuations in demand will affect the profit rate. As is commonly accepted, the slope of demand for individuals or households is negative and sensitive to price fluctuations. In other words, the quantity demanded increases as the price fall and increases as the price falls. There is a saturation point for each product, which implies that beyond this point the influence of demand on price and the quantity supplied looses its significance.

Given the price and plant-capacity, fluctuations in effective demand do affect the rate and the size of profits. To illustrate the case, let us study Figure: 5-4, where the demand schedule (**DD**) is a decreasing function of the price. Optimum plant capacity is shown by **Oq**. D_xD_x, which represents the effective demand for the output **q** while **B** denotes the break-even point where total income (**TR**) equals total costs (**TC**). In other words, q_b is the quantity, which raises just enough revenue to cover the total costs, but fails to produce any profit. q_b is a very critical point because no rational entrepreneur would continue to supply products below this quantity. The **FC**-line is constant while operating costs (**OC**) including wage costs, is indicated by a straight-line **TC** which rises proportionately. The Total Profit area is designated by the triangle **Bef** and the unit price is $p=TR_x:q_x$. Every shift in the demand curve, leads to shifts in the quantities supplied, and affects the size and rate of profits, given the price and the productive capacity.

Assume that purchasing-power falls due to a rise in income-tax. This would cause the demand curve to fall to D_yD_y. As a result, the quantity supplied falls from q_x to q_y and the profits fall to the area designated by **Bcd**, due to increasing per unit fixed costs.

Now, assume that real income increases due to wage-rises or a drop in the income tax-level, this would cause is a shift in demand curve. The new demand curve would be **DzDz**. As a result, the size of profits would increase to the area designated by **BTRTC**, while plant capacity utilization would grow to **q**.

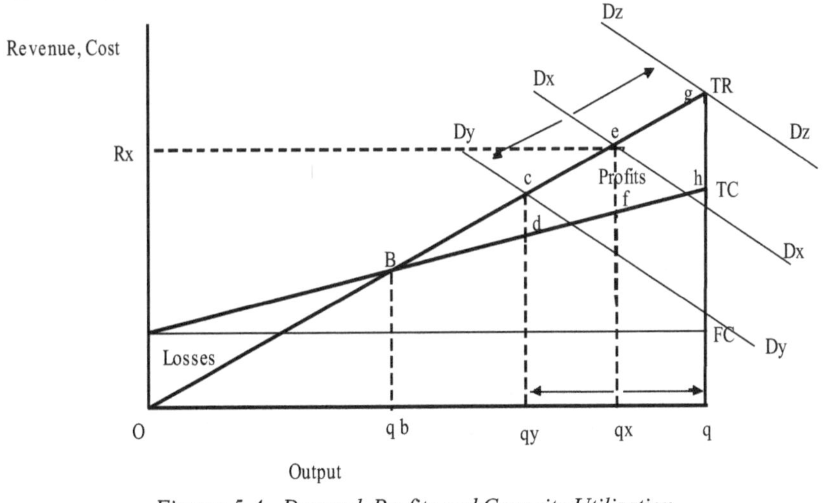

Figure: 5-4 Demand, Profits and Capacity Utilization

The firm-specific analysis made above is also valid for the entire market for a specific product. The only significant difference is the assumption that all values denote "average" hypothetical values for the market.

Long Term Individual Demand & Technological Innovations

In the long term, price, preferences and income, which influence demand, are assumed to be variable, due to the technological developments. Demand is expected to be influenced differently depending on the nature and extent of these variations. Below, we shall attempt first to analyze the impact of **cost-reducing technological innovations** on demand, then the impact of **technological innovations introducing new products on demand** and finally the impact of a **shift in income (purchasing-power) h**as on demand.

Cost-reducing Progress & Demand; "given" the product

Assume that a cost-reducing process is introduced by a refrigerator producer which involves a new per unit production cost, excluding profits, is 90 TL instead of 100 TL, which means a 10 percent reduction in cost. The new break-even point would be q2 instead of q1, closer to the origin (see Figure: 5-5:a). The firm may choose one of the following options, cet. par.:

1- Keep the price constant, thus increase the size and rate of profits; or

2- Reduce the price and improve firm's competitive position.

If the first option is preferred, there will be no change in demand, as the price is constant. However, due to falling total and average costs, profits would increase.

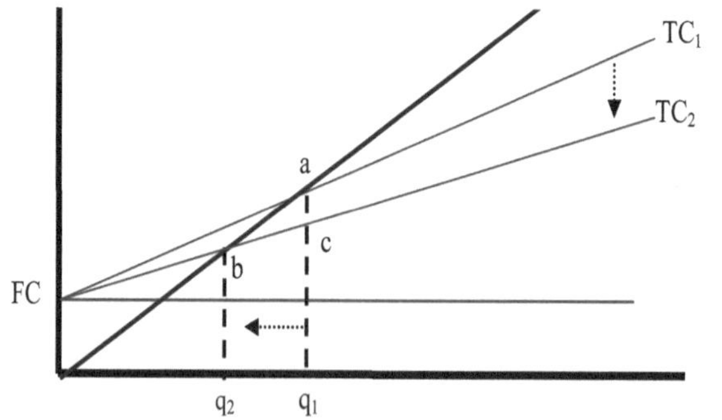

Figure: 5-5:a Impact of cost-reducing process -1 and demand

If the firm prefers second option, price will be reduced to a lower rate (see Figure: 5-5:b), while demand would increase from q_1 to q_2.

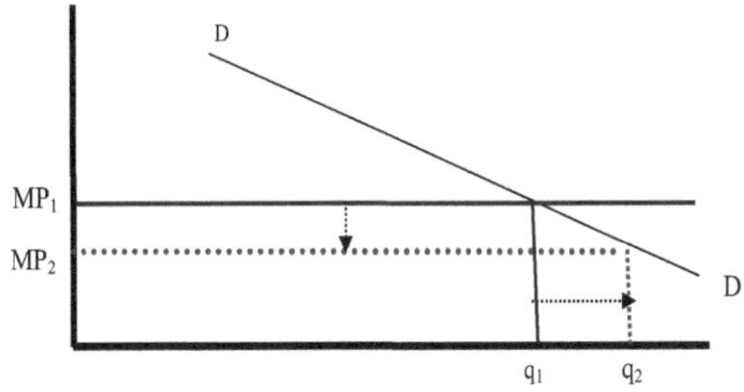

Figure: 5-5:b Impact of cost-reducing process -2 and demand

Now, assume that each consumer demands four pieces of the same product and the law of decreasing utility applies to all consumers. The market is expected to saturate at the quantity q*, at the time t. In the meantime, the enterprise is assumed to introduce cost-saving processes continually, which leads both to, reduced unit costs as well as a reduced unit price, subject to competition. How would the demand curves look like during this time span?

Figure:5-6 shows that during the time (**t**), the price line will have a downward sloping curve due to the cost-reducing processes, while at the same time marginal utility declines with successive consumption. Assume that during the time $\mathbf{t_1}$, the demand curve looks like $\mathbf{D_2D_2}$ while consumption is $\mathbf{Oq_1}$. During the time $\mathbf{t_2}$, consumption increases to $\mathbf{Oq_2}$. In the meantime, as marginal utility is decreasing, the demand curve will become relatively steeper and look like $\mathbf{D_2D_2}$. **Oq*** indicates the saturation level of markets and there will be no further increase in demand beyond this point. After this stage, the purpose of production will be to replace depreciated products.

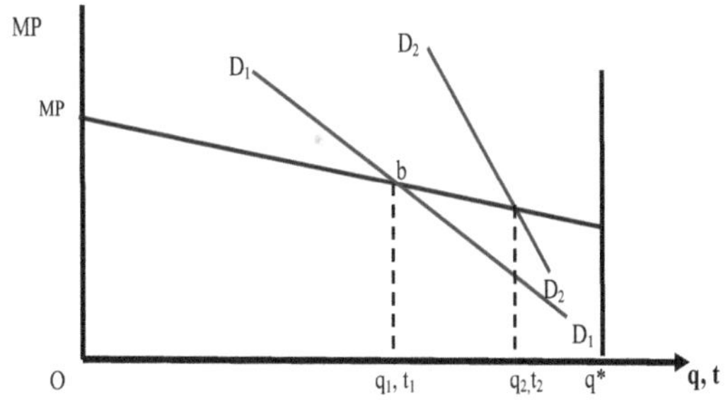

Figure: 5-6 Demand, decreasing costs and decreasing marginal utility

“New” Products & Individual Demand

When a new product is introduced, the expected consequence is the generation of a “new demand”. The strength of the new demand depends on the price and quality of the new product, cet. par. For instance, the new generation mobile-phones, which are capable of showing images of the speaker, are “new” products and the demand for them is steadily increasing. In fact, every “new” product capable of some degree of consumer satisfaction creates a “new” demand. Therefore, the expected degree of the strength of demand for new products is high. A new product involves patent ownership, which in turn, leads to monopoly profits, until the competitors catch up with similar or better products. Due to relatively high prices at the initial phase, the actual demand is expected to be relatively lower than the price and demand under more competitive conditions.

The "new" demand curve **DD** for the “new” product is likely to resemble Figure: 5-7 due to producer’s power of monopoly. Due to the monopoly position and the monopoly price, the producer would earn relatively high monopoly profits in the initial stages and demand would be lower, say at Oq_1 than the potential attainable.

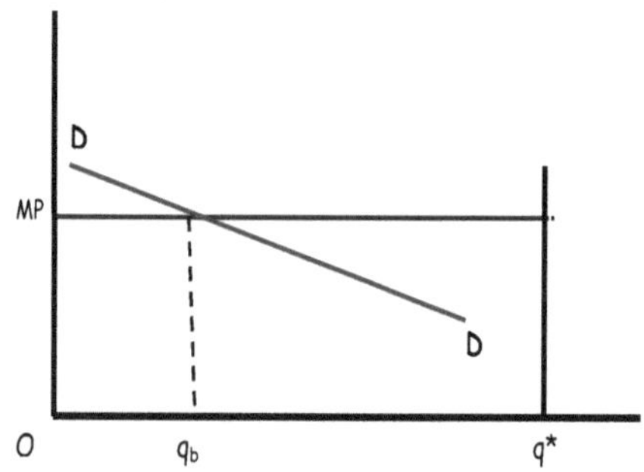

Figure: 5-7 New demand for new product

Income and Individual Demand

How would a rise in real income (purchasing-power) affect the demand on a “given” product, assuming the price, technology and the preferences remain unchanged? The case will be analyzed with the assistance of Figure: 5-8a and Figure: 5-8b.

First, let us analyze the case where each consumer buys only one piece of the product and the marginal utility of each product is constant. As a result of a rise in income, the demand curve shifts parallel to the right from $\mathbf{D_1D_1}$ to $\mathbf{D_2D_2}$

(see Figure: 5-8:a). Now, consumers can buy more of the "given" product, cet. par. As in the previous cases, **Oq*** indicates the saturation level of the market and there will be no further increase in demand beyond this point. After this stage, production will only be undertaken with the purpose of replacing depreciated products.

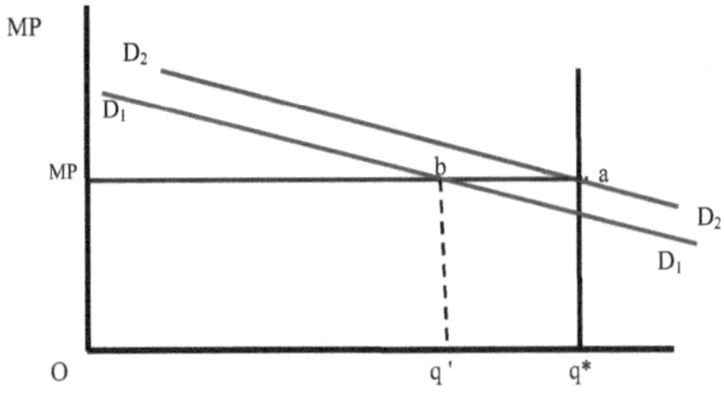

Figure: 5-8:a Income rise, constant marginal utility and demand

Now assume that in this case each consumer buys four pieces instead of one to obtain their maximum personal satisfaction level. Under the circumstances, total market saturation will be reached when all consumers have four pieces of the "given" product. As a result, as the markets saturate, the demand curve will become steeper, implying decreasing marginal utility with each successive purchase as well as price elasticity of demand. Eventually, at q* of saturation quantity the demand curve will become a vertical line (see Figure: 5-8:b).

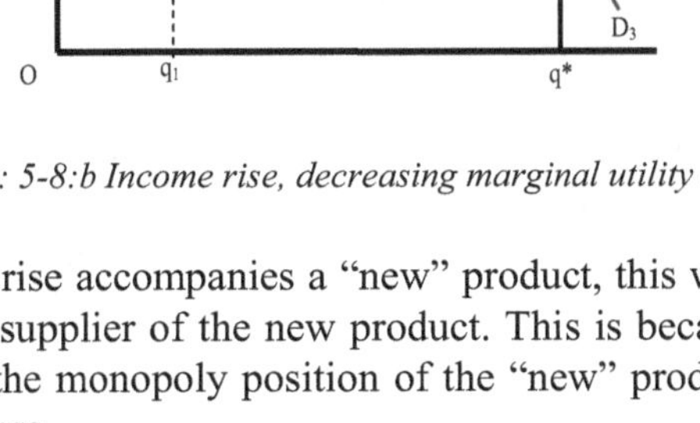

Figure: 5-8:b Income rise, decreasing marginal utility and demand

If an income rise accompanies a "new" product, this would be a golden opportunity for the supplier of the new product. This is because the realization of high profits due the monopoly position of the "new" product would likely be a much easier process.

Equilibrium: A Utopian or Scientific Concept?

A critical assumption that is acknowledged by many economists is the neoclassical doctrine claiming that there exists an "equilibrium" point. That is the assumption that the quantities demanded and those supplied are, in fact, equal. Numerous approaches have been presented by many prominent economic "scientists" in order to prove this assumption. However, even when a state of "equilibrium" emerges as a result of coincidence in a given "static" time period, it is mostly likely to occur "momentarily" and is unsustainable. For instance, supply and demand can be in equilibrium in year 2010, on 15th of January at 02:00 pm, as a result of some coincidence or other. However, this is not likely to be a sustainable position in a different time period. The probability of a sustained equilibrium in a certain time interval, say from January 2010 to March 2010, is practically zero; it has never occurred and seems unlikely ever to occur. To sustain a state of equilibrium, either supply and demand must either freeze or increase in equal proportion and in the same direction, accompanied by full employment. A decrease in supply and demand in equal proportion and in the same direction would produce partial equilibrium with less than full employment. After full-employment equilibrium, the supply has to be just sufficient to replace depreciated products and can only increase in proportion to population growth, cet. par. Otherwise, a distortion of the state of equilibrium would be inevitable. In a situation like this, due to the competitive conditions, profit rate would tend towards zero and would eventually become zero or close to zero.

However, the historical record shows the opposite of a "state of equilibrium" situation and has so far indicated no situation in which the profit rates fall to zero. The indicators clearly show that the historical process has always been dynamic and subject to economic ups and downs. The main two reasons for this are technological innovations and never ending consumer demand. Given the endless demands of consumers, the continuous introduction of "new products" and "new production processes" have always been able to sustain a dynamic fluctuating process rather than stagnating in a state of equilibrium. In order for technological innovations to be exhausted or to come to a standstill, the creative abilities of the human brain have first to be exhausted.

Since equilibrium is clearly an unrealistic assumption which only exists in the minds and studies of academicians of a neoclassical heritage, we shall adopt a more realistic assumption and make an analysis in "**economically stable conditions**" with periodic ups and downs. The concept "**economically stable conditions**" imply that:

1- Given a specified time-span, for instance a month or three months or a year, and data on some key indicators such as output level, demand level or employment level, is within "**acceptable limits**" in regard to the specific conditions of a particular country (static analysis).
2- And those fluctuations in the major specified indicators are, on average, within "**acceptable limits**" at the given time-span (dynamic analysis).

Let us compare the USA with the Western European situations. While 5-6 percent unemployment is "acceptable" for the USA, the "acceptable" rate for Western Europe is about 2-3 percent. In other words, while an unemployment rate above 3 percent is perceived as a negative sign to be corrected in Western Europe, it indicates a healthy sign in the USA. Similar differences in values and perceptions can be found in various other economic issues such as plant-utilization rate, inflation rate, and growth rate changing from country to country.

Assume that a 3 percent inflation rate, a 4 percent unemployment rate, 90 percent plant-utilization and an annual growth of 2 percent are "acceptable" values for Sweden. As long as these values remain at these acceptable limits over a given time-span, though occasionally exceeding them within acceptable margins in some instances, one can say that Sweden is economically stable.

The target of any nation should be to sustain economic stability in the long term rather than focusing on short term deviations. However, as we all know from experience, a market economy cannot always maintain stability in the long term due to the inherent features of the system. Every free market economy is and has always been, subject to fluctuations from time to time in regard to the major indicators such as inflation, growth or unemployment rate. The primary target of the economic decision-makers at such times is to revitalize the economy and put it on a "stable" path again. In other words, measures have to be taken to bring the economy back to its acceptable limits some of which prove successful while others fail to produce a satisfactory outcome. As is commonly known, various kinds of economic measures have been introduced over the years to bring the European, USA and Japanese economies into line and to put the economy back on track without much success. These prevailing long-lasting economic problems may qualify the developed nations to be considered as a "**faulty stability**", because the economies seem to be stabilized under undesirable conditions.

Concluding Remarks

Demand is an indispensable precondition of all production. In the absence of demand there would be no production of goods or services to be marketed. The magnitude of the supply of products also depends on the demand schedule. All these are the well-known facts of economic science and are quoted in economic text books. The main difference in this chapter from the mainstream approaches is the analytical approach of the demand schedule being based on technological innovation.

Chapter 6: FUNCTIONAL INCOME DISTRIBUTION

Unequal distribution of income has always been one of the major problem areas and often a cause of embarrassment for both economic science and economists. The problem does not refer only to income distribution and the related inequalities among individuals, households, and classes but also to global income distribution and inequalities among nations. Global income distribution is especially disappointing when one considers it in terms of the expectations from globalization.

So called "leftist" economists have always tended to emphasize income inequalities and supported redistribution of income in favor of less favored groups in society. The conservative right wing economists, on the other hand, tended to give priority to capital accumulation rather than income redistribution which they believed would enlarge the cake to be shared out and as a result, all income groups were expected to be better off. The critical question in regard to the long term economic interests of society is whether priority should be given to more fair income redistribution or to capital accumulation. Perhaps a combination of two policies would have a more positive impact in the long term.

The individual or household distribution of income has always been a subject of lively debate amongst economists, because the problem has always remained unresolved. It refers, basically, to the incomes of individuals and households. Functional income distribution, on the other hand, has been the subject to endless arguments ever since the appearance of economics as a separate discipline. Functional income distribution studies the distribution of income among two basic classes; workers receiving wages (**W**) and capitalists receiving profits ($\boldsymbol{\pi}$) which includes interest rate and rent.

The definition of "capital" was discussed in Part-2 where it was defined as any kind of expenditure with the purpose of producing goods and/or services in order to make profits. Capital can be expressed in terms of money, but it is not purely money. It covers all expenditures on the inputs of production ranging from patents or licenses for technology, to raw materials, semi-finished products, and energy and wages for the laborers. A capitalist assumes that he/she may risk loosing some or all of his/her expenditure and will receive, in return, some profit. Except in the minds of academicians of the neoclassical heritage, in reality there is no such thing as the "productivity of capital". It exists only in unfeasible world of utopian models, because the two sole productive factors are nature and labor-power, as discussed in Part-2.

An Ideal Income Distribution

Pareto optimum

The Pareto optimum allocation of income implies that one cannot redistribute income to make at least one individual better off without making others worse off. To put it differently, if it is possible to improve an individual's income position without worsening someone else's position, distribution is not yet in Pareto optimum.

Assumptions of the doctrine:

- A perfectly competitive market.
- Two producers and two consumers.
- A "given" technology.
- "Given" prices.
- "Given" terms-of-trade.
- "Given" tastes.
- A general equilibrium in markets.

The Pareto optimality depends on above mentioned utopian equilibrium and perfect competition conditions as well as "given" values. Many economists see some merits in such a deficient and utopian theory to explain actual economic developments. Another serious shortcoming of the theory is the lack of awareness of the impact of technological progress on income distribution.

Figure:6-1 shows with the assistance of the so-called "Edgeworth Box" where the indifference curves of two consumers ($\mathbf{O_a}$ and $\mathbf{O_b}$) are tangential. The Figure shows that there is more than one Pareto optimum points such as $\mathbf{D^1}$ and $\mathbf{D^2}$. Thus, at any equilibrium point along the **OaD** line, one should not attempt to redistribute income. **D,** $\mathbf{D^1}$ and $\mathbf{D^2}$ denote the possible equilibrium points and **TT** the transformation curve.

In fact, it seems that the Pareto optimum argument as such appears to serve the interests of higher income groups rather than aiming at a more equal income distribution, given the present situation of the unequal distribution of income. Because, redistribution of income in favor of the poorer income groups would lead to a deterioration of the high income groups' incomes, that means at least one well-off individual of the upper class income group will be worse-off after the redistribution and therefore it is better not to change the present equilibrium condition which is at the Pareto optimum, though this is not an egalitarian state of affairs.

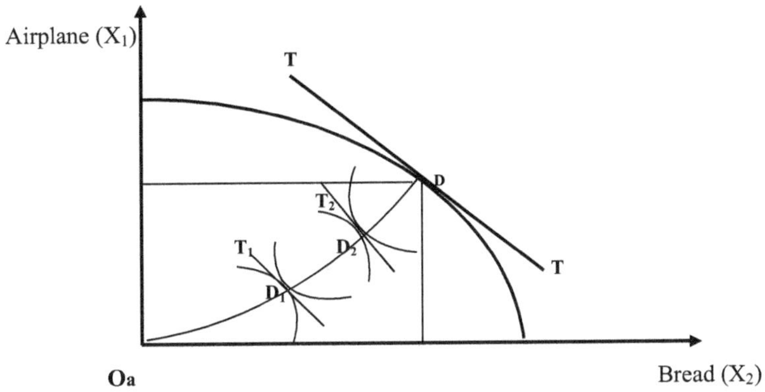

Figure: 6-1 Pareto optimum income distribution

Optimum Functional Income Distribution

The Classical economists used to divide the income receiving groups into two distinct groups in their income analysis:

1- Labor-power (i.e., laborers or workers) (**L**); and
2- Capitalists (**K**).

The successive economists of the neoclassical heritage continued to use models with the same two production factors (**L** and **K**); however, **L** was now standing for "labor" not for "labor-power". After Solow's contribution in the 1950s, economists began to use a third productive factor in their models along with **L** and **K**; i.e., technology (**T**), a critical "re-discovery" of an important input of production. Nowadays, it is popular to use a forth factor of production in equations, human capital (**H**). It would not be a surprise at all to encounter a fifth factor; for example "institutions" in the near future production analyses.

As discussed earlier, functional income consists of the wages (**w**) received by workers and the profits (π) of capitalists, including interest and rent incomes. However, it does not seem quite appropriate to consider rent and especially interest income as a sub-income of profits in contemporary income models. The reason behind this is the fact that a considerably large part of interest incomes do not come from loans for investment. There are huge amounts of financial resources looking for opportunities to exploit the position of governments or enterprises that are in financial straits. Sometimes, even enterprises use such opportunities to increase enterprise incomes. For instance, in years 2000 and 2001 a considerable part of the annual income of Turkish large-scale enterprises came from such financial transactions (see Table: 6-1). Thus, it would be an error to consider that all interest incomes come from loaned money used for investments. However, in this section, incomes from such financial transactions shall be ignored and adopt the position, like the Classical economists that functional income originates from two sources which are;

1- wages (w) received for the labor services hired; and
2- profits (π) received for the risks assumed.

The critical question here is; which kind of functional income distribution should be accepted as the optimum? In other words, what should be the optimum wages and profits?

The answer to this critical question is bound to be subjective and ideological, for it is impossible to provide an objective answer that is free of all value and ideological judgments on social, political or economic issues where two income receiving groups display diametrically opposite economic interests. One income group has to gain or lose at the cost of the other group. However, if capital ownership could be distributed equally amongst all individuals, the optimality problem would be quite different (Gürak, 2004).

Table:6-1: Non-industrial Income of the Largest 500 Private Enterprises and the Ratio of Net Profits (before tax) (000 TL)

	Other incomes (1)	Change (%)	Net profits (2)	Change (%)	1:2 (%)
1982	18,438,880	-	120,558,000	-	15.3
1983	37,782,726	104.9	192,819,000	59.9	19.6
1984	65,888,349	74.4	316,573,000	64.2	20.8
1985	104,501,915	58.6	433,462,000	36.9	24.1
1986	204,558,231	95.7	663,879,000	53.2	30.8
1987	285,321,034	39.5	1,593,763,022	140.1	17.9
1988	632,251,158	121.6	2,494,087,226	56.5	25.4
1989	1,299,143,459	105.5	4,189,117,743	68.0	31.0
1990	2,224,648,247	71.2	6,679,368,414	59.4	33.3
1991	3,721,503,901	67.3	7,282,297,783	9.0	51.1
1992	7,794,368,122	169.7	20,052,422,789	175.4	38.9
1993	17,548,778,004	125.1	43,093,652,150	114.9	40.7
1994	57,694,648,710	228.8	105,587,224,479	145.0	54.6
1995	96,191,958,000	66.7	206,857,875,064	95.9	46.5

Source: İSO, Sanayi Odası Dergisi (Istanbul Chamber of Industry), Sept.-1996, No:366, p.82

In the following sub-sections the focus will be on the functional distribution of income amongst two classes; workers and capitalists. An important detail of the analysis will be the impact of the available technologies employed and technological progress on functional income distribution.

The subjects to be discussed are:

1- Functional income distribution with a “given” technology.
2- Functional income distribution after efficiency, i.e., micro-productivity growth, “given” a specific technology.
3- Impact of technological progress on functional income distribution.
4- Global functional income distribution.

1- Functional income distribution: with a “given” technology

The functional income distribution analysis of neoclassical doctrine is based on the assumption of the marginal productivity concept of various factors. Since the assumption of the marginal productivity of capital is purely an imaginary concept, we shall instead chose a method based on the "added value produced" criterion in income distribution analysis. This approach is also used globally for national account statistics to measure growth and prosperity.

Assumptions:

- Prices for produced goods and services are a “given”.
- Technology employed is a “given”.
- No scarcity of endowed labor force required for efficient production.

Functional income in terms of the value added (**VA**) approach can be shown as below:

$$VA = W + \Pi$$

where **W** stands for total wages and **Π** for total profits. The interests of these two income groups are diametrically opposed. If the share of wages in “added value” increases the share of profits is bound to decline and vice versa.

Figure:6-2 shows this contradictory relationship between income classes at an enterprise level. Let us assume that the initial position is at **B**, the break-even point where costs equals enterprise income. Given the wage level and the price of the product, the area denoted by **TR-TC-B** indicates the total profits of the enterprise. If the wage level increases for some reason, cet. par., the total cost curve (**TC’**) of the enterprise will shift further away from the origin and the new profit area will be smaller (**TR-TC’-B’**).

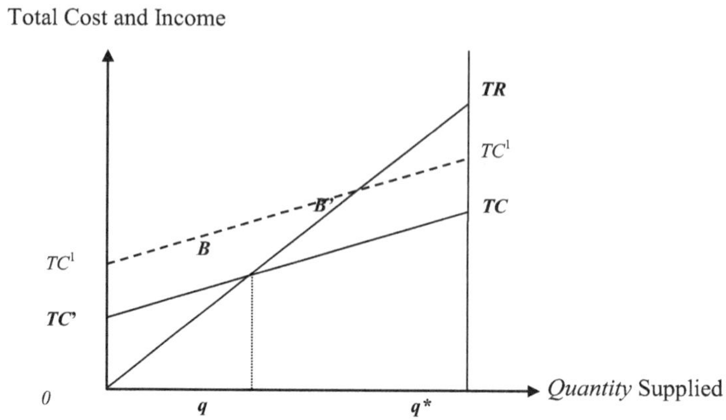

Figure: 6-2

2- "Efficiency Growth" & Income Distribution

Given the wage level, the price of the product and the technology, and assume that an improvement is made in efficiency. As a result, the relative share of the wages in total added value would decline, while the share of the profits would increase leading to the laborers being relatively worse-off in terms of income (see Table: 6-2), cet. par. In other words, capital owners receive a larger slice of the pie while the laborers would have to settle for a smaller portion, cet. par.

Given time, the employees would, quite likely, attempt to increase their wage level which is dependent on their negotiation power and the market conditions. If wages increase with a given technology, i.e., method of production, the relative share of wages would improve but at the expense of the capitalists.

The nominal wage level is likely to increase in the long run as the economy grows. What happens to the real wage level is dependent, in the long term, on the technological progress, the competitors' prices and the demand for the product along with the negotiating power of the trade unions.

Table: 6-2: Impacts of efficiency (micro-productivity) growth on income Price, technology and wage-level "given"

Cause of efficiency growth	VA:K	VA:L	π:VA	w:VA	Outcome
Restructuring production	↑	↑	↑	↓	Income distribution shifts in favor of capital-owner
Increasing capacity utilization	↑	↑	↑	↓	--- " ---
Multiple shift work	↑	↑	↑	↓	--- " ---
Reallocating resources	↑	↑	↑	↓	--- " ---
Improved education system	↑	↑	↑	↓	--- " ---
Learning By Doing	↑	↑	↑	↓	--- " ---
Improved Safety & Sanitary	↑	↑	↑	↓	--- " ---
Participation in decision-making	↑	↑	↑	↓	--- " ---

***VA:** Value added. **K:** Total costs + wages, **L:** Labor-force; employees, .**w:** Wage .**π:** Profit*

3- "Technological Productivity Growth" & Income Distribution

This section will analyze the impact of technological progress on functional income distribution. The main assumptions are as follows:

- New knowledge (new technologies).
- Constant price.
- No decline in the effective demand.

Hypothetical initial values:

$\mathbf{w_t} = 100$ TL

$\mathbf{L_t} = 500$ employees

$\mathbf{LWC_t} = \mathbf{w_t} * \mathbf{L_t} = 100*500 = 50{,}000$ TL

$\mathbf{OC_t} = \mathbf{FC_t} + \mathbf{VC_t} = 80{,}000$ TL

$\mathbf{TC_t} = \mathbf{LWC_t} + \mathbf{OC_t} = 50{,}000+80{,}000= 130{,}000$ TL

Total income (**TR**) of the enterprise:

$\mathbf{p_t} = 15$ TL

$\mathbf{q_t} = 10{,}000$ units

$\mathbf{TR_t = p_t}$ (15)* $\mathbf{q_t}$ (10,000) = 150,000 TL

Profits (**π**), profit rate (**r**) and added value (**VA**) are.

$\boldsymbol{\pi_t} = \mathbf{TR_t - TC_t}$ = 150,000 - 130,000 = 20,000 TL

$r_t = \pi_t : TC_t =$ ~% 15

$\mathbf{VA_t} = \boldsymbol{\pi_t} + \mathbf{LWC_t}$ = 20,000+50,000 = 70,000 TL

And, the functional income distribution:

$\pi_t : VA_t$ = 20,000:70,000 = ~% 28 (capitalist's share)

$LWC_t : VA_t$ = 50,000:70,000 = ~%71 (workers' share)

In the analysis below, we shall see how technological progress affects functional income distribution. We shall study first the impact of labor(-er)-saving then input-saving and finally output-increasing technological progress, in that order.

Case-1 Labor(-er)-saving technological progress

Assume that the producing enterprise introduces a new production method which increases the productivity per employee by using labor saving inputs and the number of employees declines from 500 to 300. The price of product, wage and other input costs are assumed to be constant. What would be the impact of the technological progress on the functional income distribution?

$\mathbf{LWC_{t+1}} = \mathbf{w_{t+1}} * \mathbf{L_{t+1}}$ = 100*300 = 30,000 TL

$\mathbf{OC_{t+1}} = \mathbf{FC_{t+1}} + \mathbf{VC_{t+1}}$ = 80,000 TL

$TC_{t+1} = LWC_{t+1} + OC_{t+1}$ = 110,000 TL

And,

$\pi_{t+1} = TR_{t+1} - TC_{t+1}$ = 40,000 TL

$r_{t+1} = \pi_{t+1} : TC_{t+1}$ = ~ % 36

$\mathbf{VA_{t+1}} = \boldsymbol{\pi_{t+1}} + \mathbf{LWC_{t+1}}$=40,000+30,000=70,000 TL

New functional income distribution would look like:

$\pi_{t+1} : VA_{t+1}$ = ~ % 57 (capitalist's share)

$LWC_{t+1}:VA_{t+1}$=30,000:70,000= ~ % 43 (workers' share)

Due to the decline in the number of employees who continue to produce the same amount of output, the percentage of profit in total added value (**π:VA**) increases from 37 percent to 57 percent, while that of the wage-earners' (**LWC:VA**) drops from 62 percent to 43 percent. Now, in terms of functional income, capital owners are better-off after the introduction of the technological progress while the workers are worse-off, cet. par. This outcome clearly shows why enterprises are in a constant search for new knowledge on production, i.e., new technologies, in order to reduce production costs.

Case-2 Input-saving Technological Progress

Assume that the initial values prevail and the enterprise introduces a new production method which reduces the quantities of non-labor inputs. Say that operating costs (**OC**) decline from 80,000 TL to 60,000 TL.

$\mathbf{w_t = w_{t+1}}$ =100 TL

$\mathbf{L_t = L_{t+1}}$ = 500 employees

$\mathbf{LWC_t = LWC_{t+1}}$ = 100*500 = 50,000 TL

$\mathbf{OC_t = FC_t + VC_t}$ =80,000 TL

$OC_{t+1}=FC_{t+1}+VC_{t+1}$=60,000 TL

$\mathbf{TC_{t+1}=LWC_{t+1}+OC_{t+1}}$=50,000+60,000=110,000 TL

Total income (**TR**) of the enterprise is:

$\mathbf{p_t = p_{t+1}}$ = 15 TL

$\mathbf{q_t = q_{t+1}}$ = 10,000 pieces

$TR_t = TR_{t+1}$ = 150,000 TL

New size of profits (**π**), profit rate (**r**) and added value (**VA**) would be:

$\mathbf{\pi_{t+1} = TR_{t+1} - TC_{t+1}}$=150,000-110,000 = 40,000 TL

$r_{t+1} = \pi_{t+1} : TC_{t+1}$ = ~% 36

$\mathbf{VA_{t+1} = \pi_{t+1} + LWC_{t+1}}$=40,000+50,000= 90,000 TL

And, inevitably, functional distribution of income would also be affected.

$\pi_{t+1} : VA_{t+1}$ =40,000:90,000 = ~ % 44 (capitalist's share)

$LWC_{t+1} : VA_{t+1}$ =50,000:90,000= ~% 55 (workers' share)

As a result of the new technology, the capitalist's share in total added value (**π:VA**) increases from 28 percent to 44 percent, while wage-earners share (**LWC :VA**) declines from 71 percent to 55 percent. In the meantime, the profit rate jumps from 15 percent to 36 percent. We see clearly once again why enterprises are in a constant search for some new knowledge (technology) which reduces cost.

Case-3 Output Increasing Technological Progress

Assume once again that initial values prevail and the enterprise introduces a new production method which increases the quantities supplied with given inputs and number of employees. Say that the quantity supplied after the introduction of a new technology increases from 10,000 units to 12,000 units which inevitably would affect the distribution of the functional income.

$\mathbf{\Delta q}$ = 2,000 units

q_t = 10,000

$\mathbf{q_{t+1}}$ = 12,000 units

$\mathbf{OC_t} = \mathbf{OC_{t+1}} = 80{,}000$ TL
$\mathbf{TC_t} = \mathbf{TC_{t+1}} = = 130{,}000$ TL
$\mathbf{TR_t} = 150{,}000$ TL
$\mathbf{TR_{t+1}} = 15TL * 12{,}000 = 180{,}000$ TL

Due to technological progress, capitalist's share in total added value will increase while that of wages decline, indicating a deterioration for the employees.

$\boldsymbol{\pi_{t+1}} = \mathbf{TR_{t+1}} - \mathbf{TC_{t+1}} = 180{,}000 - 130{,}000 = 50{,}000$ TL
$r_{t+1} = \pi_{t+1} : TC_{t+1} = \sim \% \ 27$
$\mathbf{VA_{t+1}} = \boldsymbol{\pi_{t+1}} + \mathbf{LWC_{t+1}} = 50{,}000 + 50{,}000 = 100{,}000$ TL

New functional income distribution would look like as follows:

$\pi_{t+1} : VA_{t+1} = 50{,}000 : 100{,}000 = \sim \% \ 50$ (capital's share)
$LWC_{t+1} : VA_{t+1} = 50{,}000 : 100{,}000 = \sim \% \ 50$ (workers' share)

Once again we observe that given the prices, wage level and demand, any technological progress produces results in favor of the capital owners, which is why enterprises constantly seek new technologies.

Wage rise in the medium & the long term & its impact on income distribution

In the analyses above we assumed a constant wage level in the short term until new wage negotiations between employee and employer were entered into. A constant wage level and technological progress seemed to erode the share of income of the employees even though the real wage may remain constant. When negotiations begin employee unions would normally demand a wage-rise while the employer unions attempt to resist this increase. The rise of the wage level depends largely on the negotiating power of the employee unions, the competitive conditions and the demand for products. Any improvement in favor of one income group would naturally imply deterioration in the relative share of the other group. However, wage negotiations, not infrequently, conclude with a percentage wage rise.

Assume that, as in **Case-1** above, the new technology reduces the number of employees and the labor-unions succeed in raising the wage level, say by 50 percent, cet. par..

$\mathbf{\Delta w} = 50$ TL (wage-rise)

New wage:

$w_{t+2} = 150$ TL $\quad (w_{t+1} + \Delta w)$

The wage cost of production would naturally increase and pull total costs upwards.

$\mathbf{LWC_{t+2}} = \mathbf{w_{t+2}} * \mathbf{L_{t+2}} = 150 * 300 = 45{,}000$ TL
$\mathbf{OC_{t+2}} = \mathbf{FC_{t+2}} + \mathbf{VC_{t+2}} = \quad 80{,}000$ TL

$TC_{t+2} = LWC_{t+2} + OC_{t+2} =$ 125,000 TL

And,

$\pi_{t+2} = TR_{t+2} - TC_{t+2} = 25{,}000$ TL

$r_{t+2} = \pi_{t+2} : TC_{t+2} = \%\ 20$

$\mathbf{VA_{t+2} = \pi_{t+2} + LWC_{t+2}} = 25{,}000 + 45{,}000 = 70{,}000$

New shares in total income:

$\pi_{t+2}\sim : VA_{t+2} =$ $\sim \%\ 35$ (capital's share)

$LWC_{t+2} : VA_{t+2} = 45{,}000 : 70{,}000 = \sim \%\ 64$ (workers' share)

Given the size of profits and the total added value, the share of the capital in total added value declines from 60 percent to about 35 percent, simply because of a wage rise while the share of the wage-earner increases to about 64 percent, cet. par. The wage rise clearly improves functional income distribution in favor of the working class and that is why enterprises always tend to resist wage rises.

4- Technological Imperfections & Global Income Distribution

It is not only the competition, productivity, prosperity and the income distribution of a country but also the global competition, productivity, prosperity and income distribution that are affected by technological developments. Per capita income as well as gross domestic product (GDP) is higher in high-technology countries compared to the technologically less advanced countries. For instance, Turkish enterprises, on average, use less advanced technologies in their production in comparison to Japanese enterprises. This is the underlying cause of lower per capita productivity and income in Turkey.

Let us analyze these global differences with the assistance of some hypothetical figures.

"Technology-intensive" & "labor-intensive" methods of production

Two products - two technologies - two countries

Assumptions:

- Two countries (the developed (**X**): the less developed (**Y**))
- Each country produces only one product.
- Developed country (**X**) employs advanced technology while the less developed country (**Y**) employs relatively less advanced technology.
- Due to technological difference, the wage level in the developed country (**X**) is, say four times, higher than in the less developed country (**Y**). In

contrast, country (**X**) requires only one tenth of the employees compared to country (**Y**) to realize efficient production.

- In each country production is undertaken by one enterprise only with "**exactly equal" sum of capital** (**K**), say 100,000 TL.

Hypothetical values:

Developed Country (X)	Less Developed Country (Y)	
$\mathbf{w^x} = 400$	$\mathbf{w^y} = 100$	
$\mathbf{L^x} = 50$ employee	$\mathbf{L^y} = 500$ employee	
$\mathbf{LWC^x} = 20{,}000$	$\mathbf{LWC^y}=50{,}000$	**(LWC=w*L)**
$\mathbf{OC^x} = 80{,}000$	$\mathbf{OC^y} = 50{,}000$	**(OC=FC+VC)**
$\mathbf{K^x} = \mathbf{TC^x} = 100{,}000$ TL	$\mathbf{K^y}=\mathbf{TC^y}=100{,}000$ TL	**(K=OC+LWC)**

Further assume that prices, quantities supplied and total incomes are as follows:

$\mathbf{p^x} = 200$ TL	$\mathbf{p^y} = 150$ TL
$\mathbf{q^x} = 1{,}000$	$\mathbf{q^y} = 1{,}000$
$\mathbf{TR^x} = 200{,}000$ TL	$\mathbf{TR^y} = 150{,}000$ TL

It is highly likely that the higher percentage share and cost of the technologically advanced inputs of production would make the ratio of non-wage costs (**OC**) to total cost (**TC**) look higher in the developed country-X than in the less developed country-Y.

$OC^x : K^x > OC^y : K^y$

On the other hand, since the technology employed in the less developed country is relatively less advanced, the ratio of non-wage costs (**OC**) to the capital invested is only 50 percent.

Accordingly, the size of profits (**π**), rate of profits (**r**) and added value (**VA**) would look like as follows:

$\pi^x=TR^x - TC^x= 100{,}000$ TL	$\pi^y= TR^y - TC^y= 50{,}000$ TL
$\mathbf{r^x} = \pi^x : TC^x = \%\ 100$	$\mathbf{r^y} = \pi^y : TC^y = \%\ 50$
$\mathbf{VA^x}=\pi^x + \mathbf{LWC^x}=120{,}000$TL	$\mathbf{VA^y}= \pi^x + \mathbf{LWC^x}=100{,}000$ TL

And income distribution:

$\pi^x : \mathbf{VA^x} = \sim \%\ 83$	$\pi^y : \mathbf{VA^y} = \%\ 50$
$LWC^x_t : VA^x_t = \sim \%\ 16$	$LWC^y_t : VA^y_t = \%\ 50$

The hypothetical figures show that 100,000 TL invested as capital in high technology produces a value worth of 120,000 TL while the less advanced technology produces only 100,000 TL worth value. By the way, not only the added value but also the wage level and profitability are higher in the more advanced technology using country.

Given the insights above, in order to reduce and eventually eliminate the global income differences, it is imperative to eliminate technological differences in production and the imperfections in the global technology markets. In other words, the technological infrastructure has to be improved and the employment of advanced technologies has to be promoted in the less developed countries in order to increase productivity.

Concluding Remarks

In the short term, given the technology and the wage level, an efficiency (micro-productivity) growth is expected to increase the total added value, cet. par. while;

1- The proportionate share of wages decline.
2- The proportionate share of profits increase.

As a result, functional income distribution changes in favor of the capitalists and against the workers.

In the long run, total added value shows a tendency to rise alongside technological progress; a process called "technological productivity growth". Given the wage level, technological progress causes a change in functional income distribution in favor of the capitalist, not the workers, at the start of the process. However, in time, how the income or total amount of added value is distributed among the income groups depends on the bargaining power of the employee and employer unions along with the prevailing competitive conditions. Any change in any direction of functional income distribution leads to a deterioration in the income of the other group.

As to the global distribution of income among countries; it is determined, to significant extent, by the technology market conditions, or to be more specific, by the imperfections in the technology market in regard to who owns and controls the technology and its distribution (see Gürak; 1990 and 2003).

Chapter 7: GROWTH

Productivity and productivity growth are two popular concepts frequently referred to, not only by academicians but also by the "man on the street" in daily conversations. Though they are the basic concepts of economics, they often mean different things depending on who is referring to it and on the subject matter in question. The concept of productivity for the economist often has a different meaning than when the same concept is used by a politician, the military, teachers or the mayor of a town. There is a huge and substantial difference between a student's productivity and a carpenter's productivity or a musician's productivity. In order to avoid confusion, it is necessary to define the concept within the framework of a particular analysis.

Productivity (V)

The concept of **productivity** simply indicates the relationship between the output and the inputs of production in terms of values or quantities. Thus, **productivity** can be defined as a "static" concept which refers to the relationships between "inputs" and "outputs" of production. To put it differently, productivity can be described as the "**capability to produce**" or rather, as the "**capability to add value**".

At an enterprise level, or synonymously for an entrepreneur, the concept of productivity normally means profitability with respect to the inputs and outputs of production. The underlying explanation of this behavior is that enterprises are established with the sole purpose of making profits, preferably the highest possible profit rate. If an enterprise is unproductive, e.g., not making profits, it loses the basic motive of its existence. In other words, every enterprise engaged in production has to be productive (profitable) for survival, as previously discussed in Section 5.

For national economies, the criterion of productivity normally means the capability to produce value consisting of enterprise profits and wages, cet. par., which has a different implication for macro-economic analysis. In other words, at the macro-economic level the concept productivity is related to the capability to add value (**VA**).

Before proceeding with the analysis, it would be useful to point out the differences between "productivity", "economic efficiency", "technical efficiency" as well as "profitability" from the perspective used throughout the analysis.

- **Productivity (V)**: Producing value.
- **Economic Efficiency (EE)**: maximizing the difference between total value of inputs and total value of outputs.
- **Technical Efficiency (TE)**: maximizing the quantity supplied while minimizing the quantities employed.
- **Profit Rate (r)**: profit : total cost of production [$\boldsymbol{\pi : (p*q + w* L)}$]

Measuring productivity

As a static concept, the analysis of "productivity" can be carried out from two different points of view:

1- Quantities; and
2- Values.

The Quantitative Analysis

The "quantitative analysis" of productivity contains some inconveniences and difficulties. For instance, assuming only one type of output, e.g., a homogeneous product, there would be no serious difficulties in measuring the productivity per employee, or "partial" factor productivity (**PFP**) in terms of "one given input". But, when heterogeneous outputs or more than one input is involved, this measurement becomes cumbersome, even unlikely. Assume that 110 tires are produced in a plant and the inputs of production are 10 workers, 20 Kg rubber, 100 KW energy and two machines. Partial factor productivity (**PFP**) with reference to employee can be shown as output per employee.

PFP= Output : Employees= 110:10= 11 Tires Per employee (1)

Or, alternatively:

PFP = 110 :20 Kg Rubber = 5.5 Tires : 1 Kg Rubber (2)

Equation (1) shows that one employee produces 11 tires, and equation (2) shows that 5.5 tires are produced with 1 Kg rubber.

But, what if the inputs are more than one? Would it still be possible to measure total or partial productivity? Equations (3) and (4) give the answer.

V=110 pieces tires:10 employees+10 Kg rubber+2 machineries= **???** (3)

PFP = 110 pieces tires : 10 employees+10 Kg rubber=**???** (4)

It would not be an exaggeration to claim that it is not possible to measure the total input productivity (**V**) in terms of quantities.

V = Quantity supplied : Employees + All other inputs = **???** (5)

Let us use some specific products in eq. 5:

V = 20 Tables : Employees + Quantities of all other inputs = **???** (5a)

There is more to it. Let us re-consider the output per employee analysis in quantities and take a look at the output of two competitive firms in the auto industry. Assume that one worker at the Mercedes plant produces 5 cars while at the Ford plant one worker produces 7 cars a day. Is the worker at Ford's automobile plant more productive than the worker at the Mercedes plant?

The answer is in the negative. It would be irrational and misleading to make such a comparison. Because, for a sound comparative analysis the output of both firms has to be the same, e.g., homogeneous and employ the same technology. This is a case encountered in the neoclassical economic analysis only.

In short, the quantitative analysis of productivity with two or more inputs of production is not of much value in analysis, while partial analysis with regard to one input only can give us some useful insights.

Measuring qualitative differences

The problem of the measurement of productivity in terms of quantities is not limited to the above mentioned problems. Let us reconsider per employee output in terms of the quantities supplied and analyze the productivity of two competitive enterprises. Assume that an employee at the Volvo plant produces five cars while at Seat the number is seven. Would it be a proper statement of fact that the employee at Volvo is more productive?

The answer is again in the negative. Given the qualitative differences, it would look like comparing oranges with apples. To make a proper and fair comparison of productivity, not only the cars supplied but also the technology employed, the quality of the inputs of production and the merits of labor-force have to be the same; that is **homogeneous**. This happens only in the scientific (?) models of the neoclassical heritage.

In short, a quantitative approach to the measurement of productivity does not seem to be enlightening.

Value Analysis of "Productivity"

Given the specific measurement problems of a quantitative approach, it seems less cumbersome and more explanatory to use an approach based on "value" or to be more specific the value added to the product (**VA**). The value added to the product is the sum of total wages (**LWC=wL=W**) and total profits (**Π**), including interest payments but excluding taxes.

$VA = LWC + \pi$

Assume that total non-wage cost of inputs is 80 TL, total wage cost 20 TL, profit 10 TL, and total revenue after sale 110 TL which provides an added value worth 30 TL. This enterprise is said to be productive both at the enterprise level and at the country level.

VA = 20 + 10 = 30 TL

The proportional productivity relation is:

V = VA : TC

where **V** stands for productivity. Even when the enterprise makes a zero profit (**π=0**) it can be regarded as productive from the national economy point of view because it pays wages and the **VA** is greater than zero.

Assume that, given the total costs including wages, the unit price increases, say due to a shift in demand, and total revenue grows from 110 TL to 120 TL. Now the VA produced is 10 TL higher, although the quantity supplied has not changed. The additional 10 TL is in fact "rent", a type of "unearned" income, e.g., not the result of the productive employment of resources.

Measuring productivity in terms of value is not free of problems, either. However, it seems to be less cumbersome, more reliable and a less complex method than to use the quantitative approach. Using the **VA** criterion, the productivity analysis can be divided into 5 broad sub-categories. The first one is "total factor productivity" (**TFP**):

1- **TFP= VA:TM** = Wage + profit : Total prod. cost

= **VA:(OC+LWC)** = **(wL+ π) : (p^i*q^i + wL)**

Partial factor productivities are indicated below:

2- **PFP= VA:L**= Wage + profit : Per employee

3- **PFP= VA :t**= Wage+ profit : Unit time employed

4- **PFP= VA:W**= Wage + profit : Total wage bill

5- **PFP= VA:OC**= Wage+ profit : Non-wage costs

TM, denotes total production costs; **L**, employees; **t,** unit time employed; **W, (L*w)** total wage bill; and **OC**, non-wage input costs.

An alternative value measurement

If the value added to the product (**VA**) is replaced with total income (**Y**) in the definition of productivity, would we be measuring productivity or something else?

V = Total income : Total expenditure = **Y : TC**

Or, alternatively;

$$= (p^f * q^f) : (p^i * q^i + wL) \qquad (6)$$

According to some economists, eq.6 measures the productivity, which is, in fact, the proportional relationship between income and expenditure i.e., costs. A closer and careful examination would not overlook that what is actually being measured is, in fact, not productivity but profitability. As discussed above, for an enterprise profitability may imply productivity but for the national economy productivity should be measured in terms of the value added where profitability represents only one component of the value added.

Let us take a closer look at eq.-6 with the hypothetical data below. Assume that

Y=110 and **TC**=100.

$$\mathbf{V} = \mathbf{Y{:}TC} = 110{:}100 = \mathbf{1.1} \quad (7)$$

Eq.-7 where **r** denotes profitability, it has exactly the same result as in eq.-6.

$$\mathbf{r} = \mathbf{Y\text{-}TC : TC} = \%\ 10 \quad (8)$$

In other words, stating that the enterprise productivity is 1.1 has the identical implication as when enterprise profitability is 10 percent. It is substantially the same for an enterprise, though not for the national economy. Eq.-9 is just a different version of eq.-7 and eq.-8.

$$\boldsymbol{\pi} = \mathbf{Y} - \mathbf{TC} = 110 - 100 = 10 \text{ TL} \quad (9)$$

Optimum Productivity

The optimum position implies that productivity is at its peak, i.e., the highest attainable level with a given technology and labor-force quality. This is the highest productivity level. For instance, given the technology and the labor-force quality, the inputs are assumed to be acquired at the lowest cost and the income obtainable is at its highest possible level while the plant capacity used and the supplied quantities are assumed to be at the maximum possible level. There is no waste of any resources. Under the circumstances, both the economic efficiency (**EE**) as well as technical efficiency (**TE**) would be at maximum levels along with the size of profits (**π**) and the profit rate (**r**).

The critical question is; is it likely for an enterprise to maintain production at an optimum level? The fact is that, generally, 80 to 90 percent utilization of plant capacity is considered a good performance. When capacity utilization shows a trend towards higher level capacity utilization supported by demand, there would be a good incentive for the enterprise either to expand capacity or to set up a new plant with new investments.

"Productivity Growth"

Productivity growth is a dynamic concept indicating an increase in regard to a specific criterion whether it is value or quantity, implying economic growth designated by "**g**". Our reference will be a value based approach to productivity. Productivity does not only improve the competitive strength of enterprises, but also helps to increase their total value added and in doing so increases the individual and national economic welfare.

The study of the causes of productivity growth is important in order to understand its short and long term developments. Thus, productivity growth will be considered in three sub-categories:

1- Efficiency (micro-productivity) growth (technology "given")
2- Technological (macro) productivity growth (new products and/or production methods).
3- Horizontal expansion (technology "given").

Growth-1: Efficiency increase

An increase in productivity does not take place through the introduction of new technologies only. Improvements in the efficient use of the available resources with a "given" technology can also lead to productivity increases. In other words, there are several ways of increasing productivity with the given technologies which shall be referred to as "**short term micro productivity growth**", or synonymously, as" **efficiency growth"** (see Tablo:7-1).

Table: 7-1 Efficiency (micro-productivity) growth

1- Economic efficiency (EE) 2- Technical efficiency (TE)	Short term	Technology "**given**" Long term

1-**Economic efficiency (EE) growth**: Given the technology, **EE** covers all attempts to reduce production costs and increase income aiming to maximize profits. **EE** can be stated as below.

$$\mathbf{EE = TR : TC = (P_sQ_s) : (wL + p_i\, X_i)} \qquad (10)$$

$\mathbf{p^i}$ denotes input prices, $\mathbf{p^s}$ output price, $\mathbf{Q^s}$ the quantity supplied, $\mathbf{X^i}$ the input quantities, **w** wage level and **L** number of employees. **EE** growth implies a positive change in its value.

EE growth = $\Delta TR > \Delta TC$ or $\Delta VA > \Delta TC$ (11)

For instance, acquiring inputs at a lower cost or a rise in the sale price of a product would imply **EE** growth.

If TC ↓ cet. par. VA ↑, π ↑ and EE ↑ (12)

Or, p^s ↑ and TR ↑ cet. par. VA↑, π ↑ and EE ↑ (13)

Or, ΔTR ↑ > ΔTC ↑ cet. par. VA ↑ π ↑ and EE ↑ (14)

2- **Technical efficiency (TE) growth: TE** is a concept related to the more efficient exploitation of physical inputs, given the technology. In other words, it refers to the efficient utilization of physical inputs and plant capacity. For instance, capacity under-utilization would imply technical inefficiency.

TE = Quantity Supplied: Supply Capacity ("**given**" the technology) (15)

When **TE** ratio is equal to one (**TE=1**), the quantity supplied is at the maximum attainable level with the given technology. When the **TE** ratio is less than one (**TE‹1**), it implies that the physical resources can be utilized more efficiently and the physical quantity supplied can be increased. As **TE** moves toward one, physical productivity will continue to improve.

The rate of profit which is the driving force of production for an enterprise will be maximized when **EE** and **TE** reach their highest possible levels. In other words, for maximum profitability level **EE** and **TE** have to be at their maximum values.

Some impacts of efficiency growth

As seen above, it is possible to increase productivity even in the absence of any technological innovation or progress. For instance, an enterprise may increase productivity by restructuring the production method, thus making more efficient use of the given physical resources. In a similar fashion, productivity with the given technology can be increased by improving the skills of the labor force or by increasing the capacity utilization level or improving health and security measures, etc. Table:7-2 shows some of the impacts of efficiency growth on the value added (**VA**), rate of profit (**r**) and the share of profit in **VA**, while causing the share of the wage (**w**) in **VA** to fall, cet. par.

However, increasing productivity (growth) with a given technology has its limits. In time, markets are bound to gradually saturate. After the full saturation of the market, the output would grow only in accordance to population growth. In other words; the growth potential of micro-productivity is limited.

Table: 7- 2 Impacts of efficiency (micro-productivity) growth

New technology	Cause of efficiency (micro-productivity) growth	VA:K	VA:L	r	π:VA	w:VA
No	Restructuring production method	↑	↑	↑	↑	↓
No	Increasing capacity utilization	↑	↑	↑	↑	↓
No	Multiple shift-work	↑	↑	↑	↑	↓
No	Reallocating the resources	↑	↑	↑	↑	↓
No	Improved education system	↑	↑	↑	↑	↓
No	Learning-by-doing	↑	↑	↑	↑	↓
No	Improved safety & sanitary	↑	↑	↑	↑	↓
No	Participation in decision-making	↑	↑	↑	↑	↓

Growth-2: Technological Productivity Growth- Long term

The process of growth supported by new knowledge (or technological progress) displays different features than growth with a "given technology". Therefore, the growth process due to the introduction of "**new products**" and/or "**new production methods**" will be referred to as **technological productivity growth** to distinguish it from the efficiency growth process with a given technology. In order to achieve long term growth targets, enterprises have to undertake new investments. There can be no long term growth process in the absence of new investments.

The most distinguishing feature of technological productivity growth is the introduction of new products and/or production methods into the markets. Technological progress is central to this process. This process sometimes facilitates the supply of "given" products at less cost per unit and sometimes increases the range of consumable products both of which lead to increased welfare. Cost-reducing technological progress is important, but the introduction of a new product or a new production method is much more important and vital in the long term. According to Drucker (1995; p.13) who employs an abstract definition of productivity and further points out that productivity has increased about 3-4 percent annually in last 125 years which has multiplied total productivity by a factor of 45 in the developed countries. The underlying reason behind the improved standards of living in these countries is this explosion in productivity. Baumol-McLennan (1985; p.5) make a similar comment regarding the role of abstract productivity growth.

Along with technological productivity growth, we observe a clear increase in the variety and quality of products as well as less working hours per employee. About 100 years ago an average employee used to work 3,000 hours in a year. Nowadays an employee works about 1,500-2,000 hours annually in the developed countries and has a much higher income and richer range of products to benefit from. A simple comparison indicates that in modern economies an employee produces 10 times more value per hour than 100 years ago.

Technological productivity growth, which is the engine of long term economic growth, will be studied under the two headings below (see Table:7-3).

Table: 7-3 Technological (macro) productivity growth.

a- A "given" product but new production method b- New product and/or new production method	Long term	**New** technology

a-) A "given" product, new production process: Medium-term growth

Given the product, the most rational and efficient behavior for an enterprise in order to improve its competitive strength and profits is to employ new unit cost reducing production methods. To serve this purpose, the new technology should facilitate production with one of the following features:

1- The same amount of **VA**, but less inputs of labor.
2- The same amount and value of inputs, but more **VA.**
3- The growth rate of **VA** is greater than the growth rate of value of inputs.
4- The rate of decline in the value of inputs is greater than the rate of decline in **VA.**

As unit production cost declines, the enterprise may reduce the sale price of product in the markets which would lead to a growth in terms of real income, cet. par. As a result, demand for the products is expected to increase. However, over time, demand is expected to decline due to market saturation, which would cause the profit rate to decline, which, in turn, would cause a decline in the investment rate.

b-) New products: Long term growth

The distinguishing feature of this kind of macro (technological) productivity is the introduction of "**new products**" usually accompanied by "**new production methods**". Long term sustainable economic growth can only be realized as technological productivity increases. Long term economic growth rate is normally subject to fluctuations, which may occasionally even reach crisis levels. Neither does the growth process cease, nor does the profit rate tend to fall to zero in the long term due to continuous technological progress. Often, the shortage or exhaustion of certain natural resources becomes the major subject of economic debates. But, nevertheless, the economic growth process continues. Moreover, in contrast to approximately 3,000 hours worked annually 50-60 years ago, an employee now works about 1,500-2,000 hours and produces a much better quality and a greater variety of products. The only reason for these developments is continuing **technological productivity growth** that is the supply of new technologies, or, to be more specific, a continual supply of **new products and/or new production methods**.

New products require new investments, which naturally generate new demands. As a result, the initial profit rate tends to be higher than the average rate prevailing in the markets with "given" products and "given" technologies. This is a natural process. Otherwise, the firms would not have any incentive to take risks and to utilize new technologies. As a result of new technologies, not only the profit rate tends to rise, but also the options for consumers increase.

In summary, the reason that the long-run profit rate does not tend to fall to zero and that economic growth is sustained is due to **technological productivity growth**. The invention and application of new technologies is an irreversible and uninterruptible process of economic life in any progressive society. Continual technological productivity growth serves not only the interests of producers but also those of the consumers. As a result of technological productivity growth, employees work less hours and produce more and better quality products. In addition, the real income per capita increases, facilitating more consumption and improving living standards. In spite of some setbacks and objections, people in general, welcome such developments.

Measuring technological productivity growth

It is imperative for enterprises to enter into a continuous search for increased productivity. Otherwise, competitors employing new technologies may gain an advantage and attempt to eliminate their rivals from the market which fits the characteristics of the so called "free market" system. This is known as "**creative**

destruction" and was pointed out by Marx and other Classical economists, long before being referred to by Schumpeter. Thus, the search for new technologies is an obligation for all enterprises under competitive conditions.

Technological productivity growth can be analyzed in two sub-categories: the value added **(VA)** and the quantity **(Q)**.

1- Quantitative growth: or
2- Value growth.

Quantitative productivity growth

A quantitative growth indicates a variation in the relationship between the quantities used in production and the quantities supplied. The remarks made on quantitative "productivity" analysis are also valid for quantitative "productivity growth" analysis. In other words, a measurement of productivity growth with regard to two or more inputs would not produce healthy and reliable results. Measurement with regard to one input only, especially in regard to the employees or the unit time employed would be possible, but the outcome is sometimes bound to be dubious, especially in regard to "**new**" **products** and "**production methods**".

Let us assume that **Q** denotes the quantity supplied **L** the number of employees and $\mathbf{X_i}$ all the other inputs of production in the production function below.

$$\mathbf{Q = f\,(L, X_i)} \qquad i = 1,2,\ldots, n \qquad (16)$$

The quantitative productivity growth can be defined as the increase in the ratio of the quantity supplied to the quantity of the inputs of production $[\mathbf{V_t = Q_t:(L_t, X_{i,t})}]$ in two different time periods.

$$g = V_{t+1} - V_t \qquad (17)$$

In ratio it can be stated as:

$$g = (V_{t+1} - V_t) : V_t \qquad (18)$$

Assume that a given quantity (**Q**) is being produced with less input quantities (**X**).

$$X_{t+1} < X_t \quad ; \quad Q_{t+1} = Q_t \qquad (19)$$

Or, assume that output supplied increases with given quantity of inputs; or

$$X_{t+1} = X_t \quad ; \quad Q_{t+1} > Q_t \qquad (20)$$

Input quantity decreases while output supplied increases; or

$$X_{t+1} < X_t \quad ; \quad Q_{t+1} > Q_t \qquad (21)$$

Assume that the growth rate of quantities supplied is greater than the growth of inputs;

$$X_{t+1} : X_t < \quad Q_{t+1} : Q_t \qquad (22)$$

In all four cases the measurement of the growth is quantitative. However, the results of such quantitative analysis are unlikely to very reliable, unless the quantities of inputs and outputs are homogeneous. Homogeneity of products would inevitably carry us to the utopian world of neoclassical economics which we hope to avoid throughout this book.

Partial factor productivity growth

Though it might seem, at least initially, less complicated to measure the partial factor productivity (**PFP**) this approach does not to seem to produce highly sound or reliable results either. For instance, unless the output supplied is assumed to be a homogeneous product, it is highly unlikely to lead to reliable results. The "homogeneity assumption", on the other hand, implies a journey into the utopian world of economic transactions of the neoclassical heritage.

Let us take a closer look at the partial productivity growth of, say "input item five" among the many other inputs of production, where t stands for time. Assume that the quantity required for the fifth input, say energy, declines by 20 percent from 100 KW to 80 KW due to a technological progress. As we see below the new input quantity of energy is 80 KW now, a 20 KW saving.

$PFP^5_{t} - PFP^5_{t+1}$

$$100\ \text{KW} - 80\ \text{KW} = 20\ \text{KW} \tag{23}$$

If input(s) and output were homogeneous, then there should not be any serious measurement problem of partial productivity growth. However, as the number of inputs subject to productivity growth due to technological changes increases, measurement problems would become inevitable. For instance, how can one make a reliable estimate in a situation where energy demand declines by 20 KW while labor input declines by 10 employees due to a new technology?

To summarize, the arguments stated in regard to the static productivity analysis above are also valid for a dynamic productivity growth analysis subject to the technological progress. In other words, making a reliable quantitative analysis of a specific dynamic productivity growth is complicated and cumbersome, if not impossible. Especially, when **new products** are introduced as a result of technological progress, any attempt to measure productivity growth are bound to be sterile because there are no products of a similar quality with which to compare them.

Value-based productivity growth

Measuring productivity growth based on monetary value, or to be more specific, on a value added criterion for national economies seems to be a much less complicated process and displays less serious shortcomings compared to a quantitative productivity growth analysis. Therefore, from now on, productivity growth will be considered only in terms of the value added (**VA**) at a national economy level, unless otherwise stated. Since labor is regarded as the only production factor capable of adding value, it would be rational to measure productivity in relation to the number of workers employed (**VA:L**) or in regard to the cost of wages (**VA:LWC**).

Is a "value" criterion a perfect choice?

A productivity growth analysis in terms of value is, certainly, not free of controversy, but it is more likely to produce reliable results when compared to a quantitative analysis. Here are some examples of the shortcomings.

Case-1

Assume that a technological progress in an intermediary sector reduces the input quantities that are required for the final output, cet. par. To be more specific, assume that now 10 KW of energy is required instead of the 20 KW because of an energy-saving technological progress, cet. par. Further assume that the price of energy (p^e) remains constant. How would this development affect the total value added?

As a result of input-saving technological progress the total value added would increase due to a rise in total profits, cet. par. Yet, there is no increase in the total quantity of the supplied final product.

Case-2

The increase in the amount of the total value added might be due to a wage-rise or increased employment, cet. par. Yet, there is still no increase in the total quantity of the final product that is supplied. This new development would cause deterioration in the economic efficiency (**EE**) and the technical efficiency (**TE**), though the total of the value added (**VA**) would increase.

Case-3

Assume that an enterprise with a monopoly or a few enterprises constituting an oligopoly determine the market sale price of a product and decide to increase the market sale price of the product concerned, while demand remains unchanged. Although the quantity supplied has not changed, the total amount of the value added would increase, cet. par., and appear to be a productivity growth in terms of value.

Case-4

Assume that for some reason the value of the national currency is reduced against other currencies. A comparative analysis of income with another country after the devaluation would give the impression that this particular country has suffered some loss from its previous economic position, although the total quantities supplied in both countries remain unchanged.

In spite of the shortcomings stated above, a value-based productivity growth analysis seems less complicated and more reliable compared to a quantitative analysis.

"New products" and productivity growth

Technological progress is the single most important feature of economic and social development. One significant contribution of technological progress is the facility to produce "given" products at less unit cost while another and more significant contribution is the introduction of "new products" often accompanied by "new methods of production". This dynamic process sometimes slows down and sometimes speeds up but never ends.

As the products are "new" with different designs and/or new features, it is difficult to compare them to previous products. Thus, it seems like more rational to attempt to measure the productivity growth of "new" products in terms of a value added criterion.

For instance, total productivity (**V**) with regard to all inputs is:

$$\mathbf{V} = \mathbf{VA} : (\mathbf{LWC} + \mathbf{p^i X^i}) \qquad i = 1,2,.....n \qquad (24)$$

$$= \mathbf{VA} : \mathbf{TC} \qquad (25)$$

Partial factor productivity (**PFP**) of the fifth input;

$$PFP_5 = VA : p^5X^5 \qquad (26)$$

Wage productivity per employee ($\mathbf{V_{LWC}}$);

$$V_{LWC} = VA : LWC \qquad (27)$$

Growth-3: Horizontal investments & growth

Technological progress is the key to development but countries as well as enterprises can continue to grow for a considerable period of time by making "horizontal" or "expansionary" investments with "given" technologies. For example, production may be initiated at one given plant in a given location. In time, however, as demand for the product grows, it can be profitable for enterprise to make additional investments in order to expand the quantities supplied which in addition contributes to the expansion of total amount of the value added. Foreign direct investments can be considered under the same category as horizontal investment with given technology.

However, since the product concerned is a "given", sooner or later, the markets will gradually saturate and the growth process will come to end which means that future growth, from an economic point of view, using horizontal investments is limited.

An Inter-Country Productivity Comparison

The "value added" criterion is the most used common criterion when comparing international economic indicators. However, these methods can sometimes provide misleading results. For instance, the 0-16 age group in Turkey is larger than in Sweden. Therefore, an inter-country comparison between Turkey and Sweden based on the per capita value added might be deceiving. A comparative study based on per employee value added seems to produce more healthy results.

The amount of the value added is the most common criterion used in the comparison of international economic indicators. For instance, two frequently used criteria are;

1- the per capita value added (**GDP : Total Population**); and
2- the per employee value added (**GDP : Total Employees**)

to measure and compare productivity. However, these methods can sometimes provide misleading results. For instance, the 0-16 age group in Turkey is larger than in Sweden. Therefore, a cross-country comparison between Turkey and Sweden based on per capita value added might be deceiving. A comparative study based on per employee value added seems to produce more healthy results.

Another interesting issue in any inter-country productivity comparison arises in conjunction with direct foreign investments. Let us consider the inter-country productivity in the automobile sector. As is well known, the more sophisticated and high-technology parts are being produced in the relatively more developed countries, while the developing countries are, in general, assigned to undertake the production of the more labor-intensive parts at a lower wage. In such cases, it would perhaps be more rational to make global profitability comparisons of globally operating enterprises because global production is shaped by their global interests.

Concluding Remarks

One of the most distinguishing factors in this book is the emphasis placed upon the close and direct relevance shown between the creative mental contributions of the labor-force and technological innovation. Since economic growth is one of the most important and lively discussed topics in economics, special emphasis was put on technological innovation in regard to the growth process both in the short and the long term. Naturally, it is not the first time that a relationship between economic growth and technological innovations has been considered. As it is well known, the so called "classical" economists like A. Smith, Ricardo and Marx, amongst others, have already pointed out the importance of technological innovation for economic growth. However, ever since the 1870s, with the rise and gradual domination of the "neoclassical" doctrine, the role of technological innovation began to lose ground. However, Schumpeter did make some serious contribution in highlighting the importance of technological innovations once again about 70-80 years later.

However, the vital role played by technological innovations was not acknowledged by neoclassical economists until Solow **"rediscovered"** the role of technology in economic growth in the 1950s. Nowadays, every economist acknowledges the role of technological innovation in the growth process in spite of some differences in their approaches.

The main difference in this discussion has been the "redefinition" of some critical concepts and assumptions that have been used and accepted as "a priori" by mainstream economists and have been used by them as the "basic undisputed principles" in their economic analyses. It has been shown that long-term economic growth has always been due to technological innovation which has introduced new products which in turn were brought about by creative mental labor assisted by physical labor.

Chapter 8: GLOBAL TRADE

> While the comparative cost concept and other basic concepts have rarely failed to provide some help, they have usually carried the analyst only a little way toward adequate understanding.
>
> Vernon, 1966,p.190

Concept Confusion

The title of this section might give the impression, at first glance, that two different trade types were to be discussed. The simple reason behind this misconception is the play on words which leads people to assume that "global trade" and "international trade" are two different types of trade. It should not come as a surprise to encounter a third word implying the same thing; "world trade". Yet, the fact is there is no difference at all in regard to substance.

Since the subject matter is economics, we will be discussing "**global**" or "**world**" or synonymously "**international**" trade and we shall use these terms interchangeably. Therefore, it would be misleading to use these concepts as if they are substantially different. Global trade refers to the export and import of products taking place on our planet not only "within" but also "among" the economic agents. Long before the use of the concept "global" in economic jargon enterprises were engaged in international or, synonymously global trade. In other words, "international" trade refers exactly to the same economic transactions that are found in "global" trade transactions. The interesting question is; why was the concept of globalization introduced as if basically different economic transactions were taking place, suggesting that world economic relations were undergoing a substantial change?

The answer is simple; Anglo-Saxon ideologists have a tendency to give a new name to an old town, as the Turkish idiom says, "unwelcome innovations are rarely well received[3]". For example, countries were labeled as "**developed**" and "**undeveloped**", for many years. Understandably this was not happily accepted by the countries which were labeled as "**undeveloped**". The term was perceived as abusive. Then, the term was replaced by "**developed and developing**" which seemed less abusive than the former. For a while the term "**digital-divide**" was introduced which did became somewhat popular. Soon after, a new and less objectionable term was introduced to please the relatively better-off developing countries; "**emerging**" countries.

---

3 The original version of the Turkish idiom is: "Eski köye yeni adet getirmek".

The relevant critical question is; has anything substantially changed in regard to the global income disparities or the widening global gap? Still, a larger share, about 80 percent, of the world's population is relatively poor while a minority of about 20 percent enjoys a much higher standard of living. Changing the concepts has not been able to change inter-country inequalities and global poverty.

The main purpose of this section is to focus analysis on two important issues:

1- Global trade.
2- Global growth.

Attempts will be made to find answers to these basic questions: What are the underlying causes of global trade? What are the impacts of global trade on national economies? Why do enterprises undertake intra-firm trade? What is the nature and impact of intra-firm trade on national economies?

There is no need to ask whether global trade contributes to economic growth; this is a fact acknowledged by probably all economists around the world. However, the impact of global trade seems to be a critical question, in view of the present global economic structures, relationships and courses of development. The following sub-section will focus on these issues looking for appropriate answers to global economic issues.

Global Trade and some Theories

Global trade has been going on for thousands of years. The earliest and most attractive trade centers and regions were located in the Middle East and Asia. In modern times, the "largest share of total global trade" is being realized by the enterprises of the developed countries; either amongst the developed country enterprises or in the form of intra-firm trade of globally operating enterprises. The underlying forces which produced this situation are, due partially to a successful adaptation to new socio-economic changes but, are due, mostly, to a past economic growth process based on technological progress, which are the products of creative mental labor.

From the perspective of consumer benefits, global trade helps to increase potential consumer satisfaction by facilitating increasing alternatives for end-users. Global trade also contributes to increasing the incentive to undertake the production of various products that have not been previously produced locally.

For the enterprise, global trade implies, on one hand, alternative sources of inputs at globally competitive markets prices which could help reduce production cost and thus its global competitiveness. On the other hand, global trade opportunities give rise to new markets for the products supplied. Increased global competition would also imply increased incentives to develop and introduce new technologies in order to reduce cost and/or offer new products.

When reviewing global trade, we observe the following: The richest and the industrially advanced countries have eliminated almost all the barriers of trade between themselves. Most barriers on imported industrial goods from a large number of the less developed countries into the developed countries have been eliminated. In addition, member countries of the World Trade Organization (WTO) accepted a resolution in 2005 to diminish and eventually eliminate all trade barriers. Judging from these developments, we observe that **global trade in industrial goods** increasingly exhibits the characteristics of "**intra-country**" trade. We also observe that attempts to increase the **trade in global services** are rapidly gaining in importance. There are presently also many attempts to increase global trade in agricultural products.

The removal of trade barriers leads to increased global competition. There would be no need for a foreign trade theory to explain why enterprises engage in global trade, in countries or regions which already have eliminated all trade barriers. The same motives and rules apply to all enterprises located in a free trade area of specific products. In countries where the same or a similar level of standards prevails in regard to development level and incomes, elimination of all trade barriers would increase the benefit for consumers as well as producers.

Unfortunately, most of the enterprises in developing countries do not enjoy the same standards as the enterprises of the more developed countries in regard to infrastructure, labor-force qualifications and competitive strength. Therefore, the precautions taken by developing country decision-makers are vital to the future progress of their countries' enterprises. Especially, the protection and promotion of infant industries deserve close and sensitive treatment.

There is, of course, another option for the developed country decision-makers; they might prefer to rely entirely on the blessings of liberal market forces. The most serious disadvantage of generous liberal economic policies in regard to a less competitive enterprise is the risk of a take-over by a globally operating "giant" enterprise which are increasingly shaping and controlling global production and distribution.

The benefits of global trade

The major potential global benefits of global trade can be classified under the following headings:

- Increased competition.
- Increased output/consumption.
- Scale economies.
- Increased employment.
- The transfer of embodied technology.
- Access to products not available before.
- The global division of labor.
- Increased capacity utilization.

On Trade Theories

Economic theories on global trade, or alternatively, international trade or world trade or foreign trade, is believed to start with A. Smith's view of an "absolute advantage" principle followed by Ricardo's "comparative advantage". Classical era theories on production were, predominantly, based on the labor-power value principle. The succeeding economists who felt that there were some shortcomings in those theories, they made attempts to make refinements or extensions. The major contributions were the "offer curves", "opportunity cost" concept and "factor endowment" concept that were introduced into trade theory. Later we see further contributions from prominent economists like Singer-Prebisch, Bhagwati and Lewis introduced into the international (global) trade theories. Attempts to introduce extensions or refinements based on concepts like "technological differences", human-capital", "product cycle" or "revealed comparative advantages" continued.

However, none of the preceding international trade theories seem to have succeeded in presenting a comprehensive theory capable of reflecting actual economic relations and transactions. Since the initial starting point was, in general, based on unrealistic assumptions of economic models, they could not go beyond being relevant and explanatory in the utopian models with the utopian relationships of some academicians. Classical and Neoclassical economists were referring to trade between different countries in their analysis. By doing this, they were also making a significant mistake; in reality, **"countries" do not engage in trade but "enterprises" do**. Trade between countries can only mean trade between enterprises of the different countries.

Enterprise and trade

All products, whether a commodity or a service exchanged (traded) in markets are produced by commercial units called an "enterprise" or a "firm". When this transaction takes place between the enterprises of different countries, it is called global or international trade. In principle, there is no difference in the nature of these transactions whether intra- or inter-national, in pursuit of profit. For example, the nature and principles of exchange taking place whether it be between Istanbul and Izmir or Rome and Milan or Turkey and Italy or Azerbaijan are the same; the driving motive is the maximization of profits. And the terms of trade is based on the principle of "**absolute advantage**" as once clearly stated by many of the founders of economics in the Classical era which applies not only for the price but also the quality and design of products.

The distinguishing feature of trade between countries or intra-country is the rules and regulations placed on these transactions, or foreign trade policies, imposed by the different country decision-makers. When a country introduces restrictions on international trade such as a quota or customs duty, the quantity of traded products would inevitably be influenced. In the absence of restrictions on trade, there would be no substantial difference between the global inter-country trade and the intra-country trade amongst enterprises, cet. par. For instance, because all trade restrictions for industrial goods are eliminated completely between some European Union countries, the rules and regulations of trade are the same for all transactions. Let's take a look at the trade between Italian and Swedish enterprises; there is no difference between inter-country trade between Italy and Sweden and intra-country trade, whether it takes place in Italy or in Sweden.

Economists have been introducing various types of "international trade theories" to explain the nature and principles of transactions. As a consequence, many paradigms have emerged with a great variety of features. The most widely acknowledged paradigm of international trade is based on the principle of "**comparative advantage**", i.e., the comparative abilities of nations according to "**opportunity costs**". An ideology-free approach would clearly demonstrate that the most rational and realistic paradigm is based on the law of "**absolute advantage**", i.e., the comparative abilities of enterprises according to "**absolute costs**". There is no need for a comprehensive and in depth trade analysis in order to be aware of this fact; simply ask any enterprise manager engaged in international trade.

The following relevant questions might pop up:

1- Assuming that the inadequacy of foreign trade theories based on comparative advantage is obvious, as claimed above, how come nobody has discovered that before?
2- Why should the use of the term "international trade" be considered a mistake, since the export earnings realized are registered in the trade balance sheets of countries?

The answer to the first question is simple; in most of the economics departments of universities around the world the Anglo-Saxon ideology is dominant. A. Smith had focused his trade theory on an "absolute advantage" principle but in the case that one of the two trading countries has an absolute advantage in both sectors, as occurs in reality, there would be no motive for the disadvantaged country to enter into trade relations with the other. Ricardo's law of "comparative advantage" arrived just in time to rescue the foreign trade theory of the Anglo-Saxon ideology. Now, even in the case that one country has absolute advantage in both sectors, in a two-country, two goods model, the comparative advantage principle would make foreign trade, at least in theory, look like a rational and mutually beneficial process. The neoclassical ideologists highly admired this approach and dedicated themselves to the promotion and expansion of this new "law of comparative advantage". However, the fact that it is enterprises not countries that engage in trade, in a multi-country, multi-product world, is still waiting to be discovered.

Evaluating the foreign trade theories in retrospective, it would not be an exaggeration to point out Vernon's contribution as the closest in reflecting actual economic transactions. According to Vernon, technological progress, scale economies and uncertainty are the essential factors determining the production cost and its location (Vernon, 1966; p.190) which are, in turn, expected to influence the size and nature of the inter-country trade decisions made by the enterprises.

In conclusion; there is an essentially important law which affects the exchange relationships of products between enterprises, i.e., the **"law of absolute advantage".** It applies not only to price but also to quality and design.

As to the second question in regard to the dichotomy of whether it is enterprises or countries that engage in trade: Trade between countries is undertaken by enterprises but the data on the results of this trade or the "trade figures" are announced in the countries' trade balance report. Countries can always influence the size, nature, price, quality and direction of trade by imposing "country specific" trade policies. However, influencing trade is one thing and actually executing trade another thing. Failure to see this basic distinction has led many economists in the wrong direction which has impeded the development of more realistic trade theories.

The value of exports from Turkey was about 100 billion TL in 2005 while the import value of the total products reached 140 billion TL. These national statistics on trade reflect how much Turkish enterprises succeeded in exporting and importing various products based on the "**absolute advantage** principle", not on the "comparative advantage" principle, as some economists claim. The same applies to all enterprises and countries pursuing liberal market policies in accordance with Western values.

Major Determinants of Global Trade

The driving motive for an enterprise to engage in foreign trade is the unsatisfied demand for a product. The major grounds can be classified as follows:

1- The product is not supplied locally.
2- Demand is in excess of supply.
3- The available domestic products fail to meet consumer tastes and/or preferences.
4- Price differences.

Major factors influencing the consumers' demand decisions can be classified as follows:

1- Price.
2- Preferences for diverse qualities or designs.
3- Income and/or wealth level.

1- Price and Trade

Price of a "given" product in a competitive market is determined by the cost of production, competitors' prices and the expected profit rate of the enterprise, cet. par. Production cost consists of wage costs and input costs, including plant site, insurance, etc. The technology employed in the production process is important in determining the production cost and end-user price. Assuming that there is no idle plant capacity, the production method which minimizes production cost in the market is expected to give an advantage to the enterprise in price competition compared to enterprises not employing the most efficient method of production. A lower unit cost than one's competitors accompanied with price flexibility leads to a greater competitiveness for the enterprise as well as a greater income potential.

2- Preferences for Diverse Qualities & Designs

By assumption, quality and design diversities were ignored in the above section when considering a "given" product. Yet, we know that many products with the same or similar use for consumers which have diverse qualities and/or designs do influence the decisions of consumers. The car market is like an excellent example to use in order to highlight the importance of diverse qualities and/or designs. The basic use obtained from cars is, no doubt, the same for all; the transportation of human-beings from one location to another. Yet, different individuals prefer a different quality and differently designed cars in order to obtain the same service from their cars. In a similar fashion, wrist watches all perform the same duty; showing time.

Now, let's give an example from the service sector, practically all men go to a hairdresser for a hair cut once in a while. Yet, some prefer luxury barber shops in fancy areas while others are satisfied with a normal and everyday service. Again, some parents prefer high cost private schools for their children with the expectation of a higher quality of service while many attend public schools. The standards of the technology used and the laborers employed are the main factors that determine quality and design diversities.

3- The Impact of the Level of Income on Global Trade

A nation's total or per capita income level directly related to its level of general development, which includes the level of technological development level and the level of qualification of the labor force. The more advanced a country, the more likely its citizens enjoy a higher per capita consumption which leads to a potentially higher share of global trade. For instance, in some developed countries per capita income is around 40,000 US $ while in some others the per capita income does not exceed two or three thousand US $. Such global income inequalities inevitably lead to inequalities in global consumption.

Types of Global Trade

Global trade shall be analyzed under four headings.

1- Between developed country enterprises.
2- Between developed country enterprises and developing country enterprises.
3- Between developing country enterprises.
4- The intra-firm trade of globally operating enterprises.

Let us begin by specifying the assumptions.

- Global trade is always between commercial enterprises.
- The prices, qualities and designs of globally traded products are not identical, e.g., no homogeneous products.

- The law of "absolute advantage" is valid in trade between enterprises, except for intra-firm global trade.
- There are no major disparities between developed countries in regard to income, labor force skill level or technological advancement.
- There are significant disparities between the developed and developing countries in regard to income, labor force skill level and technological advancement.
- Final-consumer tastes are similar.
- Transportation costs have an important influence on product costs which in turn can influence global trade decisions.
- The patent owner of a new technology enjoys a "monopoly position" in the market until the competitors develop similar products.

1- Trade between Developed Countries

Assume that among developed countries there are no major disparities in regard to income, labor force skill level or technological advancement. Similar cultural values and institutional efficiency are also assumed. Further assume that there are neither market interventions nor barriers to trade of any kind. Thus, all enterprises are assumed to perform under the same competitive conditions.

The markets and conditions described above more or less reflect, the situation prevailing in the founding six countries of the EU and in the Scandinavian countries. Given these circumstances, it does not really matter where the plant is located, as long as its performance is economically and technologically efficient. The enterprise supplying products with the lowest cost and price would have a greater advantage over its competitors who produce and trade similar products. Marketing skills and the quality of the after-sale service would also make a difference in the level of competition but by assumption there are no significant differences among the countries concerned. There are two aspects to which deserve closer scrutiny.

Aspect-1: Free global trade between countries at the same or a similar level of development would contribute to economic growth in the **importing country**, cet. par.

For example, if consumer products are being imported, the consumers in the importing country would, most likely, improve their living standards by having access to either;

1- Cheaper products; and/or
2- Better quality products; and/or
3- Better (preferred) designs.

When the imported product is used as an input to produce anther product, then the following results might be obtained which would increase competitive strength.

1- Increased productivity (lower unit cost); or

2- Better quality output and/or better design.

In both cases, the enterprise as well as the national economy would benefit from the free global trade of these products, cet. par.

Aspect-2: Free global trade between countries at the same or similar development levels would contribute to economic growth in the **exporting country**, cet. par.

Assuming no domestic economic disturbances or imbalances, the exports would make positive economic contributions to both, the exporting enterprise and the national economy. Even when domestic markets suffer from demand insufficiency, exports could facilitate a further supply of products and an economic growth. In the long term, however, economic growth would be solely dependent on the nature of the technological progress, because the markets are bound to saturate sooner or later, cet. par.

2- Global Trade between Developed & Developing Countries

According to the "comparative advantage theory" of the trade between two countries of two goods, constant opportunity costs and the perfect mobility of the factors of production; everyone gains from the trade even if one of the trading enterprises has an absolute advantage in both sectors. It would be irrational to ignore the potential benefits to be gained from global trade. However, the actual economic relationships are quite different from those models set out to describe. First of all, global trade transactions take place between enterprises, not between countries. Thus, a trade theory based on two-country transactions only is bound to be inadequate, without taking into consideration the shortcomings of the simplistic utopian assumptions of the "comparative advantage theory".

We can compare the free trade transactions between a developed country's enterprises (**GEs**) and developing country's enterprises (**LDCEs**) to a competition between two Sumo wrestlers one weighing 200 kilos (**GEs**) and the other weighing a mere 50 kilos (**LDCE**). The only thing that is "equal" or "just", are the rules of the game. Everything else is "unequal" or "unjust" and the winner is quite obvious in advance, unless a miracle occurs.

The factors making one wrestler (**GE**) look much more superior to the other one (**LDCE**) can be summarized as:

- The quality of the labor force.
- The development level of the national technological infrastructure.
- The level of the technology used in production.
- R & D facilities.
- Organizational abilities.
- Country and enterprise specific administrative skills.
- The institutional and/or the cultural infrastructure.

The qualitative and quantitative disparities outlined in the sections above would inevitably lead to qualitative and quantitative disparities in the goods and services supplied by a developed and a less developed country's enterprises. The natural outcome of these disparities is clearly seen in contemporary relationships; developed country enterprises tend to specialize in high-technology sectors that require highly-skilled labor-power, while a developing country's enterprises seem to specialize in relatively lower level technology and sectors that require less-skilled labor-power.

As we know wages tend to be lower in the less developed countries. Yet, the value added per worker in developed countries tends to be much greater than the value added per worker in the developing countries. In addition, products which require a higher-technology and a better-skilled labor force generally tend to be of a higher quality and of a better design, so naturally demand is much greater for this kind of products. Access to more advanced and dynamic technologies along with a highly skilled labor force seems to pave the way for profitable and sustainable potential economic growth.

Workers in sectors using dynamic and advanced technology such as the electronics, Smart TV-set, luxury automobile and biology tend to produce more added values in unit time than workers using less developed technology in labor-intensive sectors producing, for example, t-shirts, cotton pants, ready-made clothing, etc. The global competition between high technology using enterprises and low technology using enterprises only leads to an "unequal" and "disadvantageous" competitive position against the interests of the latter, that is, in practice, for the developing country's enterprises. In time, the more advanced technology using enterprises would get stronger and widen the technological gap, unless measures are taken to strengthen the technological position of the developing country's enterprises.

3- Global Trade between Developing Countries

Developing country's enterprises (**LDCEs**) and their national economy displays quite distinctive economic, institutional, technological and political features in regard to the developed ones. Due to the variety and nature of these features, it would be over optimistic to expect the same results from free trade as is expected between the developed countries. However, the design and implementation of specific development policies which make the best use of diversities might create synergy, and thus free global trade might pave the way to achieving the desired economic growth. Wherever there is a significant divergence in the degree of labor force skill, enterprises that are relatively better endowed than the competitors would benefit more from free global trade and it is highly likely that they would grow faster.

One should not overlook the influence of an important factor when analyzing the global trade between the enterprises in the developed countries. The subsidiaries of these developed country enterprises which operate in the developing countries are constantly increasing their share of global trade as a result of foreign direct investments (**FDIs**). That means, in the future, more and more subsidiaries will be in control of global production and trade, making critical decisions subject to global interests of headquarters, which are not expected to be in the interests of that particular developing country. This is an important issue which should not be forgotten in any economic analysis.

4- Intra-Firm Global Trade

According to the conventional textbooks, foreign trade theories study, in general, the exchange relationships between two countries producing two-products, based on the law of comparative advantage. Yet, actual economic relations display some distinct features, as has been mentioned previously. Neither is the assumptions of conventional trade theory based on comparative advantage realistic nor are the exchange relations described. First of all, global exchange takes place between enterprises, not countries; exchange does not take place according to the law of comparative advantage but according to "absolute" advantage criterion. In addition, a constantly growing amount of global trade is taking place intra-firm (**IFT**) that is among the enterprises scattered around the world belonging to the same headquarters.

Assuming that states do not interfere in market transactions, as some archaic trade theories assume, there will be no difference between global or domestic trade if all foreign or domestic enterprises compete under the same conditions. As we know, enterprises are driven by the profit motive in the long run. A competitive enterprise would attempt to buy inputs from the lowest cost source and sell products to the highest bidder, cet. par. The law of exchange is "absolute advantage" in price and/or quality and/or design. However, whenever country decision-makers impose restrictions on imports, they can easily influence:

1- Price.
2- Quantity imported.
3- Quality; and
4- The source of imports.

They can achieve these objectives by using one or more of the following measures:

1- Customs duties.
2- Quotas.
3- Subsidies.
4- Non-tariff barriers.
5- Foreign currency regulations.

Definition of Intra-Firm trade (IFT)

Intra-firm trade refers to exchange transactions among enterprises which belong partly or wholly to, in general, one globally operating enterprise (**GE**). The purpose of these transactions can be divided into two categories:

1- **Production oriented IFT**: the trade of the products used in production, such as raw materials, machinery, tools, intermediaries, etc., between the parent-firm and the subsidiary or between subsidiaries.
2- **Distribution oriented:** the distribution of products produced by the parent-firm or a subsidiary in another country.

Our emphasis will cover trade between, for example, an automobile manufacturing unit in Turkey and the company's sales agent in Rome, or trade between the intermediary-goods supplying subsidiary and the final-product producing parent-firm or another subsidiary.

The Table: 8-1 provides some data on the size and extent of **IFT** on US economy. According to OECD data, the share of exports from US-based parent-firms to their subsidiaries of total exports reached to 32.1 percent and the imports to 46.7 percent of total imports.

Table: 8-2 shows data on intra-firm trade with a partner region. Just as in the case of the US enterprises, intra-firm trade displays rapid and steady growth. According to data for 1999, **IFTs** account for about 14.8 percent of imports and 28.6 percent of exports. Table: 8-3 shows the dimensions of **IFTs** in some dynamic sectors. The main cause of rapid expansion of **IFTs** seems to be the restructuring of global production and distribution methods through the global operations of the **GEs** in accordance with their global interests.

Table: 8-1 Intra-firm trade of the US, with selected trading partners (As percent of all goods trade with partner country)

Imports	Level 1999	Change 1992-1999
Japan	73.7	-1.3
Mexico	66.4	3.1
Korea	49.3	22.5
Canada	43.1	-2.9
Eastern Europe	32.1	20.1
Taiwan	20.8	4.9
China	17.6	7.1
Total	46.7	1.7
Exports		
Mexico	44.3	5.6
Canada	42.4	-2.9
Japan	36.3	0.1
Taiwan	16.0	6.0
Eastern Europe	12.3	2.6
China	11.6	5.0
Total	32.1	1.2

Note: Partner countries shown are those with the highest level of intra-firm trade in 1999 or the largest increase over the period 1992-99.

Source: US Department of Commerce, 2001: in: OECD, 2008, VI. Intra-Industry & Intra-Firm Trade & the Int. of Prod., p.165, Tablo:VI.4

Table: 8-2 Intra-firm trade of Japan, where parent company is Japanese, with main trading blocks (As percent of all goods trade with partner region)

Exports	1990	1999	Change in %
Total	14.5	28.6	14.1
Rest of Asia	10.1	22.4	12.3
North America	20.9	36.8	15.8
Europe	12.0	29.0	17.0
Imports			
Total	4.2	14.8	10.6
Rest of Asia	6.3	22.5	16.1
North America	3.1	6.8	3.7
Europe	1.1	3.9	2.9

Source: Japanese Ministry of Economy, Trade and Industry: in: OECD, 2008, VI. Intra-Industry & Intra-Firm Trade & the Int. of Prod., s.165, Table: VI.3

Table: 8-3 US trade in products with a high degree of intra-firm trade (Percent)

	Share of total imports: exports	Intra-firm trade
Imports		
Transportation equipment	17.7	75.6
Computer & electronic products	20.8	66.3
Chemicals	6.4	59.3
Machinery except electrical	6.6	50.3
Electrical equipment, appliances & components	3.3	50.0
Exports		
Transportation equipment	15.6	41.2
Plastics & rubber products	2.2	40.7
Chemicals	9.9	39.3
Computer & electronic products	20.7	36.9
Electrical equipment, appliances & components	3.3	35.1

Source: US Department of Commerce, 2001: in: OECD, 2008, VI. Intra-Industry & Intra-Firm Trade & the Int. of Prod., p.166, Table: VI.5

Motives for IFT

The driving force behind **IFT** is the maximization of the global profits of the **GEs**. As well-known, nowadays practically all decision-makers in all countries are in a kind of race to attract more **FDI**s by various types of promotions including generous financial and other type of incentives. Not infrequently we observe that "**tax havens**" are created for the foreign investments of the **GEs** while quite often local producers complain about high taxes on locally supplied products.

Generous incentives along with the presence of relatively lower wage costs, attracts many **GEs** to move their production plants to developing countries in order to obtain mostly the low-technology and labor-intensive components required in production. Through this, they attempt to maximize global profits and gain a cost and/or price competitive advantage against their rivals. Even simply moving a plant site that requires cheap labor-services would be a sufficient incentive for a **FDI** and would lead to increase global profits, cet. par (Gürak; 2006-c).

The Products & Sectors in which most of the IFT takes place

Potentially, **IFT** can take place in all sectors and with all tradable products. In practice, the **GEs** tend to carry out production that requires a high-quality labor-force, products using dynamic and advanced technology in their parent-firms' home countries while in developing countries they tend to use relatively low-technology and employ a low-skill labor-force to supply their products. The **GE**s normally possess the patents of their own high technology products which endow them with a monopoly power in the markets which is most often encountered in the most dynamic sectors such as communication, biology, pharmacy, space technologies, etc.

The Turkish automotive sector is an excellent example of how the global division of supply and distribution takes place with **IFT**. According to export data, Turkish made automobiles rank at the top of the exported products from Turkey. Yet, there is not one single automobile plant "owned" and "controlled" by Turkish citizens. What really happen are the parts that require the most advanced-technology are produced in other countries while production of the most laborer-intensive parts take place in Turkey where wages are comparatively lower, and production is supported by generous incentives for the foreign investor. Eventually, automobiles produced in Turkey are exported to other countries under the Ford, Hyundai, or Fiat brand names.

What happens if the real wage level begins to rise in those developing countries which offer attractive low-wage production costs, in addition to other incentives? According to the Turkish newspaper "Sabah" on 29-October-2005, if the Trade Unions kept on demanding higher wages, the management of the well-known tire producer Pirelli would not hesitate to move its plant to another country.

The conventional trade theories are unable to offer any remedy to such practical global problems.

Major Benefits of IFT

The major benefits arising from the **IFT** of **GEs** can be classified, briefly, under five headings.

1- Increased productivity due to a global division of labor.
2- Starting the supply of products not produced before.
3- Increased employment.
4- Improved organizational and institutional skills.
5- Foreign currency earnings from exports, (if any).

Major Objections to IFT

There are many serious objections or criticisms to the global consequences of **IFT** practices which should not be neglected. Some of the criticisms are:

- Global production and trade is increasingly being shaped by **GEs** in accordance with their global interests, undermining the developing country interests.
- The underlying reason for the move of some production plants to developing countries is the opportunity to exploit a cheap labor-force.
- Many foreign enterprises do not, in fact, undertake any new investment which may add to productive capacity of the recipient country or creating new employment. Not they prefer to take-over the existing plants of production which simply means a change of ownership, not a real contribution to the productive capacity of the developing country.
- Practically, **IFT** does not make any significant contribution to technology transfer (discussed in Part-9).
- New global production relationships restructured by the **GEs** in accordance with their global interests do not indeed make any serious contribution to global competition. A given number of **GEs** continue their competition with products supplied from plants scattered around the globe, but this does not mean global competition is increasing. In order for global competition to increase, the number of independent profit units has to increase, which is not the case regarding the **IFR** transactions.
- Due to the prevailing imperfections in technology markets, the trend does not indicate any signs of improving the technological and labor-force abilities of the enterprises in the developing countries. Under the present global circumstances, it seems highly unlikely for the developing countries and their enterprises to close the income, industrialization or the development gap.

IFT and the Ownership of Enterprises

Most of the **GEs** engaged in **IFT** originate from developed countries. Thus the global production and distribution is being shaped according to the interests of enterprises of these developed countries. At first glance, this may not seem problematic. However, when viewed from the point of view of global income distribution, it might well be a different matter. Let us review the situation in more detail. As we know, the national income of a country consists of wages and profits, including interest rate, which we called the "value added" (**VA**).

Assume that 25 percent of all the value added by foreign controlled enterprise is profit and this profit is transferred to the country designated by the headquarters which would quite likely be a developed country. This would imply a transfer of income from the developing to the developed country which would contribute to the income growth of the developed country while diminishing the developing country's share of global income.

We assumed that 25 percent was the officially declared profit rate realized. However, we also know that **GEs** have all the facilities and abilities to make clandestine income transfers from the developing to the developed parts of the world (see Gürak; 2003). Unfortunately, there is no way to estimate the exact amount of this income transfer through "official" channels. In fact, it is an implicitly accepted taboo to comment on the adverse effects of **FDIs**. The **GEs** with global interests do not welcome such criticism in regard to what really happens in the markets and do their utmost to prevent it. This can be considered as a natural reaction because of the amount of transferred income received by **DCs** via clandestine channels is known to be a huge amount when compared to the net income generated by the **FDI** in the host country. This would be subject to global debate and criticism. Therefore, the expectation that data on present day clandestine income transfers would be made public appears to be a highly unrealistic expectation. However, we can get a clear picture from the past data already published concerning these practices (Gürak, 1990). The On the other hand, in order to have a less unequal and less unfair world, we need more and accurate information about the channels and size of "unofficial" transfers and reliable data on the extent of it.

Some Criticisms of "Liberal" Trade Policies

There are a large number of economists advocating more liberal trade policies which they claim would be in the best interests of consumers and producers. On the other hand, there are some criticisms of liberal trade policies that point out some potential disadvantages. The major objections of the opponents of liberal trade policies can be classified as follows:

- The development of infant industries might be retarded or prevented.
- The "terms of trade" are highly likely to deteriorate for the developing countries due to the presence of huge disparities in labor-force qualifications and the technological development stage.
- Due to the technological disparities, the developing country enterprises might become dependent upon the developed country enterprises for technology transfer.
- Balance of payments might deteriorate in the developing countries which might result in financial dependence.

While evaluating the potential benefits and the disadvantages of global trade, it is imperative to take into consideration the criticisms mentioned above. As a matter of fact, the observed data on globalization, the nature of global transactions and especially the "restrictive practices" of globally operating enterprises, provides solid grounds for suspicion.

A Skilled Labor-Force, Technological Progress & Global Trade

Since the close relationship between the skills of laborers and advances in technological progress has been already discussed in Sections 2 and 3, there is no further need to repeat it here. However, it might be useful to remind ourselves that "new products" and "new cost reducing methods of production", which are the products of creative mental labor always make a positive contribution to global trade.

Global Competition

Let us begin this section by asking a critical question: Do we really have access to a global market where all enterprises compete under the same "fair" conditions?

In order to have "fair" global competitive conditions, all enterprises from all countries should have, more or less, the same or similar technologies, e.g., production methods as well as access to a labor-force endowed with the same or similar qualities for similar products. Yet, we know very well from our observations that enterprises around the globe are not endowed with similar competitive qualities. There are enormous gaps between technological structures, financial facilities, institutional efficiencies and labor-force qualities of the developed and the developing countries and their enterprises. And this global situation tends to deteriorate, unless the existing data deceives us.

Taking measures to improve the quality of the labor-force is, primarily, a matter for the local rulers, and decision-makers. With appropriate and efficient programs in basic education problems such as increasing the rate of literacy or improving general education facilities can be easily achieved. However, improving the education or training infrastructure in developing countries to endow the labor-force with the necessary skills to efficiently use contemporary technologies, as found in the developed countries, requires a lot of time and effort, as well as the ability to establish the appropriate institutions and financial infrastructure. In the absence of a labor-force endowed with contemporary skills, it is practically impossible to use modern advanced technologies efficiently and supply products that are compatible in all the global markets. Eliminating, or at least reducing, global disparities in the skills of the labor-force should be given top priority.

Assume that all the disparities in the skills of the labor-force were eliminated with the wave of a wand; then would it be possible to have fair global competitive conditions amongst enterprises?

Given the present global economic circumstances and the structure of global institutions and their control by developed nations, it would be highly unlikely to find many high technology products and globally competitive enterprises originating from the developing countries which own and control the technology, although there might be some exceptions. The underlying reasons for this are present global economic circumstances and the imperfections encountered in technology markets. Enterprises from the developed countries, possessing high technology and operating globally, would not welcome any attempts to share their own "patented knowledge", e.g., technology, with "independent" enterprises from the developing countries (for a more detailed analysis see H. Gürak; "Hidden Costs", **www.hasmendi.net**).

In order to have independent and global competitive strength, the enterprises in a developing country might pursue a policy to develop their own technologies and own their patent rights themselves, which would provide them with a greater flexibility to make their own decisions. As we know, Japan and South Korea had implemented a similar technology and science policy in the past. However, this is a costly and risky process. It is not simply sufficient to have a high quality labor-force that makes efficient use of the present technology. There would be a great need for "creative mental labor" along with an appropriate technological infrastructure, institutions and financial facilities. Assume, for a moment, that all these conditions are met; who can guarantee success in a global competitive market when confronted with giant and well experienced enterprises. Besides, it would be difficult to defend a technology policy to "re-invent" the already produced technologies which are presently in the hands of developed countries' giant enterprises. In a way, it would be like trying to re-invent the wheel; a useless waste of time.

Given the global economic circumstances in regard to the imperfections found in the technology market and the ability of the developing countries' enterprises to change all these, the so called development experts from global economic institutions and the developed countries, strongly advise the transfer of technology from the developing countries by the elimination of all barriers and encouraging foreign direct investments (FDIs). We can clearly see that the number of countries with generous FDI incentives is increasing constantly.

Global Competition & FDIs

Let us evaluate global competition from the point of view of the **FDIs** and global production. As indicated before, increasingly more developing countries are pursuing increasingly more liberal and generous economic policies in favor of **FDIs** which they hope will contribute to their economic growth rate. Yet, global income and wealth disparities seem to widen in time, instead of diminishing. The crucial related question is; what happens to global competitiveness? Does it show a tendency to increase over time?

Unfortunately, it is impossible to give a positive answer? It is true that the number of laborers endowed with improved abilities is expanding, but that does not mean global competitiveness is increasing. To give an example, let us take a look at the automotive sector in Turkey again. As we know, Turkey has a large automotive sector with a substantial amount of exports to the developed as well as developing countries. Yet, there is no automobile producing enterprise owned and controlled by Turkish citizens with a Turkish trade-mark or own technology patent. The cars produced by brand names such as Fiat, Renault, Hyundai and Toyota are actually owned by the **GEs** of developed nations which also control both global production and distribution units. Their production plants in Turkey operate only as "**subcontractors**" and have no say in regard to crucial issues regarding the type of automobile, quantities produced and exported, etc. These critical decisions are made in the headquarters of the **GEs** with respect to their global interests. İrmiş (2008) describes position as;

> "... a completely hierarchic vertical organization with developed country enterprises on the top placing of orders and subjacent developing country enterprises looking forward to carry out orders at predetermined prices." (İrmiş, 2008; p.4-5)

Given the nature of the subcontracting system, the huge financial, organizational and technological gap between the developed and developing country enterprises is bound to produce serious problems. One of the forth coming problems is pointed out by İrmiş (2008):

> "This weakness and isolation of developing country enterprises against developed country enterprises is subject to exploitation by developed country enterprises, especially in "cost-reducing." (İrmiş, 2008; p.5)

For instance, assume that the concessions granted by the Turkish government are considered insufficient or unsatisfactory compared to another country's more generous concessions, or that the "real" wage-level in Turkey rises above "acceptable" limits, then subcontracted production can be moved partly or wholly to a country best serving the **GE**'s' global interests.

Is it logical and rational to refer to a system based on low-wage utilization as promoting global competition? A positive answer to this question seems unlikely. For example, it is true that the nature of global competition is changing in regard to automobile production. The productions of low-technology components are located in relatively lower-cost countries which promote **FDIs** with generous policies. Would it be rational to say that global competition in automobile sector is growing?

In order to say that global competition is growing, the number of independent profit making automobile producers has to increase. Under the circumstances described, the subcontracting of production does not seem to make any positive contribution to increased global competition. What the system does is the struggle to reduce cost which helps to increase global profits.

Global Trade & the Convergence of Wages & Prices

There is no doubt that global trade makes many positive contributions to national economies. For instance, under "fair" competitive conditions both individuals and national economies enjoying similar technological and institutional development levels would benefit highly from global trade in terms of price, quality and the variety of products, cet. par. The relevant and important question is what would the benefits of increased global trade be for all national economies in regard to the huge global disparities in income, technological and institutional infrastructure and competitive strength? Would it be a rational expectation for wages, prices and incomes to converge, under the present nature of global relationships?

According to some of the proponents of the neoclassical doctrine, provided the assumptions and the conditions of their theories are fulfilled, free global trade is expected to lead to the convergence of global wages and prices. Yet, the data and the experience gained from actual global transactions indicate that just the opposite is happening. As the barriers of global trade diminish, the income gap does not tend to close, but in reality becomes greater (Gürak, 2006). Besides, historical facts and experience tell quite a different story in regard to economic development, in contrast to the liberal trade policies advocated by the developed country institutions and the extension of these institutions; the international institutions.

Given the present nature of relationships, it is highly utopian to expect wages and prices to converge. The following seem to be major obstacles in achieving this goal:

1- The nature of global supply, distribution and technology transfer relationships.
2- Disparities between general development levels.
3- Disparities in labor-force qualities.
4- Global imperfections in technology markets.
5- Poverty.
6- Corruption and bad governance in the developing countries.

Instead of closing the global income and development gap, the present nature of global economic relationships tends to produce the following results.

- Wages and prices in the developed countries might converge or get closer.
- The global prices of industrial products in all countries might converge, but not the service sector prices, at least not in foreseeable future.
- The qualitative differences of consumer products might diminish or even disappear completely in both, developed and developing countries; but the quantity of per capita consumption is unlikely to converge.
- It seems like a purely utopian expectation for the developed and the developing countries' wage-level to converge, at least under the present global economic conditions.

Concluding Remarks

Let us present the major findings briefly:

- There seems to be no significant difference in the nature of the trade relationships between national enterprises in the domestic markets or between enterprises at a global level, given "fair" and equally competitive conditions and regulations for all the enterprises concerned. Naturally, there should be neither any enterprise with a monopolistic or oligopolistic power in the markets nor any visible or invisible barriers to trade.

- Global economic trends show that trade barriers hampering global trade in industrial goods are diminishing progressively.

- Elimination of all trade barriers among countries with the same or similar development levels would make a positive contribution to global trade.

- Elimination of all trade barriers among countries with the same or similar development levels would contribute to the maximizing of consumer benefits.

- Protection of the "infant" sectors for a pre-determined time-period is highly likely to make a positive contribution to global trade and to global economic growth. Because, infant sector enterprises mature over time as global competition increases due to the participation of more competitors in the global market which also would effect consumers in positive way.

- Enterprises lagging behind in contemporary level of technological advancement cannot survive the long-term challenge of their rivals in competitive markets. Therefore, all competitive enterprises have to strive to keep up with the technological changes. However, as indicated in Section-7, there are serious imperfections in the global technology markets to the detriment of the "technological" late-comers. The present nature of the technology markets, the consequent global economic relationships, together with historical developments, does not seem to make a positive contribution to global competition. For instance, scattering the automobile production plants around the globe by using the wholly or partly owned subsidiaries of a "given number" of Globally Operating Enterprises would not really increase global competition. To increase global competition, the number of independent automobile producers who seek to maximize their profit margins has to increase. To overcome this obstacle, the imperfections in the technology markets have to be eliminated or, at least, the transfer conditions of technology have to improve in favor of the developing countries' enterprises.

- The share and significance of intra-firm trade (**IFT**) has been constantly growing. In principle, growing global trade is a good sign responsible for global economic growth. However, it is also liable to lead to some undesirable economic consequences, especially in the more "**clandestine income transfers**". For example, assume that a foreign-owned enterprise-"A" undertakes an investment in Turkey to produce automobiles. Further assume that some of the inputs used in the supply of the automobiles are imported from a source and at a price determined by the parent enterprise. The inputs imported may be available in the global markets at global competitive prices. But, although the global prices for the imported inputs might be much lower, the plant in Turkey has no choice but to purchase these inputs from the parent company's sources and at a price predetermined by headquarters, in accordance with the global interests of the parent enterprise. This decision from "headquarters" may result in, or may be used for, a **"disguised transfer of profits"** to a pre-determined source, in accordance with its global profit policy.

- The global interests of enterprises engaged in **IFT** are more important for the foreign-owner than the potential benefits or damages to the host-country's economy, and not infrequently, these interests are incompatible.

- **IFT** transactions may lead to the economic dependency of the host-country's economy on the foreign global enterprise, e.g., the **GE**.

Chapter 9: TRANSFER of TECHNOLOGY

> The institution that most changes our lives we least understand, or, more correctly, seek most elaborately to misunderstand.
> That is the modern corporation.
>
> K. Galbraith;
> The Age of Uncertainty, p.275

As empirical evidence on the global economic performance indicates, there is a widening gap in the economic welfare and technological advances between the so called Developed Countries (**DCs**) and Developing or Less Developed Countries (**LDCs**). Neither the popular import-biased economic growth strategies of the 1950s and 1960s nor the highly praised export-biased growth models have been successful in transforming the **LDCs** from the ranks of the less developed into the levels of the developed welfare state prevailing in Western industrialized countries. As a recent World Bank study indicates:

> "The last decade of the 20th century saw great progress in parts of the world. But it also saw stagnation and setbacks, even in countries that had previously achieved the fastest rates of economic growth. These gaping differences and sharp reversals teach us much about what contributes to development. At the center is economic growth, not just its pace but—as important—also its quality." (World Bank,2000; p.XXIII)

The World Bank claims that there is often inadequate attention paid to certain crucial aspects and recommends the broadening of the policy framework to include some qualitative aspects. Accordingly, the World Bank focuses on four dimensions of quality which contribute to the growth process;

1- Improving the distribution of opportunities;
2- Sustaining natural capital;
3- Dealing with global financial risks; and
4- Improving governance and controlling corruption.

The term "quality" is an ambiguous and subjective concept. While improved sanitation and health conditions might be considered as a qualitative change for the citizens of Country-X, present family relations in **DCs** might be considered as reduced quality for the citizens of Country-Y. Yet in another community, the quality might imply egalitarian income distribution or better gender and racial equality while for people in poverty it might imply better nutrition and improved shelter conditions. Thus, given the disparities in the economic, social, cultural and institutional environment, the concept of "quality" would necessarily lead to different interpretations and implementations. Each nation will find its own subjective and specific qualitative patterns as economic growth takes place. The four dimensions of the World Bank outlined above can only serve as a set of guidelines.

As the World Bank states; for developing countries: "**At the center is economic growth.**" Therefore, at the expense of other "qualitative" aspects, the emphasis in this section will be on the analysis of inappropriate conditions for economic growth and continual social change. To be more specific, the focus will be on the global technological aspects, with the purpose of shedding some light on the "adverse" impacts of technology transfer through the medium of direct foreign investments (**FDIs**) to the **LDCs**. As technological changes take place, socio-economic changes inevitably follow which, in turn, changes the qualitative aspects of life, both in the developed as well as the less developed nations. The key to both qualitative and quantitative progress, given the proper economic policy and the institutional and cultural environment to go with it is the resource arising from the advancement in human knowledge and abilities (Gürak, 1999; 2000-a; 2000-b).

The present analysis draws extensively from a particular study by Gürak in 1990 which focuses on the "**hidden**" costs arising from the use of the "**restrictive clauses"** contained in "**package deals**". But first concepts such as "development", "growth", "new technologies" and the "channels of technology transfer" will be briefly reviewed.

Economic Growth & Development

It is difficult to draw a distinct line between growth and development. For some researchers growth means increased per capita growth of income while the concept development means much more, i.e., economic growth plus the institutional, social and cultural changes in the society. In regard to the circumstances in LDCs, development would suggest, in addition to per capita income growth, improvements in areas ranging from educational opportunities, income distribution, housing conditions, infant mortality, and life expectancy to the political and judicial system.

As a World Bank study explains:

"Development is about improving the quality of people's lives, expanding their ability to shape their own futures. This generally calls for higher per capita income, but it involves much more. It involves more equitable education and job opportunities. Greater gender equality. Better health and nutrition. A cleaner, more sustainable natural environment. A more impartial judicial and legal system. Broader civil and political freedoms. A richer cultural life. As per capita incomes rise, several of these aspects improve in varying degrees—but others do not." (World Bank: XXIII)

According to the statements above, the following proposition would not be inaccurate; "all national economies, whether DC or LDC, grow as well as develop in time".

There is a close correlation between technological progress and economic growth and development. As more firms introduce new technologies in order to control and to change the economic circumstances, they also, indirectly, induce socio-economic change. In other words, new technologies lead to inevitable modifications in the institutional setting and the cultural values. Continual technological changes constantly change our socio-economic life. One of the most recent and drastic examples of this is the widespread application of computers and Internet Developments in the realm of information technology (IT) which have not only made communication easier, generated new employment opportunities, opened up new markets but also raised social and political awareness as well as expectations. A related recent change is, nowadays citizens of the DCs demand a broader participation in the decision-making concerning both local and national issues. Since all economies, one way or another, continually undergo technological progress and technological progress leads to socio-economic changes, then all countries are, at the same time, growing and developing.

Technology & Technological Progress

Technology is knowledge that changes and controls our environment. In this study, as we focus on "commercial technology transfer", the term technology will be used as the set of "**productive knowledge**" applied in order to produce commodities or to render services that meet the needs and wants of society. It is the *"key to the progress of mankind"* (UNCTAD, 1983, p.41) and paves the way for economic development along with social-political change. (Gürak, 2000-a; 2000-b)

The invention-innovation process of a new technology is a costly and risky process, which is predominantly undertaken and controlled by globally operating enterprises (**GOFs**). New technologies require the engagement of highly skilled human labor as well as financial resources, as well as the appropriate technological, organizational, institutional and cultural infrastructure. The determining factor of firms engaging in such a costly and risky process is to obtain the maximum compensation or return on investment in the long run. To achieve this goal, the new technology must be able to make the owner more competitive and profitable either in terms of lower unit costs by introducing a "new production method" for a "given" product or by introducing "new products and production methods" which usually facilitate the realization of above average profit rates, until the competition catches up.

In a market economy, the patent rights system guarantees the reward for the technology owners' effort in the form of returns on their investment. The owner of the new technology (productive knowledge) is thus granted the right by the authorities to enjoy the fruits of owning a new productive knowledge until the competition develops similar products. The patent system does not only stimulate research for new productive knowledge but also eliminates unnecessary effort in the same field as others would discover that their idea has already been developed. As the patent is disclosed in a public document, it is said to stimulate further improvement (development) in the patented technology by other enterprises.

The **GOFs** possess an immense pool of productive knowledge, as well as widespread experience and managerial and organizational skills. Global inequality in the distribution of wealth is expected to narrow by transferring technology to the **LDCs** mainly through the **FDIs** of the **GOFs**. Empirical evidence indicates that the most dynamic industries of the global economy are those in the research-intensive sectors where technological change is a never ending ongoing process. Therefore, it is no surprise that globally operating GOFs are, in general, found in those dynamic, research-intensive industries, which sometimes requires funds greater than the total national income of some nation-states.

Transfer of Technology

To meet the desired development targets, the LDCs are faced with two alternatives:

1- Encouraging indigenous technological efforts from R&D to product development; or
2- Transferring the already existing and tried and tested technologies from the DCs.

In our age of a rapidly and continuously advancing technological environment, consumers' preferences both in the developed and developing countries are shifting towards more sophisticated and technologically complex products, especially in dynamic sectors such as communication, biology, space industry, etc. On the other hand, regardless of present rate of economic growth and the level of development, the **LDC**s, in general, seem to be in short supply of an essential element of development, i.e., a skilled labor force with appropriate endowments.

Having access to an appropriate technological and institutional infrastructure along with a labor force endowed with appropriate skills is a prerequisite in order to invent and develop a new technology; there is also a need for large investments in R&D and access to markets for the new products and/or production methods. The **LDCs** are short of all these ingredients necessary for the development of a new technology. Therefore it seems more rational for the **LDCs** to acquire the new technology through a transfer from the developed countries in the form of **FDIs** accompanied by a "package deal". Common sense would suggest that using the **LDCs** scarce resources to produce something that already exists in the **DCs** is not only risky and highly costly but also irrational.

As is commonly acknowledged, technology transfer has many positive impacts on the economy of technology importing countries. Access to new and advanced know-how, in addition to increases in domestic productive capacity and the generation of employment are just a few of the advantages. But the technology market also contains many imperfections. Various factors seem to restrict the full-utilization of the transferred technology. In other words, FDIs do not only mean benefits but also lead to some adverse impacts on other important aspects such as income distribution, employment and foreign currency reserves. There are even claims that the overall costs by far outweigh the benefits.

Channels for the Transfer of Technology

The channels of technology transfer can be classified in three groups:

1- Transfer of Informative Knowledge.
2- Transfer of Products; and
3- Transfer of Production Method.

The Transfer of Informative Knowledge

The scope of the transfer of informative knowledge ranges from the flow of publicly available knowledge such as patent disclosure, professional books and journals to the education and the training of manpower. However one has to determine, that what is to be transferred is **not** "productive knowledge" on "how to produce", but rather the information on the "product itself" such as what it is, where it is used and how it is used. The patented knowledge available at patent offices may seem at first glance as an opportunity to copy the productive knowledge and use it in the production process. But this is not what happens in reality. A patented knowledge cannot be commercially utilized by other enterprises unless the owner allows its utilization through a contractual agreement.

As such, informative knowledge is beyond the scope of this paper.

The Transfer of Products

The transfer of products is also referred to as the "Direct Transfer" of technology, and takes place when a commodity containing the "features of a specific technology" is transferred or imported to another country as a finished or semi-finished commodity. It is important to note that what is transferred is still **not** productive knowledge about "how to produce" a commodity but "a commodity" embodying the in-built features of a specific technology in a "disguised" form. In other words, there is a simple transaction, e.g. sale or purchase, of a commodity. A great deal of global trade consists of finished and semi-finished commodities. In this sense, a massive amount of technology transfer takes place every day, but the subject is not within the scope of this paper, either.

The Transfer of Production Method

The transfer of technology should involve, as UNCTAD postulates:

> "... the transfer of systematic knowledge for the manufacture of a product, for the application of a process or for the rendering of a service and does not extend to the transactions involving the mere sale or mere lease of goods." (UNCTAD, 1983, p.2)

We refer to such a technology transfer as "the transfer of production method". The means for this kind of transfer ranges from the establishment of a subsidiary wholly owned by the host-country to patent or license arrangements, joint ventures, turnkey arrangements or profit-sharing arrangements. The transfer of production method often introduces new products that have no previous counterpart in the importing countries, especially in the **LDCs** by introducing:

1- A new production process for an existing product; or
2- New commodities and/or services; or
3- Both.

The channels of the transfer of production method can be subdivided into two further groups:

1- The sale or purchases of licenses or patents; or
2- Foreign direct investment (**FDI**).

Given the appropriate conditions, the LDCs could save a lot of time, money and human resources by transferring technologies from the DCs. There is of course a price for the technology to be transferred, which ought to be lower than the costs of local-development or the re-invention of the desired technology. The focus, in this section will be on the "hidden" costs arising from **FDIs**.

What Should the Price Be?

If there were perfectly competitive markets as the Neoclassical theory predicts, the price of new technology would equal the marginal costs of distribution. Because, once a new technology (productive knowledge) is developed, its exploitation by others does not diminish its availability to others. Thus, to acquire the **optimum** utility from the new technology, its price ought to be set at the marginal costs of distribution for other potential users. But, this represents a "utopian" case in contrast to the common business practices in the global economies. In real life, there is a price determined by the technology owner which has to be paid by the technology buyer in excess of its diffusion costs.

The Actual Cost

It is not an easy task to evaluate the actual costs of technology which the technology importing enterprise accrues. Some costs are statistically measurable but some occur in a disguised form, such as the "**transfer pricing**" of imports and/or exports, or costs arising from restrictive practices on imports, exports, etc. Such indirect costs involve both conceptual and verification problems. UNCTAD suggested distinguishing the direct costs from indirect ones in the manner described below.

> "Direct costs:
>
> (a) Charges for the right to use patents, licenses, know-how and trade-marks;
>
> (b) Charges for technical knowledge and know-how needed both in the pre-investment and in the investment stages and in the operation stage.
>
> Indirect costs:
>
> (c) Charges through overpricing of imports of intermediate products and equipment ("hidden" costs or "price mark-ups"), some of which may not have market price;
>
> (d) Charges arising through profits on capitalization of know-how (equity participation in place of, or in addition to, other means of payments for the transfer of technology); dividends on these equity holdings are, therefore, to be regarded as, in part, payments for the transfer of technology;
>
> (e) Charges in the form of some portion of repatriated profits of wholly-owned subsidiaries or joint-ventures the establishment of which does not make specific provision for payments for the transfer of technology;

(f) Charges through imports of capital and other technical equipment, the price of which usually allows for the exporters' valuation of the cost of technology." (UNCTAD; 1972,p.24)

Hidden Costs of Technology Transfer

Without doubt there is a sufficiently large quantity of literature and comments on the positive impact on the economy of the host country of technology transfer through foreign direct investments such as its contributions to;

- Domestic employment.
- Foreign currency inflow through investment and exports.
- Foreign currency saving through local production instead of importing.
- Increased production capacity.
- Increased productivity.
- Access to "new" superior productive knowledge.
- Tax revenues; etc., etc.

But, as mentioned before, there are also some serious demerits, i.e., "**hidden costs**" involved in the system which cost the host countries dearly and are sometimes to the detriment of their economic and technological development, in contrast to their expectations. Costs like the repatriation of profits, royalty payments, and management salaries are measurable quantities and the cost to the host country can easily be evaluated. But the so-called "hidden costs" which might amount to huge sums are difficult to reveal and to measure.

The following subsections will focus on these hidden aspects of technology transfer, the costs of which accrue to the host countries and are practically impossible to measure in their full extent due to the inherent feature of the system; that is being "hidden", but which ought to be dealt with if a better and fairer global economic, social and political order is desired.

The General Circumstances

In general, the LDCs offer a variety of generous financial and non-financial incentives and concessions with the hope to attract more FDI, hence to accelerate the domestic economic growth, increase employment, and solve other related problems. But, these incentives and concessions are not always compatible with the development plans and aspirations of the developing countries. Not infrequently, there are even conflicts of interest between the **GOF**s and the host country. It has often been observed that the foreign investors enjoy monopolistic or oligopolistic advantages in the host country in regard to the quantity and the quality of production, distribution, the sources of the inputs and the finance, prices, quantity and type of exports, as well as the method of production. These monopolistic or oligopolistic advantages may cause serious adverse effects on the economy of the recipient countries, such as an imbalance-of-payments, "non-transfer" of technology, a deterioration of income distribution or the introduction of inappropriate e.g., luxury products. It is also a great concern to many that the globally operating corporations might take too much and leave too little, thus the costs to the host country might far exceed their initial financial benefits and their expectations as technology markets are prone to the imperfections which work to the detriment of LDCs.

At first sight, the sources of advanced technology seem to be plentiful and this fact seems to place the technology-importing firms in a more advantageous position when compared to that of the technology sellers. But there serious problems, for example; a country with a low technological absorption capacity would not know what alternative technologies are available, or what are the most suitable for local production, or which are the best transfer channels or how to bargain effectively about the transfer terms.

If the developing countries could agree on certain basic principals to act collectively against the **GOFs**, their bargaining power and the ensuing benefits would improve significantly. In practice, however, it is the **GOFs** that have the upper hand, especially when technologically more complex projects are involved. The more complex the imported technology for the buyer the weaker the bargaining strength of the recipient tends to be and the more the costs tend to accumulate. The **GOFs** are normally in a strong bargaining position and usually dictate the terms and conditions of technology transfer in conjunction with their own global interests. Thus, the complexity of the technology markets and the relative bargaining powers of related parties appear to be the major initial causes of the imperfections in technology markets.

What are the specific circumstances leading to these undesired hidden costs?

"Package Deals" with Restrictive Clauses

Package deals can contribute to the acceleration of economic development in developing areas by providing a secure flow of the vital inputs of production. But they can also become impediments to economic and technological progress. As we observe, the **GOFs** not only respond to the local market imperfections such as inefficient economic policies, but often generate these imperfections themselves and package deals containing various kinds of restrictive practices are common practice. It seems likely that many **FDIs** would not have taken place in the developing countries in the absence of restrictive practices which redistribute income in favor of the industrialized countries, thus adversely affecting the global income distribution pattern.

There are three major reasons for packaging a certain technology;

1- packaging enables the **GOF** to exercise a considerable degree of control over key issues such as price, source of inputs, exports, quantity, etc.;
2- packaging minimizes the risks of technological and organizational inefficiency in the operation of the subsidiary and guarantees a certain degree of quality in order to protect the image of the "trade-mark"; and
3- the **GOF** would be reluctant to see the unchecked diffusion of its technological and managerial skills that might lead to the creation of local competitors.

In contrast to the direct foreign exchange costs and tax-concessions, costs arising from package deals are rather cumbersome to measure, if not impossible. In the case of a joint-venture it is expected of the **GOF** to make an explicit written agreement specifying the nature and the extent of any transactions. But, if the subsidiary is a wholly-owned or controlled subsidiary of the GOF, such explicitly written contractual agreement would be superfluous, since the subsidiary would receive all instructions directly from **GOF** headquarters. There would be no need for formal documents because the **GOF** is in complete control of all operations anyway. As a result, there would be no "visible" restrictions to be criticized and estimating "hidden costs" would become impossible.

Institutions in developing countries urgently have to find and impose counter-measures to minimize these hidden costs, which lead to;

- loss of tax revenues to the host state;
- higher consumer prices (when the imports tend to be over-priced);
- less dividends for the local share-holders (in the case of a local partner);
- deteriorating foreign exchange reserves (over-priced imports or under-priced exports); and,
- loss of export earnings (if exports are restricted).

The Classification of Hidden Costs

The "hidden" costs can be analyzed in the following major groups:

1- Transfer Pricing ("Under-pricing" exports or "Over-pricing" of imports).
2- Export Clauses.
3- Import Clauses.
4- Production Clauses.
5- Management Clauses.
6- Intra-firm Loan Clauses (Excessive interest-rate on intra-firm loans).

7- Grant-back Clauses (Reverting the product improvements to parent-firm).
8- Technological Dependence.
9- Economic and political dependence.
10-Brain drain.
11-Corruption.

1- Transfer Pricing (Over Pricing Imports, Under Pricing Exports)

A significant share of global trade takes place intra-firm that is between the subsidiary and the parent firm, which provides an appropriate climate for a **transfer-pricing** mechanism in transactions with the Parent Firm. Probably the most efficient means of the clandestine transfer of company revenues (e.g. **invisible profits**) from the subsidiary to the parent firm is through the transfer-pricing mechanism. **GOFs** possess the necessary facilities, experience and expertise to manipulate the intra-firm prices in accordance with their global strategies, especially in developing countries. Unfortunately, making a sound estimate of such costs is difficult due to the commercial secrecy of these strategies and a reluctance to publish such data. They are assumed to be of a significant amount.

A transfer-pricing mechanism, accompanied by restrictive clauses, obliges the subsidiary to;

1- buy the necessary capital goods and the other inputs of production from a pre-determined source, and at the prices, determined by the technology supplier, i.e., **over-pricing**; and/or
2- sell the subsidiary's output to the customers, and at the prices, determined by the technology supplier, i.e., **under-pricing**.

The empirical data indicates that the provisions of contractual clauses are used mainly for over-pricing purposes, rather than under-pricing. (Gürak; 1990) While the over-pricing of input and capital goods in intra-firm trade contributes to the maximization of global earnings for the **GOFs,** it represents the loss of an already scarce source; the foreign currency reserve of the host country. For instance, for some specific input, say the doors for Fiat automobiles, as there is no international market for them, the source of supply is normally determined by **GOF** headquarters at a pre-determined price to be paid by the subsidiary. There is no way to estimate the rate of over-pricing and the ensuing clandestine revenue transfer correctly.

According to a recent but naive approach by UNCTAD, transfer-pricing methods are introduced as a response to tax policy inadequacies, such as double taxation. (UNCTAD; 1999-c,E.99.II.D.8) The recommended remedy for this problem is to restructure the international tax laws and other such arrangements including mutually acceptable transfer pricing methods. New global tax arrangements might indeed serve to eliminate double taxation but would hardly be sufficient to eliminate the transfer pricing mechanism and the evils caused by it.

Given the global strategies of the **GOFs**, the motives for the Parent Firm that supplies the technology to prefer a transfer-pricing mechanism can be summarized as follows;

1- to avoid double taxation or any taxation levied by the host country;
2- to maintain a pattern of "image" in the host country by keeping declared profits or royalties low;
3- to maximize the profits in predetermined "profit-centers"; and
4- to overcome host country controls and regulations on remittances.

The firms are reluctant, by nature, to pay taxes (item-1) and this factor may induce the Parent Firm to search for some means to avoid or minimize these payments. Instead of paying the full amount taxes, the Parent Firm may transfer earnings to a preferred center, by means of the over-pricing mechanism.

For some people, especially in the developing countries, **FDIs** represent a new form of economic imperialism and thus exploit the indigenous endowments. To avoid further antagonism in the host country or in the international arena, the Parent Firm may pursue a policy of "low profits" in the developing host countries. Thus, while preserving its image as a good "corporate citizen" (item-2) it can continue its operations, including its transfer-pricing, smoothly and comfortably.

In the case of joint ventures, the Parent Firm can increase its share of the profits by reducing the profit rate at the subsidiary level through transfer-pricing (item-3). And finally, the stringent foreign exchange controls and regulations by the host country (item-4) may induce the Parent Firm to resort to means other than transferring royalty payments or profit remittances from the subsidiary firm.

Transfer pricing is not a dilemma that only affects a developing country. It also occurs in the intra-firm trade among developed countries. The most striking example of over-pricing, to our knowledge, is the case of Hoffmann-La Roche. The U.K. subsidiary of the firm had declared profits at around 5 percent while The Monopolies Commission in the UK claimed that the return on the capital earned over the period from 1966-1972 was, in fact, over 70 percent (Franco,1976,p.227). Similar cases occur throughout the world, but, not infrequently, the developing host countries, although certainly not unfamiliar with this problem, are unable to cope with it efficiently.

2- Export (Non-competition) Clauses

The main purpose of such clauses is to preempt the possibility of a competitor of the subsidiary from entering the global markets and delivering the same products as the Parent Firm. Although this appears to be a rational behavior from the point of view of the Parent Firm, these export clauses lead to a "potential" loss of foreign exchange earnings for the developing country.

Export clauses appear in various forms ranging from the use of the direct prohibition of exports, the limiting of the quantity of exports, the restriction of the number of export zones to the subjecting of products to strict quality controls. The prohibition of the use of trademarks in third world countries and the export of "similar" products are other serious obstacles to exportation which work to the detriment of the **LDCs**.

Nowadays, there is a widely acknowledged and highly praised tendency towards globalization of production and distribution that is shaped by the GOFs. At first glance, one might get the impression that products are being produced at the sites of least cost and flowing freely to the international markets and as a result, global competition is really growing. Thus, for some readers the subsidiaries may appear as globally competing production centers. Unfortunately, this is not the case! Subsidiaries are not "independent" profit centers, but the frontier fortresses of the oligopolistic combatants, and are used in order to maximize the profits in pre-determined profit centers in conjunction with global interests and strategies of the GOFs. Implicit or explicit export clauses serve the global interests of the GOFs. For instance, no matter how competitive in global markets, Fiat vehicles made in Turkey cannot be exported without the prior approval of the Parent Firm in Italy.

3- Import Clauses (Tied-inputs)

The distribution of tie-in clauses on inputs differs from country to country and demonstrates various levels in attempting to tie the purchase of "certain" inputs to the Parent Firm and/or to the sources determined by it, depending on its global strategies. In the case of wholly owned subsidiaries, there is no need to specify such restrictions because the Parent Firm determines the guidelines of the operations of these particular subsidiaries. But in case of a local partnership, implicit and/or explicit restrictions pop up like mushrooms. Quality control clauses can reinforce the position of the Parent Firm by determining the "additional" tied-in items that must be purchased from pre-determined sources or by restricting the purchase of inputs from "other" sources.

4- The Production Clause

Restrictive clauses on production would aim to predetermine the quality as well as the minimum and/or maximum quantities to be produced by the subsidiary which might serve to maintain the quality and the domestic or global prices at the desired level. Quality controls, as mentioned before, can easily be used to tie-in imports while quantitative controls are, not infrequently, designed to preempt the possibility of exportation.

In addition, the Parent Firm may prohibit the subsidiary importing competing products or production processes or any sort of cooperation with a third party. Restrictions on the production of "similar" products using the imported technology are a different but a no less significant matter. Production clauses are definitely not in conflict with the global interests of the Parent Firm. But, depending on their nature and extent, production clauses may become serious obstacles to increased global competition and economic efficiency, again to the detriment of LDCs.

5- Management Clauses

Technology selling firms are always anxious to maintain and consolidate control on the local firm by applying clauses on the key decision-making processes like planning and strategy, by appointing personnel trained and loyal to the Parent Firm. The key word is loyalty to the Parent Firm and its global strategic targets.

6- Intra-Firm Loan Clauses

High interest payments on **intra-firm loans** represent another form of the clandestine transfer of resources, i.e., foreign exchange which flows from the subsidiary to the parent firm. Data presently available indicates that on occasion the volume of foreign private loans coming from the home countries exceeded the volume of total direct foreign investment originating from the same countries over a given period. (Gürak; 1990)

7- Grant-Back clauses

Such clauses require that any technological improvement made locally by the subsidiary has to revert back to the owner of the said technology, i.e., the **GOF**. Such clauses deprive the host country of the potential benefits of technological improvements made in the host country, while consolidating the position of the Parent Firm in the global markets.

8- Technological Dependence

Large scale technology transfer may become an impediment to the development of local technological capabilities and infrastructure, thus perpetuating technological dependence on the **GOFs**. In addition, Parent Firms are always keen on the further use of its productive knowledge after the expiration of any contractual agreements and usually attempt to prohibit the further use of imported technology after its expiration. To extend the further use of such technology, a new agreement has to be designed which enables the Parent Firm to continue more control over the subsidiary. Such restrictions along with the "grant-back" clauses involving locally made improvements which perpetuate technological dependence on the Parent Firm are definitely not in the interest of **LDCs**, nor in the interest of global competitiveness and efficiency.

The duration period of contracts is another problem area. The longest duration period possible would be the most desirable solution from the point of view of the **GOF**. But the interests of the host country point to the opposite direction, e.g. the shortest possible duration.

9- Economic & Political Dependence

Ownership and accordingly, the control of critical economic units by foreign investors are highly likely to result in the economic and political dependence of the investment receiving country. For instance, an economically heavily US-dependent Canada or Mexico would find it difficult to challenge or be in conflict with US economic and political interests on critical issues. A country that is economically dependent, in some way or another, cannot really be independent nor can it pursue its own interests. When a dependent country attempts to challenge the interests of another country, it will sooner or later have to face the consequences. History is full of numerous examples proving this point.

10- Brain Drain

Brain-drain in general is the migration of individuals with a **skill, knowledge** and **experience** to countries other than their own in order to hire his/her labor services. In addition, another form of brain-drain occurs when the foreign investors set up a plant in another country and hire the labor services of highly skilled, educated and/or trained individuals for the sole interests of the investors. For instance, when the native qualified labor force invents a new product or process for a foreign owned enterprise, the patent right of the new knowledge is likely to be possessed by the said foreign enterprise. The benefits of this new knowledge would likely serve the foreign enterprise's interests.

In addition, the transfer of skilled native personnel to economic units in "third" world countries would again serve the interests of **GOFs** which leads, in a sense, to a drain of brain power from the native country. The beneficiary of the services of the skilled personnel is no longer the native country but the foreign investor.

11- Corruption

The negative impacts of corruption on developing countries are immense. Often, it is rather difficult to get a job done without the assistance of politicians or local administrators in return for a "favor". This behavior prevents the development of fair competition and causes the misallocation of resources. Foreign investors often exploit this weakness to solve their problems, get things done and to promote their own interests, which often work against the local interests. Dura's (2010) work provides us with some useful insights into this problem by showing how far the foreign enterprises are willing to go to reach their own targets.

Summary of the Findings

The growing dominance of the **GOF's** global transactions has led to different responses. The proponents of the new global division of labor have discovered many world wide benefits in. **FDIs**, which they claim, bring into the host country not only foreign exchange, and superior managerial qualities and better organizational ability but also new technologies which were unknown before the **FDI** arrived. Thus, the **GOFs** with their enormous facilities and global opportunities are seen as the units of real integration in the global economy.

Critics often draw attention to aspects such as economic and technological dependence, the inappropriateness of the technology imported, misallocation of resources as well as adverse income distribution effects. It is true that these adverse affects of foreign investment are, to some extent, due to the prevailing economic policies in **LDCs**. But it is also true that the way the technology markets work, especially in regard to their restrictive or abusive practices, is the cause of the many evils that occur in the global market.

The global operations of the **GOFs** are restructuring the division of production and income distribution while increasing the interdependence of nations. In this process, the **FDIs** seem to be the principal mechanism which links national economies and trade. Global prosperity is increasing, but there is a disturbing and widening gap in the economic welfare between the few **DCs** and the many **LDCs**. The rate of economic growth can, no doubt, be accelerated by the transfer of technology from the vast pool that has already been accumulated. But, the global strategies of the **GOFs** and imperfect technology markets do not seem to be a proper cure for these problems. In fact, the present globalization process seems to aggravate global inequality and perpetuates its dependence upon external influences. The **GOFs** seem to be; *"... able to manipulate prices and profits, to collude with other firms in determining areas of control, and generally to restrict the entry of potential competition...."* (Todaro; 1977;p.342). The prevailing conditions seem to prevent the extensive utilization of the available technologies by the developing countries.

The major findings of this section can be summarized as follows.

- **FDI** improves the foreign exchange reserves of the host country initially. But what is taken out of the host country in terms of royalties and profits, both official and clandestine, over along period of time (years) tends to greatly exceed the initial inflow by "a long chalk". The "transfer-pricing" mechanism seems to be the principal source of these clandestine profits, i.e. the foreign exchange costs.

- If the subsidiary is established to benefit from cheap labor in order to service foreign markets only, there is the risk of the "non-transfer" of technology.

- Tax-concessions deprive the developing host countries of vital revenues that could be utilized to promote indigenous capabilities. Unfortunately, developing nations seem to compete with each other in order to provide more generous tax-concessions.

- Restrictive or abusive practices, whether implicit or explicit, constitute a serious impediment to global competition and development. Such practices range from the prohibition of exports to tying the imports to a particular source or to qualitative and/or quantitative restrictions, which are generally predetermined by the **GOFs**.

Developing nations owe the acquisition of many new technologies to FDIs. Nevertheless, one should not fall into the trap of assuming that the **GOFs** make use of **FDIs** in order to comply with the national objectives of a particular nation. The **GOFs** only pursue their own global interests and are ultimately responsible to their shareholders.

Some Policy Proposals

Developing countries still have a lot to learn from the experiences and expertise of the **GOFs** in terms of technological know-how, marketing skills, managerial efficiency, etc. If the right steps are taken in the right direction, there is a great potential contribution to be made by technology transfer. For the sake of global prosperity and stability, such improvements are imperative. Otherwise, the global income disparity will continue to get worse and many people in **LDCs** will continue to emigrate to the **DCs** as economic refugees even using illegal means in order to receive a slice of the globally produced cake. This international, illegal, undesired but inevitable mobility of the labor force, is also referred to as "the voyage to hope", and perpetuates the many social problems in the **DCs** while solving none in the developing world.

Here are some proposals that may relieve some of these problems in the short- and long term.

Developing Indigenous Capabilities

1- Education and Training

New technologies are the product of the creative mind, e.g., mental labor, and are the genesis and a consistent source of long term growth. (Gürak; 2000-a) But, given the prevailing conditions of human development and the technological gap, a large number of the LDCs can achieve growth without having to engage in the costly and time-consuming process of producing a new technology. Because, there is already an immense pool of productive knowledge existing in the relatively more developed countries. A large number of the "known" technologies are, in fact, "new" technologies for the **LDC** firms. Assuming the elimination of all imperfections in the technology markets, this situation presents a great potential for economic growth for the **LDC** firms. What is required is the creation of the appropriate conditions for technology transfer.

An indispensable prerequisite of a successful technology transfer is, preferably an up-to-date **qualified, i.e., educated and trained human resource**, to find out **what** and **where** is the best suitable technology, **to adopt** and eventually **to further develop** this technology. The key phrase is "a **qualified labor force**", with up to date skills, i.e., an increase in the quality and quantity of the human resources. The initial cost of the investments in human resources may be high and take a long time to recoup, but the potential benefits for the country would be tremendous in the long term. If technology is the key to development, skilled manpower, given the appropriate infrastructure and economic policies, is the key to its successful application, adaptation and further development in the **LDCs** (Gürak, 2000-a; 2000-b).

2- Economic Policies

It would not be unrealistic to claim that many **LDCs** pursue inappropriate and inefficient economic policies. There are many social, historical, cultural and political reasons for this. But the decision-makers have to find out and apply appropriate economic measures that are most suitable to their country's specific conditions. There is no universal remedy for these problems. But, at least four universal areas could be considered;

1- The reallocation of resources to higher-productivity (value-adding) sectors;
2- promoting competitive conditions;
3- preserving the environment; and
4- preventing corruption by increasing economic and political transparency.

In order to reach development targets, decision-makers should prepare the conditions for the replacement of low-productivity firms and sectors, including Public Enterprises (**PEs**), by more productive firms and sectors in a fair competitive environment. For instance, it is common knowledge that **PEs** are usually run inefficiently, and are not infrequently used as a means to provide "illicit" profits for certain privileged individuals or firms close to the decision-making circles. State owned banks are another striking example of how resources are being misallocated in many developing countries. Yet, the governments are reluctant, for several reasons, to change the status quo.

Many **LDCs** encourage output in labor-intensive sectors such as ready-wear, clothing and textiles. This could be a fruitful policy in the early stages of development. But, as development reaches the higher stages, it would be in the best interest of the working people and the country as a whole to reallocate resources to the higher productivity sectors. Policies protecting the labor-intensive sectors in the long run are bound to be counter-productive. After all, there are plenty of other **LDCs** with relatively lower wages looking for an opportunity to get a slice of the market. Turkey is a good sample of this; the ready to wear, clothing and the textile sectors earn about $ 10 billion in foreign currency per year. But in order to be competitive, the wages have to be kept permanently low, except for high quality products. There is a significant gap between the wages in the low compared to the high-productivity sectors. A smooth and gradual transfer of human and financial resources to the high productivity sectors would benefit not only the workers but the country as a whole. An irreplaceable and indispensable prerequisite to reach the universal targets in regard to development targets is the presence of an up to date **qualified human resource**.

Cultural values, the institutional setting, fertility rates, political pluralism, social mobility, etc. all are critical aspects influencing economic growth and development in the long run. As human and economic development increases all these factors would change over time and would become suitable to the specific needs and conditions of a particular country. Therefore, once again, investment in human resources appears to be the best remedy in the long term.

On Supervising Agencies

Given the specific nature of the transactions in technology transfer and the urgent need for accelerated economic growth, one of the objectives of the developing countries should be to set up competent authoritative International and National Agencies, responsible for the proper guidance of technology transfer. There ought to be an "International Code of Conduct" (**ICC**) to which all countries as well as **GOFs** are subject to. An **ICC** could eliminate or, at least, relieve many of the problems and also the market imperfections. Whilst the **ICC** defines the general framework of technology related matters, a National Agency could see to it that globally accepted guidelines are not violated in the national market. In addition, a National Agency should assist local firms in their search for appropriate technologies and in their negotiations with the technology sellers. A further objective should be to encourage the efficient use of imported technology.

In 1983, the U.N. introduced a "Draft International Code of Conduct on the International Transfer of Technology", (UNCTAD,1983) which was given its final shape in 1985 at the close of the sixth session of the conference (TD/CODE TOT/47). Unfortunately, since then there has been no new initiative in this respect in spite of some radical changes in the political, economic and technological areas. Given the present nature of global interests and technology markets, the efficient operation of the International Authorities seems highly utopian, at least for now.

Encouraging Joint-investments without Abusive Practices

Complete control of a subsidiary's business transactions and its related decisions involve various disadvantages for the firms and the national economy of the host countries. After all, a wholly foreign owned subsidiary would be entirely subordinate to the global interests of a Parent Firm which pursues a global strategy of profit maximization. Without resorting to any explicitly written arrangements, the Parent Firm can exercise a complete control over key decisions concerning price, quality, quantity, exports, imports, as well as the very existence of the subsidiary plant itself, all of which could be disadvantageous to the interests of the host country. In order to increase the benefits from technology transfer, "joint-venture" investments, preferably with at least 50 percent ownership by the host country ought to be encouraged. After all, a joint-venture does not mean only cost sharing but also the sharing of technological and managerial skill between the partners, at least in theory, and as such reduces, if not eliminates, the risk of foreign control and transfer pricing.

In addition, encouraging the foreign investor to buy locally produced components would significantly increase the contribution of the imported technology for the host country.

Encouraging & Promoting License Arrangements

A license arrangement permits the recipient to have access to certain productive knowledge developed by the technology supplier. It saves the cost of producing a similar technology, thus freeing up resources for alternative uses. Therefore, license arrangements could be an efficient alternative to the technology transfer through **FDI**. Japan has been quite successful in the acquisition and adaptation of imported technology through such license arrangements and developing countries could learn a lot from the Japanese approach and experience. The key factors of this Japanese success were the availability of highly skilled manpower, and importantly the relatively narrower technological gap between Japan and the other industrialized countries (see Appendix-A).

Restructuring the International Intellectual Property Rights System (IPRS)

Technology, or alternatively, the "Knowledge of Production", is the key to progress for all nations, both in terms of economic growth and development. Because, technological advances change our economic life which, in its turn, changes our social-political life. As UNCTAD quite rightly points out, in an article (Global Entitlement to Knowledge, 1999-c), that technology transfer and diffusion, is essential for global economic growth and development. But, what UNCTAD appears to infer is that "Global Entitlement" covers all aspects of "informative knowledge" only, except for the proprietary knowledge, which is the "**knowledge about production**", that is "**productive knowledge**" or synonymously, "**technology**".

Yet, the sensitive and critical issue, the heart of the matter, is the diffusion of proprietary knowledge, i.e., the knowledge protected by intellectual property rights. Most of the evils and the imperfections in technology markets are due to prevailing **IPRS** conditions which definitely serve the interests of the **GOFs.** "*A scheme for the global mobilization of non-proprietary technology*" would certainly make a significant contribution, but is bound to have limited impact unless complemented by *a new scheme for the global utilization of proprietary knowledge* (**UNCTAD**; 1999-c).

Final words; a number of measures were outlined above to meet the standards of the **DCs** which is not an easy target under the prevailing conditions.

There is no miracle cure which can overcome all the obstacles in the path of increasing development.

Increasing the quantity of the qualified human resource is, no doubt, at the heart of the matter and the best remedy to all these problems, in the long run. Thus, the design and application of **appropriate education and training policies** along with all **other related economic, social and political policies** is imperative.

In the short term, most **LDC** firms are in need of more expertise and experience in order **TO USE** rather than "to produce" technologies. On the developmental path, in order to reach the determined targets, the **quality of governance** is also of vital importance.

Appendix (A)

Japanese government's guidelines for the foreign investors. *

1. Seek co-existence and prosperity with Japanese enterprises through joint ventures on an equal partnership basis.
2. Avoid concentration of investment in specific industries.
3. Avoid suppressing small enterprises when entering into industries characterized by small firms.
4. Co-operate voluntarily with the Japanese effort to maintain proper industrial order.
5. Avoid entering into unduly restrictive arrangements with parent companies abroad, and do not resort to unreasonable restrictions concerning transactions or to unfair competition.
6. Take positive steps toward developing Japanese technology, and do not hamper the efforts of Japanese industries to develop their own technology.
7. Contribute to the improvement of the nation's balance-of-payments through exports and other means.
8. Appoint Japanese to the board of directors and top-management positions and makes shares of company stock available to the public.
9. Avoid closures of plants, or mass dismissal, and unnecessary confusion in employment and wage practices by paying due regard to the prevailing Japanese practices.
10. Conform to the government economic policy.

* Foreign Investment Council's recommendations to the Finance Minister on June 2, 1967, approved on June 6, 1967.

Appendix-B

UNCTAD, E/CN.16/1999/4 and Corr.1,26 March 1999

A COMMON VISION ON SCIENCE AND TECHNOLOGY FOR DEVELOPMENT

5- We believe that one of the central issues of the coming millennium will be the need to build capacity in developing countries so that they can adapt to the challenges of continuous change. In pursuing this goal, the United Nations Commission on Science and Technology for Development (CSTD) is committed to the common vision of a **global entitlement to knowledge** and to the benefits of **science and technology** for development in the twenty-first century.

6- To achieve this, it will be necessary to formulate national policies and establish international arrangements that safeguard and protect the interests of all people on the planet as well as those of future generations.

12- The world of the twenty-first century will be one in which **knowledge generation** increasingly takes place within the networks of **large transnational corporations**. In such a world, there will be opportunities for the **monopolization of scientific and technological knowledge** and the potential to restrict the free flow of information. It will be necessary to provide greater support for research in the public sector particularly in the areas of health and agriculture, in order to make sure that local interests and needs are acted upon, to encourage the further development of indigenous knowledge systems, and to **increase capacities for the assimilation of transferred technology**. Research institutions, however, cannot be expected to play both a long term public research function and an entrepreneurial role aimed at short term objectives. It will be necessary to **create and support intermediary institutions, in order to build linkages between the users and producers of knowledge in developing countries**, where enterprises are small, their capacity to seek and evaluate information weak, and their in-house development capabilities limited. National and local Governments all have a role to play in this process, as do international educational and research networks.

13-In the world of the twenty-first century, nations and their economies will be more than ever embedded in a vast array of **international institutional arrangements** and economic, scientific, technological and social interactions. **These, we believe, are critical vehicles for acquiring the knowledge and information required for development**. As only a small minority of developing countries have succeeded in attracting significant inflows of foreign investment, more attention will need to be given to **alternative channels** for acquiring know-how from external sources, such as supplier-customer linkages, licensing, alliances, partnership arrangements and networks for joint research and development, production and distribution. Thanks to these linkages, exporting has proved a highly effective means of acquiring technological capabilities. The international community has a role to play in creating new mechanisms to support the flow of technology and in assisting developing countries to become more attractive both to foreign investors and to potential trade and technology partners.

14- To build local technological and productive capabilities, **greater flexibility** will be needed in international trade, investment and **intellectual property agreements.**

Chapter 10: INSTITUTIONS & ECONOMICS

At discussions on economic issues and developments, economists, especially those of a neoclassical heritage, in general overlook or ignore the role and importance played by the institutions, decision-makers and culture. Yet, institutions along with culture practically always and inevitably influence what sort of economic process we pursue and its future implications. For instance, in the absence of institutional decision-makers endowed with contemporary skills, dedication and experience, all or most of the promising targets are bound to remain sterile or inefficient. Because in the end it is the decision-makers' qualifications which generally shape the very structure and progress of their institutions.

There is no doubt that the specific social, cultural and technological development stage of a country heavily influences how efficiently the institutions are exploited by the decision-makers. For instance, when the socialist economic order was overthrown in the former Soviet countries and Eastern Europe, it left behind a very large well-educated labor force ranging from engineers to scientists and managers along with an institutional structure. In many former socialist- oriented countries the proportion of engineers and scientists in the labor force was higher than that in many developed Western countries. However, this highly qualified labor force in terms of its educational skills was not endowed with the "appropriate" qualifications which would allow it to adapt to Western institutional standards and run them efficiently, at least not in the initial phase of the transition period. The practices of the capitalist order were quite different from the practices in the so called socialist countries. As a result, institutions' decision-makers had to change in order to comply with the new standards to be efficient.

Experience clearly shows that the socio-cultural and technological development stage heavily and directly influences the shape of the institutions as well as the qualifications of the labor force in general. However, it is not the purpose here to study the potential impacts of socio-cultural environment and developments neither on the institutional framework nor on the qualifications of the labor force. Since our main subject is economics, we shall focus our attention on the economic institutions, in general.

Institutional Economics & Institutional Structure

Let us begin with the definition of an "institution". An "institution" can be defined as a collection of principles, patterns, structures, agreements, and regulations influencing as well as shaping the behavior of individuals and societies. Some institutions originate from traditional societies while some are the result of new contemporary conditions. In addition, some might be formally designed and some informally without any written agreements. As examples of written or unwritten agreements, we can mention traditions, property rights, religious practices, traffic regulations, etc.

Some of the economic institutions are for example The Central Bank, The Ministry of Commerce, employee and employer unions, OECD and last but not least the markets themselves. As Özgüven (2007; p.17) puts it, economic order can be defined as "**an institutionalized process**."

Markets as Institutions

For the proponents of the so called scientific (?) Neoclassical doctrine, under perfectly (?) competitive conditions, due to the inherent features of the system the markets will be in equilibrium. At this point, the quantities supplied equals the quantities demanded and prices are determined by perfect competition conditions. Equilibrium continues until some external force disturbs it. In other words, the markets are expected to solve all their problems by the principles inherent in this specific system, assuming complete absence of any external intervention.

However, this neoclassical claim has no resemblance in reality. First of all, a social doctrine which ignores the events and the impacts of historical developments does not deserve to be considered as "scientific". Besides, there has never been an economy nor is there ever likely to be an economy which operates completely independently of any external intervention. The last global scale market intervention occurred during the 2008 to 2010 crises due to the inherent deficiencies of this highly praised market system. Therefore, it would not be an exaggeration to state that there has always been some degree of market intervention which has, in most cases, been demanded by market forces in order to overcome critical problems in the market. To put it differently, market forces have a tendency to "demand" **institutional intervention** whenever they feel in trouble.

Evaluating the impact of institutions and institutional relationships independently from technological developments would be a serious mistake. Institutions as well as institutional relationships have always, directly or indirectly, been influenced by technological change. For instance, if transport vehicles had not been invented and used, there would be no need for traffic regulations. In a similar fashion, if computers, the internet, or mobile phones had not been invented, there would be no need for any related regulations and our means of communication would be quite different. In short, technological progress does not only affect our economic behavior by the introduction of new physical products but also affects our social behavior and habits through the medium of institutional change.

Economic institutions can have a big influence on the nature and outcome of economic relationships, either directly or indirectly, or positively or negatively. For instance, The Central Bank can directly influence the size and nature of new investments by changing the discount rate. Or, the employee or employer unions can influence the political and bureaucratic institutions' decisions in accordance with their own economic power. Some of the unions' demands may not always be beneficial for an entire community. However, preventing excessive demand is again a matter to be dealt with within the institutional structure. Nations which encourages a better performance rate among their own institutions, in accordance with contemporary standards, would be in a more advantageous position compared to the other nations.

According to institutional economists, the economic growth performance is directly influenced by the institutions. If the influence on economic growth is positive, Acemoglu–Johnson– Robinson (2004; p.9) consider it a "good" institution. Being "good" or "bad" is a purely subjective evaluation. For Acemoglu–Johnson–Robinson (2004; p.9), "good" institutions are those; *"... that provide security of property rights and relatively equal access to economic resources to a broad cross-section of society."*

It is, however, a rather critical question as to how one can distinguish the "good" institutions from the "bad" ones and what criteria are to be used for such an evaluation, with due regard to both the historical developments and contemporary global conditions. Would it be fair to call the Western institutions which traded slaves and exploited the local resources and riches of the Indian subcontinent "good" institutions? These types of markets are today condemned by practically all nations and individuals. But, was it not these "good" Western institutions' performance which paved the way for today's' institutions and conditions?

According to Rodrik (2002) too, the major force behind long term economic growth is the institution. However, having "good" institutions or a good institutional infrastructure may not always be sufficient to have a developed and efficient society. North (2002; p.139) defends a similar view.

For Rodrik (2002), investment and entrepreneurship are not sufficient for long term growth. To maintain the momentum of growth and to build resilience against shock events, four types of institutions are required.

1- "*Market creating institutions (property rights and contract enforcement)*
2- *Market regulating institutions (to deal with externalities, scale economies, informational incompleteness)*
3- *Market stabilizing institutions (for monetary and fiscal management).*
4- *Market legitimizing institutions (social protection and insurance; redistributive policies; institutions of conflict management, social partnership).*" *(Rodrik, 2002,p.6)*

> Good Institutions & Bad Institutions
>
> How to distinguish a "good" institution from a "bad" one? What should the criteria be for comparison and qualification? Which developed country institutions are "good" ones?
>
> It does not seem unfair to claim that the early "good" institutions of the West began to emerge with the Protestant movement and Calvinism. Luther had begun to challenge some of the doctrines and practices of Roman Catholic Church which resulted in a new and reformed religious institutional settlement and practices. It was no longer undesirable or considered a sin to accumulate personal wealth.
>
> The institutions of the "chosen" people of Christian faith engaged in many controversial practices around the world in past. For instance, the British East India Company had restructured the Indian institutions to make them "good" ones in accordance with the sublime British interest. As a result, Britain and her enterprises "successfully" exploited Indian resources for centuries, generally through the performance of these "good" institutions that is by a "good" dose of blood and coercion. These so called "good" institutions were contributing to the economic growth of Britain but at the expense of the Indians, just like today's "good" institutions.
>
> History tells us that another significant "good" performance of the Western "good" institutions which contributed to economic growth took place on the African continent. Millions of native people were enslaved and forced to work in accordance with the principles of these "good" institutions. Meanwhile, the "good" institutions of the West continued to contribute to their economic growth by exploiting Africa's riches.
>
> There are countless examples of the good performances of the Western "good" institutions.

As we have seen in previous sections, the source of long term economic growth is **technological innovations** which are the product of mentally creative laborers. Regardless of how efficient the institutions a country may be, long term economic growth cannot take place in the absence of **creative mental labor.** Thus, "good" institutions can only contribute to long term economic growth to the extent that they promote education and research and the implementation of new technologies. Otherwise, the contributions will be only, at best, short term. In the long term it would be a formidable error to overlook the importance of "creative mental labor" along with a labor force endowed with appropriate skills in order to use the created technologies efficiently.

Different Countries, Different Institutions

Different countries have different levels of development. Looking from a global perspective, we can easily notice which countries are better off and which ones are relatively worse off. The question is: Which are the forces that may be held accountable for such differences between countries? Or, to put a question more specific related to the subject matter of this section, can the development stage of the institutions cause such divergences? Do the developed countries (**DC**s) owe their present situation to the practices of the "good" institutions? Which criteria can be used to estimate the degree of "goodness" of these institutions? Do such objective global criteria even exist? Which institutions can be considered as "good" ones in the developing countries (**LDCs**) and which ones can be classified as "bad"?

Institutions that are a written and/or verbal collection of principles, patterns, structures, agreements, regulations, do not emerge in the form of manna from heaven. There are always some historical underlying causes and conditions behind the initial emergence of institutions unless they are imposed manna from heaven by some forces.

The emergence of "economic institutions" practically always aims to stabilize and secure economic efficiency and development, in general. Some related institutions emerge as a result of pressing conditions while others are introduced by the conscious plans and attempts of the decision-makers. And, today, we, not infrequently observe, the imposition of some institutions at the specific demand of such "good" Western institutions as the IMF and The World Bank.

Every development or change of institutional structure is subject to the contemporary global economic conditions and is also always liable to change because of the continuously changing conditions. However, one should not overlook or ignore the fact that there are no globally acknowledged criteria to define the most appropriate conditions for ideal institutions. Each country has a unique and specific historical, cultural and economic background that must be taken into consideration.

The distribution and ownership of wealth and property are also important factors which influence, if not determine, the structure and nature of institutions. Regardless of how developed and democratically run a country may be, economic wealth, and consequently economic power has always been concentrated in the hands of a small income group. This economically powerful and politically influential group has a disproportionate influence on the emergence and the functioning of the economic institutions which are given the name of the "liberal economies".

It is a globally acknowledged fact and beyond any doubt that economic power has a lot of say in shaping domestic and international institutions. And, again it is a globally acknowledged fact and beyond any doubt that the globally operating giant Western enterprises have the greatest global economic power in our age. Therefore, how the institutions in **LDCs** are shaped, is to a great extent, determined by the conditions imposed by the Western enterprises and Western oriented decision-makers. If **LDCS** do not wish to be left outside global transactions, especially with regard to new technologies and products they must act in accordance to the dictates of the Western enterprises.

If the West owes its present development stage to "good" institutions, how come the developing countries almost never succeed in transforming the level of their own institutions to the levels of the Western institutions? Is it because developing countries are inherently incapable of developing "good" institutions or is it because of some "other" obstacles hindering their development?

China and Institutions

It is a rather interesting fact that China has been growing rapidly in the last 20 to 25 years and yet her institutions do not seem to meet, to significant extent, the basic requirements in order for it to be considered on a par with the Western countries. In fact, the institutions in China can easily be considered as "bad" ones. In spite of this critical fact China's economic performance has been hailed as a "miracle" by most economists. While the world economy still struggles to recover from the 2008 recession, China still performs at an extraordinary economic level in the year 2010.

As a matter of fact neither Japan nor South Korea, the developmental latecomers had imitated the Western institutional practices until reaching a certain stage of development. In fact, not infrequently they were subject to heavy pressure by Western institutions to change their stubborn "not so good" practices and to comply with Western institutional standards. Therefore, it is difficult to distinguish "good" institutions from "bad" ones according to some specific objective criteria which are applicable to all countries. However, we can easily claim that long term economic growth cannot be sustained unless it is supported by technological progress and by the constantly improved education of the labor-force.

There is no doubt that countries such as the EU, USA, Japan, Canada, and Australia owe their status as "developed" to a large extent due to performance of their “good” institutions in the past. Let us ignore this historic fact and say that present Western institutions do have the most suitable and efficient infrastructure for contemporary economic transactions. Accordingly, assume that the best institutions to imitate are considered to be found in the West. We know very well that global institutions like the IMF, The World Bank, and the WTO, are doing their utmost to bring the institutions of the developing countries into line with Western values, infrastructure and standards. That means the number and impact of the so called “good” institutions has been growing in relatively less developed countries. Yet, the data on global income distribution indicates that the income gap has been widening, rather than converging. How can we account for this fact? Is it possible to offer any logical and rational argument without referring to the imperfections in technology markets and the obstacles that are placed in the way of global knowledge diffusion?

The present global economic structure with a clear Western institutional domination of all global economic relationships and their future direction, including the imperfections in technology markets, do not seem to contribute in any way to increased global competitiveness. On the contrary, instead of the increase of global competitiveness among the independent profit units, we observe a continuation of global competition among the giant enterprises by a cost reduction due to generous incentives granted by the developing countries in order to attract more foreign direct investment. Therefore, the developing country decision-makers have to pay the utmost attention to the following details.

- Instead of attempting to introduce replicas of the DC institutions, LDCs should strive to form new institutions best suitable to their own conditions and interests.
- New global and local institutions should be established with the specific purpose of eliminating the imperfections in technology markets, thus increasing the diffusion of knowledge and global competition.
- Institutions alone cannot challenge present global shortcomings and faults unless due and diligent attention is devoted to the imperfections in technology markets and the diffusion of knowledge (for a more detailed analysis on this aspect see Gürak, 1990, 2003 and 2009).
- Institutions should emerge according to the specific needs and projections of countries subject to their specific conditions. As North (2002,; p.12) put it; institutions are created by human beings. In time, they evolve and are subject to incessant change.

Role of Institutions in Retrospect

Case study: The institutions of Ottoman Empire?

The role played by institutions in the past was as significant as it is today. The analysis of the Sumerian, Persian, and Roman or in fact any other civilization which had a deep rooted impact on historical developments would be incomplete without an accompanying study of its institutions. The Turkish Ottoman Empire was one of these civilizations which have influenced the developments of three continents, Europe, Asia and Africa for about 600 years before disappearing from the historical scene after the First World War. The Ottomans had the potential to become one of the more industrially developed countries due to its huge domestic markets, the extent of economic activities and freedom of trade. For instance, there were many established industrial production units ranging from mines to the manufacturing of various products which could have easily paved the way to an advanced industrialization process. However, it did not happen. The Ottoman Empire lagged behind in terms of economic development instead of becoming one of the pioneers of industrialization process.

Which forces could have prevented the Ottoman Empire from industrializing just as their major rivals, the European countries or their empires did in the 18th and 19th centuries? Could the general institutional structure of the Ottoman Empire be accountable for the retardation or the slow progress of its industrial change? Could there be some other critical aspects other than the institutions and liberal markets with free trade which hindered faster economic growth in the Ottoman economy? What could these factors be? Could the "good" institutions of the West be accountable for these obstacles, at least to some extent?

Judging from the considerations of North (2002), Rodrik (2002) and Acemoglu–Johnson–Robinson (2004), the institutions of the Ottoman Empire seem to be rather "good", especially in the 15th Century, compared to other nations; although "not good" in the same sense as the Western institutions were. The Ottomans had at that time, a set of highly sophisticated and progressive regulations, especially in regard to the production quality of goods and consumer protection. There were large domestic markets and population for economic growth. There was no need for external markets or colonies for economic exploitation. In addition, there was a huge demand for armaments, military equipment and uniforms by the armed forces. Private property rights except for the land ownership were protected by Islamic principles (Inalcık, 2000; p.83). All citizens, regardless of their ethnic origin or religious persuasion, could engage in trade and making profits was permissible. Even the property rights of the other nations' entrepreneurs were under the protection of the Turkish Emperor.

It was common practice among Ottoman institutions to consider the welfare of citizens and to secure product quality, protect consumer rights and to regulate the market price of basic needs. Obligatory alms giving or "zekat" was, and still is, a common practice which helps to redistribute income in favor of the lower income groups. A charitable establishment called "imaret" had the duty to provide food for the hungry and needy. The giving of alms to the needy or to beggars was another common institutional practice demanded by the religion (Inalcık, 2000; p.84). In short, securing basic public needs and maintaining stability were given top priorities by the Turkish rulers and their institutions.

Another significant institution which contributes to economic growth is the access to the markets, to be more specific, the size of the markets. The Ottoman Empire had large domestic markets and a large population especially in the 15th century. There was no need for external markets or colonies for it to exploit. In addition, there was a huge demand for armaments, military equipment and uniforms by the armed forces.

The approach of the Ottoman states and its institutions to international trade was quite liberal even in terms of the standards at that time. The restrictions on the export of basic foods aimed to meet and secure the citizens' needs, as the welfare of the citizen always had priority. Custom duties on imported goods were kept at a relatively low level, around 3 to 5 percent. Therefore, we can easily claim that the Ottoman state had liberal policies in regard to global trade, except for the Darülharp[4] countries.

If Ottoman Empire had all the basic institutional structure and the markets required how come it did not succeed in making, like Britain or Holland the transition to capitalism, the newly emerging "good" system with a "creative destruction" mechanism i.e. technological progress?

Was there something missing in the institutional set up?

Or perhaps, weren't the institutions "good" enough for this transition?

These are the critical issues that will be left to economic historians to deal with. As a hint to economic historians, we can point out to two striking reasons for the failure to transform the Ottoman economy into a modern one with advanced technologies and qualified labor:

1- The approach of the Ulema[5] and the decision-makers to technological innovations.
2- The lack of a progressive, widespread and secular educational system.

4 A Darülharp country: according to Islamic law is a country with which there is no signed peace agreement or a country ruled by an "infidel" ruler.

5 Ulema: The educated Muslim expert on the Islamic religion.

A "good" (?) Turkish institution: The Lonca (guild system)

"Loncas have never hesitated in giving disciplinary fines to its members. The disciplinary fines are equivalent to the consumer protection practices frequently encountered in contemporary nations. Some of the sanctions are as follows.

***Advice**: Summon the tradesmen displaying unethical behavior in order to give advice.*

***Cereme (cerime)**: The tradesmen who behaved contrary to sale or trade procedures and who sold defective goods, had to pay a fine called "cereme", a sort of reparations expenditure, in addition to returning the unearned income in cash or in kind.*

***Closing the shop**: Those tradesmen who insistently continued to behave contrary to tradition and consciously keep selling defective goods would, by the Lonca management's decree, have to close the shop for up to three days.*

***Beating**: This had a more frightening purpose to deter rather than to put in practice; there used to be a bastinado stick hanging on the wall of the "kethüda" (the chamberlain's) room.*

***Social and economic exclusion**: One of the harshest punishments applied to the tradesmen who showed no improvement. Depriving them of certain rights, like fund benefits and treating them as if they were non-members of the guild. This punishment was applied to tradesmen who showed no improvement and were recalcitrant.*

***Dismissal from the guild**: Those who made a habit of fraud and failed to comply with tradition, along with burglars, the dishonest and murderers used to be expelled form the guild."*

Source: http://tr.wikipedia.org/wiki/Lonca_Te%C5 %9Fkilat%C4%B1, 2009-03-16

What should be the Long Term Targets of Institutions?

The distinctive features of the theories emphasized by institutional economists are "**private property rights**" and "**liberal competitive markets**". Global institutions shaped and controlled by Western countries also put a heavy emphasis on these two issues. However, it is a well-known historical fact that neither Britain, nor the USA nor late-comer Japan paid much heed to the so called "**liberal competitive markets**" argument until they reached a certain level of development. How come the economists who give priority to the institutional structure as a tool for economic growth overlook or ignore such historical facts? As the matter of fact, it would not be incorrect to claim that even in our age contemporary developed countries do not completely fulfill the standards of "**liberal competitive markets**" in many aspects. In regard to private property rights, many developing countries have more or less similar laws as in the developed countries. Yet, these rights do not seem to secure long term economic growth or to close the global income gap.

The Turkish government entered a customs union with the EU countries in 1995 and she is the only EU-candidate which signed such an agreement before full membership. In addition, private property rights have a long history as far back as the time of Ottoman Empire. In some years the Turkish economy grows annually by high rates such as 7 or 8 percent while experiencing low or negative growth rates in other years. If "**private property rights**" and "**liberal competitive markets**" were sufficient for long term growth, how come Turkey does not seem to close the income gap with countries like Sweden, Germany or France? Could there be some critical aspects other than institutions, private property rights and liberal markets hindering the faster economic growth of Turkey? If so, what are they? Could the "good" institutions of the West and the present global economic condition shaped by Western enterprises be accountable for this situation, at least to some extent?

There seems to be two major reasons coming to the fore for the failure to close the income and development gap in regard to the developed countries.

1- The scarcity or insufficiency of a qualified labor force that can employ contemporary technologies efficiently.
2- The ownership pattern of advanced technologies as well as the global imperfections in technology markets.

Any institutional theorem or argument disregarding these two aspects or reducing them to a lower level of priority are bound to give rise to serious shortcomings and would fail to fully grasp the problem. The contemporary global "good" institutions have to take into consideration the following suggestions to secure a long term sustained growth process. Institutions should;

- Promote and encourage the qualification and the number of the labor-force in order to facilitate the most efficient use of contemporary advanced technologies.
- Promote and encourage creative mental labor and R&D for new technologies.
- Reorganize the global technology markets and the diffusion of knowledge in favor of the developing countries (see Gürak, 2009).

In regard to the first and second aspects, there should not be any conflict amongst economists. However, changing the global imperfections in technology markets in favor of the developing countries would, highly likely, meet strong resistance from the developed countries and their enterprises. After all, they are clear beneficiaries of the present system.

Another important issue is related to the global institutions' role in the global development process for a better global economy. Global institutions are, in general, created by Western institutions in accordance with Western values and interests. Expecting radical changes from these institutions which would undermine the global interests of developed country enterprises is doomed to failure.

Concluding Remarks

1. Institutions are important for economic growth. They should give priority to the education and training of the labor-force to endow it with contemporary qualifications (**efficiency growth with given technology**; Gürak, 2009).
2. Institutions should promote and encourage technological progress and pursue technological independence policies to secure long term growth (**technological productivity growth;** Gürak, 2009).
3. Domestic institutions should take precautionary measures to minimize costs arising from "transfer pricing" in technology transfer.
4. Global institutions should take global measures to minimize costs arising from the imperfections in technology markets.
5. Global economic institutions are, predominantly, founded by developed countries with developed country values and interests in mind. Attempts should be made to alter the present structure in accordance with developing country interests or restructured on "equality" basis.
6. Private property rights are "not" an indispensable factor for economic growth; example; China.
7. Having Western type replica institutions is not a precondition for economic growth; example, China.
8. When referring to the "good" institutions, one should not overlook the historical experience, practices and purposes of these institutions before giving too much credit to them. The riches of the Indian subcontinent were rubbed out by these "good" institutions which also sold opium by force to China, enslaved Africans, massacred American Indians, employed child labor in mines and pushing small children up chimneys in order to clean them, just to mention a few "good" incidents for which these "good" institutions were responsible.
9. Ruthless exploitation of environmental resources in the past was also undertaken by the "good" institutions of the West. Most of the contemporary environmental problems have their origins in extravagant exploitation by "good" institutions in the past and even today.

To summarize; attempts to solve the domestic and global economic problems and to secure long term economic growth in developing countries by replicating Western institutions seems naïve and inadequate. Because, the present global economic problems owe their emergence, to large extent, to "good" practices of institutions of the West.

Chapter 11: WHERE IS THE GLOBAL ECONOMY HEADING?

In our age, the global production and distribution of products is realized, to a large extent, by so called “Multinational” or “Supranational” enterprises of developed countries scattered around the world and some of which have more annual revenues than the national income of many developing countries. We refer to them as Giant Enterprises (**GEs**) or Globally Operating Enterprises (**GOEs**) on the grounds that they, predominantly, are owned and controlled by one nations’ citizens, although there are a few exceptions with a two or three country ownership like Royal Dutch Shell and Unilever, both British-Dutch owned. Thus, the terms “Multinational” or Supranational” enterprises do not completely reflect reality. Owing to their enormous economic power, these **GEs** also possess and exercise great political power around the world. Their operations are nowadays referred to using the concept of “globalization”.

Globalization is a relatively new concept in economics which economists began to use increasingly after the collapse of the former Soviet Union to describe “new” (?) economic relationships. However, the inherent nature of global economic transactions is not new at all. In fact, using an analogy, it is just a new name for an old and well-known town. Image-makers of the West often make use of such concept changes to give the impression that a “new” stage is in progress. For instance, once there were concepts like “**developed-undeveloped**” countries which were, later changed to “**developed-developing**” then to the “**digital divide**”. A related popular concept is “**emerging countries**” referring to countries that are in a process of relatively faster economic growth and development. All of these concepts refer, in fact, to one big simple reality; the world is divided into two: poor and rich countries. Playing with words will not change this fact.

A similar game is being played with reference to environmental problems. Well-known, global climate problems are referred to as “**global warming**” by many scientists in Turkey and Europe while the USA decision-makers prefer the concept “**climate change**” which gives the impression that it is a “nature-oriented” problem not a “man-made" one. The latter term makes it look like the developed countries’ ruthless and extravagant consumption behavior does not have much responsibility for the present situation. Dura (2009) warns his readers against the risk of using concepts or definitions introduced by the developed countries without using a "mind filter" whenever they are used by the developing country economists. He says:

> "...blindfold imitation of the West has been producing more damage than utility for us: The question is about reckless devotion, blindfold obedience or total submission; the common mentality and practice are: "Whatever the West thinks, says, writes is true or does is good." I believe that this level of submission is one of our biggest problems. Indeed, our people, primarily the intellectuals, display incredible and shameful degree of submission." (Dura, 2009)

The concept of globalization in economic jargon is a relatively new one referring to old and well-known economic transactions, as stated above. For instance, people have been trading for thousands of years, foreign direct investments (**FDIs**) have been taking place since the 1850s, the "brain-drain" has been taking place from time immemorial, etc. The international transfer of monetary capital in the form of precious metals or currencies is an ancient and a well known transaction. What is left there to refer to "globalization" as a new or recent economic process or brand new stage of development?

The flowing texts will attempt to seek answers to two questions with reference to **globalization** or equivalently, **internationalization** of economic transactions.

1. How does the globalization process effect production and trade?
2. How does the globalization process effect global income distribution?

> Different Expressions for the Same Thing
>
> Barber? Hairdresser? Hair designer? Tonsorial artiste?
>
> To those who think globalization is an entirely new process with distinctive features, we can give the simple example of the "haircut".
>
> About 20 to 30 years ago whenever a man needed a haircut, he would say either "I'm going to the barber" or ""I'm going to the hairdresser". Nowadays, there is a new term, "hair designer" who does exactly the same job as the barber or hairdresser.
>
> There is no basic difference in what a barber or hairdresser or hair designer does; he/she cuts the hair. There might be some treatment in addition to the haircut but a "haircut is a haircut".
>
> Globalization as a concept is like a haircut; a rose by any other name is still a rose.

Global Production

Global production or to use the old terminology, world production has been moving ahead in its own natural process which means men have been continually creating new knowledge (new technologies) increasing their material well-being and improving their social conditions at the same time. By the way, it is not the globalization process that constantly improves the standards of living but technological progress by introducing new products and production methods. Certainly, the globalization process contributes to improved global standards in the sense as the spreading of investments until markets saturate with a "given" technology. But long term global growth can only be attained the use of the "new" products (see Gürak, 2006-a).

Figure: 11-1 shows the proportional distribution of global production in 1995 and 2006. There is no change in the share of the Middle East and North Africa along with Sub-Saharan Africa (two percent of the total) during these 10 years while Europe and Central Asia appear to have increased their share from seven to eight percent. In the meantime, the share of Latin America and the Caribbean Countries declined from nine to eight percent while East Asia and the Pacific increased their share from nine to fourteen percent. We observe a significant percentage decline in the share of the high-income countries from 66 to 59 percent. All this data indicates that there has been some changes in the structure of global production between 1995 and 2006 but the wide gap still persist between the rich and poor countries. To put it another way, the globalization process does not seem to have shifted positions significantly. When analyzing this data one should not overlook the fact that it only shows the regional distribution in terms of the value added. However, how the distribution of production affects the global income distribution after transfers is more important and is the subject of the following analysis.

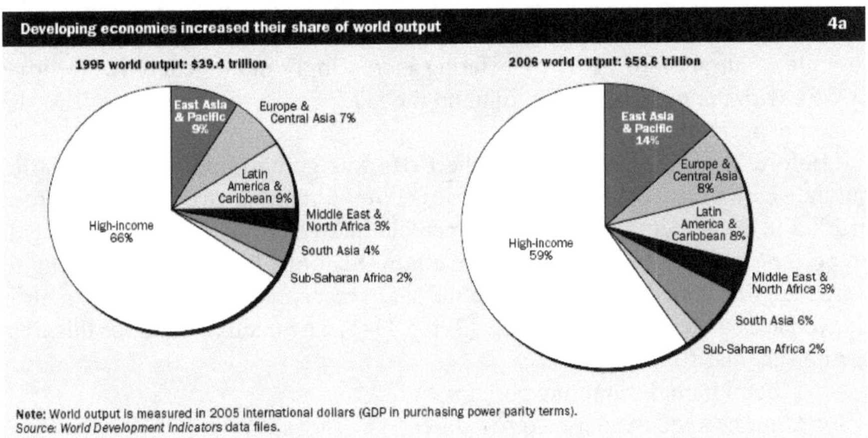

Figure: 11-1 Global distribution of production (GDP at 2005 purchasing power parity (US $)
Source: World Development Indicators, 2008-a

On Growth

In Latin America, only three countries have grown faster during the 1990s than in the 1950-80 period. One of these three was Argentina, a country whose hopes of economic salvation through financial integration with the world economy now lie in ruins. A second was Uruguay, also in deep trouble. Only Chile looks like a long term success. Among the former socialist economies, real output still stands below 1990 levels in all but four of them. And poverty rates remain higher than in 1990 even in Poland, unquestionably the most successful of the East European countries. In sub-Saharan Africa, results remain very disappointing, and far worse than those obtained prior to the late 1970s.

D.Rodrik, 2002, After Neoliberalism, What?

http://ksghome.harvard.edu/~drodrik/after%20neoliberalism.pdf

Foreign Direct Investments (FDIs)

Globally Operating Enterprises (**GEs**) do indeed influence the structure of global production through their foreign direct investments (**FDIs**). However, **FDI** is not a new process; it has its roots as far back as 1850s. At that time the underlying cause for **FDI** was to secure a long term supply of the necessary inputs from colonies for industrial output in the Western countries. In our age, **FDIs** are presented and acknowledged by many countries including China, as essential elements for economic growth and development and the developing countries often struggle to attract more **FDI** by offering increasingly more generous incentives to **GEs** with the purpose of climbing up the ladder of development. At least that is their expectation.

Before 2005 a large portion of the **FDIs** was going to developed countries, but the share of the developing countries shows a rapid growth from 22 percent in 2002 to 31 percent in 2003 and 39 percent in 2004 while declining slightly to 36 percent in 2005. In the year 2005 the lion share of **FDIs** was still heading towards the developed countries while the share received by developing countries showed a tendency to grow steadily (Table:11-1).The main reasons for this trend can be stated as follows:

- Liberal global economic policies.
- Diminished bureaucratic procedures.
- Generous investment concessions.
- Generous tax concessions-subsidies.

Table: 11-1 Distribution of FDIs by groups of countries (in billion US $)

	2002	2003	2004	2005
Total	716	557	711	916
Developed Countries	547	358	396	542
	76 %	64 %	56 %	59 %
Less Developed Countries	155	175	275	334
	22 %	31 %	39 %	36 %

*Source: YASED, 2008, **www.yased.org.tr**,_2008-06-05*

Top ranking countries with foreign investments are the USA, Japan, Germany, Holland, Switzerland and Britain which are, at the same time, top foreign investment receiving countries (Table: 11-2). Turkey has also experienced a relatively higher **FDI** period in 2005 (9.7 billion US $) and 2006's performance is known to be better. However, in the case of Turkey, most of **FDIs** seem to prefer a "take-over" rather than to invest from the ground up, i.e. setting up new production plants. Given this specific fact, the contributions of the **FDIs** to the Turkish economy seem highly controversial.

*Table: 11-2 Ranking of **FDIs** receiving countries (2005)Billion US $*

1- Britain	164.5
2- USA	99.4
3- China	72.4
4- France	63.6
5- Holland	43.6
6- Hong Kong	35.9
7- Canada	33.8
8- Germany	32.7
9- Belgium	23.7
10 Spain	22.9
22- Turkey	9.7

Source: YASED, 2008, www.yased.org.tr, 2008-06-05

As discussed before, global production structure and distribution channels are increasingly being shaped and restructured by the **FDIs** owned and controlled by the "Giant Globally Operating Enterprises" (**GEs**) of the West. This development should worry the economists as well as other social scientists and be subject to an objective analysis from the developing country point of view as to its positive or negative impacts on economic growth and development. It is important to note that **FDIs** of **GEs** are not non-profit "charity" organizations of growth and development and they have never had such motives in the past and never will have in the future. The only objective and driving force behind all local or global investments is the maximization of profits in the long term although there might be some other objectives as well in the short or medium term.

It is probably in the best interests of all nations, developed or developing, to have independent profit maximizing global enterprises, or **GEs**, with a global competitive strength and similar technologies, as the former French Minister of Reform J.J. Servan-Schreiber once wished for France (see the box).

> On the Need for Globally Competitive Enterprises
>
> *"... a country (continent) without its own multinational corporations will become a colony. If Europe does not create corporate capitals to match the American giants it will be reduced to playing a secondary, colonial role, not just in the economic sphere, but in the political, social and cultural spheres as well."*
>
> Source: J.J. Servan-Schreiber; Cited in; Kindleberger, C.P. (Ed) (1970) The Multinational Corporation, s.58-59.

Do FDIs Help to Increase Global Competition?

Global trade seems to constantly grow along with increasing **FDIs**. However, the growing global trade originating from **FDIs** or the intra-firm trade of **FDIs** does not necessarily lead to growing global competitiveness. The reason of this is that intra-firm trade among subsidiaries or between the subsidiary and the parent firm is not based on independent competition principles as is the case in trade between independent profit maximizing units. The reason is **GEs** aim to maximize their global profits subject to the global opportunities and would not welcome any kind of competition among or from the subsidiaries. This is controlled by "**restrictive clauses**" imposed on subsidiaries with a partnership and is not required if the subsidiary is totally parent-firm controlled (Gürak, 2003).

Labor-power Intensive Sectors, FDIs & Global Competition

The real wage level is an important and often the main determining, factor influencing the **FDI** decision, given the required level of qualification of labor-force, cet. par. It is a well-known fact that **GEs** tend to produce labor-intensive components in the cheap-labor countries, thus avoiding the high wage costs as well as the regulations prevailing in developed countries. Thus, they do not only increase profits but also the global competitiveness of certain products (Gürak, 2006-c). The generous grants, subsidies, concessions made by the **FDI** receiving country also play a significant role in the decisions of the **GE**-management seeking to maximize global profits.

To increase the income level of individuals or households the real wage rate has to increase over time in the developing countries. Yet, any real wage rise would be against the interests of those countries attracting **FDIs** because of their low wage level. It would discourage other **FDIs** or upset the present ones and encourage them to move the plant site to other competing low-wage countries which would be contrary to the interests in question in **LDCs** (Gürak, 2006-c).

Workers revolt

Hugo Boss preferred "Turkey" and Cleveland's people rose in revolt

Giant fashion ready-made wear manufacturer Hugo Boss, announced it will be closing down the last plant in USA and continue its production in Turkey. 375 workers who will be loosing their jobs have been protesting this decision in front of plant.

The company had said if workers accept to reduce hourly wages from 12.8 dollars to 8.3 dollars, it would continue production. However, when workers refused this offer in last December it announced the shut down of the plant on 27 April 2010.

Labor-force is cheaper in Turkey

Workers United union announced that: "They want move production to Turkey where labor-force is cheaper."

- The brand decided to run its management and growth plans itself from the base in Izmir starting from February 2010.

- Hugo Boss plant with 3,000 employees which is located in Izmir's "Aegean Free Trade Area" will export ladies and sports' wear, ready-made men's suit, shirts around the world, including USA and China.

- The plant in Izmir has an annual capacity to produce 500,000 suits and one million shirts.

Source: http://www9.gazetevatan.com/Isciler_ayaklan di/ 295896/2/Ekonomi, 2010-03-25

The inadequate level of awareness or the sagacity of the developing country's decision-makers in regard to environmental pollution problems seems to be another important motive for some **GEs** to carry their production plant to developing countries. Thus, the output of the subsidiary would not only benefit from cost-reducing conditions in order to improve the competitive edge of its products, but also to find, an opportunity to escape from the strict environmental regulations in the developed countries.

Global Income Distribution

Reviewing historical processes we observe that different countries have performed at different rates of growth. As a result, the income gap among nations widened over time. This income gap amongst nations is just as significant today. However, there was not such a big income gap about 300 years ago. From 1700 to 1820 global per capita GDP did not change much. However, from 1820 until now, we observe a rapid growth in per capita GDP (see Figure: 11.2) accompanied by a widening of the income-gap between countries.

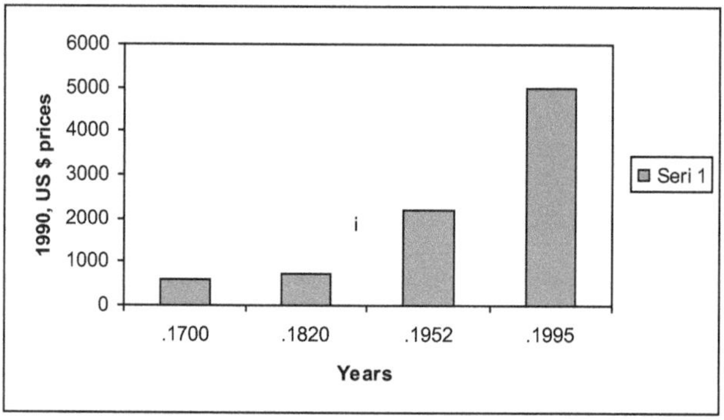

Figure: 11-2Per capita GDP at world[6]

One can clearly see on Table: 11-3 that in the 1700s and 1800s per capita income gaps valued in US $ among nations were much smaller than today. For instance, around the end of the 1800s per capita income was about 190 to 230 $ in Sweden, 160 to 200 $ in Japan, 170 to 210 $ in Egypt, 130 to 160 $ in India and 240 to 280 $ in Jamaica in 1832.

The growth rate differences among national economies seem to be significant in the 1700s. Soon after, Europe and the USA doubled their per capita incomes compared to China, Russia and Japan. And the economic booms of the 20th Century improved the living standards in Europe three times and in the USA four times (Vasquez, 2003: p.90). Table: 11-4 shows how the per capita national incomes widened between 1750 and 1977. While the ratio of the richest group to poorest group was 1.8 times in 1750 it rose to 29.1 times in 1977. During the 127 years the gap had grown enormously into a chasm. Since the year 2000 this chasm widens and per capita income differences reached 100 times.

6 A. Maddison, Monitoring the World Economy: 1820-1992; **in** Vasquez, I.0 (2003), Kapitalizm ve Küresel Refah, p.90, Figure: 5.1.

Table: 11.3 Per capita GDP estimates in some countries before industrialization process (1960 prices in US $)

Present Developed Countries	Period	Per capita GNP
Britain	1700	160-200
USA	1710	200-260
France	1781-90	170-200
Russia	1860	160-200
Sweden	1860	190-230
Japan	1885	160-200
Present Developing Countries		
Egypt	1887	170-210
Ghana	1891	90-150
India	1900	130-160
Iran	1900	140-220
Jamaica	1832	240-280
Mexico	1900	150-190
Philippines	1902	170-210

Source: P. Bairoch; ***in*** *C. Freeman-L. Soete (2003) Yenilik İktisadı, p.364, Table:13.1*
Note: Probably, incomes before these years were more or less similar.

Various factors ranging from historical developments, knowledge accumulation to the economic policies applied and several others played an important role in the widening of the welfare-income gap between the developed and the less developed countries. However, these are not the only factors causing this gap. The role played by the colonial policies and the exploitation of the less developed countries' resources should neither be overlooked nor understated. In other words, the present wealth of the developed countries is not based only on the nature of the Western values, personal abilities or institutions but also on the exploitative policies practiced in the past.

Table: 11.4 Widening per capita GDP incomes between 1750 and 1977

Years	Devel-oped	Countries	Third	World		Deficit
	(1) Total (billion $)	(2) Per Capita	(3) Total (billion $)	(4) Per Capita	(5) = (2):(4)	(6) Ratio of richest to poorest
1750	35	182	112	188	1.0	1.8
1800	47	198	137	188	1.1	1.8
1830	67	237	150	183	1.3	2.8
1860	118	324	159	174	1.9	4.5
1913	430	662	217	192	3.4	10.4
1950	889	1054	335	203	5.2	17.9
1960	1394	1453	514	250	5.8	20.0
1970	2386	2229	800	380	7.2	25.7
1977	2108	2737	1082	355	7.7	29.1

Source: P. Bairoch (1981); quoted from G. Dosi, et. al. (1992); ***in*** *C. Freeman-L. Soete (2003) Yenilik İktisadı, p.365, Table:13.2*

Table: 11-5 GDP as share of global world GDP by the largest economies.

Share of global GDP	PPP-based (percentage)	Market exchange rate (percentage)
USA	22.5	27.9
China	9.7	5.1
Japan	7.0	10.3
Germany	4.6	6.3
India	4.3	1.8
United Kingdom	3.5	5.1
France	3.4	4.8
Russian Federation	3.1	1.7
Italy	3.0	4.0
Brazil	2.9	2.0
Spain	2.2	2.5
Mexico	2.1	1.7

Source: http://siteresources.worldbank.org/ICPINT/Resources/icp-final.pdf; 2010-04-01, p.11,Table :1;PPP:PurchasingPower Parity

The World Bank's 2005 International Comparison Program (**ICP**) presented world wide data comparing the real domestic product between 146 national economies which accounts for more than 95 percent of the world's population. The distribution of global **GDP** was divided into three groups, low, middle and high-income countries using **PPP** (Purchasing Power Parity) and average exchange rates. According to the 2005 **ICP** results, the disparities among countries are striking.

> "Low-income economies, which include 35 percent of the world's population, produce 7 percent of global GDP. Middle-income economies, with 48 percent of world's population, produce 32 percent of global GDP. The GDP of high-income economies account for 61 percent of the world economy, received by only 17 percent of the world's population." (World Bank)

In spite of the optimistic expectations of some traditional economists, the "convergence of incomes over time" still seems to be a fantasy, as the actual data indicates developments in the opposite direction. Figure: 11-4 indicates these global income disparities in 2005 very clearly.

> "In 2005 PPP GDP per capita in high-income economies was more than five times higher than that in middle-income economies and more than 19 times higher than that in low-income economies. At market exchange rates the inequalities would have been greater." (World Development Indicators; 2008-a; p.4)

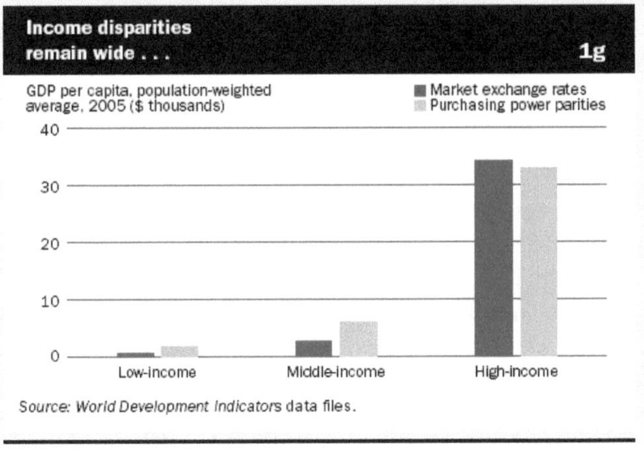

Figure: 11-4 Global income disparities World Development Indicators,2008-a, p.4,1g

Some global facts

At least 80% of humanity lives on less than $10 a day.
More than 80 percent of the world's population lives in countries where income differentials are widening.
The poorest 40 percent of the world's population accounts for 5 percent of global income.
The richest 20 percent accounts for three-quarters of world income.
According to UNICEF, 24,000 children die each day due to poverty. And they "die quietly in some of the poorest villages on earth, far removed from the scrutiny and the conscience of the world.
Around 27-28 percent of all children in developing countries are estimated to be underweight or stunted. The two regions that account for the bulk of the deficit are South Asia and sub-Saharan Africa.
Nearly a billion people entered the 21st century unable to read a book or sign their names.
Less than one per cent of what the world spent every year on weapons was needed to put every child into school by the year 2000 and yet it didn't happen.
Almost two in three people lacking access to clean water survive on less than $2 a day, with one in three living on less than $1 a day.
Some 1.8 million child deaths each year as a result of diarrhea.
Children out of education worldwide: 123 million.
1.4 million children die each year from lack of access to safe drinking water and adequate sanitation.
In 2005, the wealthiest 20% of the world accounted for 76.6% of total private consumption. The poorest fifth just 1.5%.
For every $1 in aid a developing country receives, over $25 is spent on debt repayment.

Source: Shah, A. Poverty Facts and Stats, www.globalissues.org/article/26/poverty-facts-and-stats; 2008-10-02.

Some Proposals for Future

There are many things developing countries can learn from the experiences of the developed countries in order to grow faster, improve productivity and competitiveness, thus achieve a higher standard of living. For instance, if appropriate technology policies are implemented, developing countries can successfully transfer, adapt and even further develop the developed countries' technologies which are essential for increased global productivity and competitiveness. In addition, lessons can be learned which will improve the skills and education of the labor force required for the efficient application of these technologies.

If the necessary precautions are not introduced to reduce the present global income distribution disparity, the system will be maintained as will all of its shortcomings. Potential economic problems would grow both in extent and importance and make it more difficult to find suitable remedies. It is socially and economically impossible to leave the present global problems unresolved any longer without causing a level of economic distress for the developed countries. For a sustainable global peace, comfort and stability, changes have to be made in regard to global disparities and inequalities.

What kind of measures can be taken to reduce, if not eliminate, this global disparity? Attempts will be made below to provide some suitable answers to these critical questions under the headings, of "local" and "global" measures.

Local (intra-country) Measures

1- An Educated and Skilled Labor Force

The main cause of long term growth was technological progress which is a product of **creative mental labor** (Gürak; 2006-a). Developed countries (**DCs**) have access to both, a creative labor force to invent or develop new technologies and a well educated and skilled (qualified) labor force which can use the available technologies efficiently. In addition, the **DCs** have a well developed technological and scientific infrastructure along with well developed educational or training facilities. Furthermore, the largest and economically strongest enterprises belong to the **DCs.** As a consequence, it is not surprising to find that the enterprises with the greatest potential to create new technologies lead to a monopoly in the markets due to present patent rights system until the competition catches up.

We have already considered the global imperfections in technology markets and how they affect the developing country (**LDC**) economies in Section-7. It would not be an exaggeration to re-emphasize the importance of the obstacles in accessing these technologies. In this context, emphasis will be placed on the importance of the quality of the available labor force in the **LDCs** and the measures to improve it.

One of the biggest problems encountered in the **LDCs** is the lack of the up to date education or training facilities and the skilled labor force required to use technology efficiently. We know that even in the absence of the imperfections in technology markets, many **LDC** enterprises are not in a position to produce high technology products efficiently and at the required quality. It is absolutely essential to improve the quality of the **LDCs'** labor force, but this is easier said than done. It requires long term planning and investment. No country can improve its labor force's qualifications over night, nor in the short term with the flick of a magic wand. However, in order to overcome this major developmental problem, the **DCs** could use their accumulated knowledge, expertise and human as well as their financial resources to provide help. For instance, they can help organize and finance general and specific education and training in **LDCs**.

One of the biggest obstacles to the increased numbers of a highly qualified labor-force in the **LDCs** is the "brain-drain" to the **DCs.** As we all know the **DC** institutions and their decision-makers do their utmost to prevent the immigration of ordinary **LDC** citizens to move into the Western world. But, we also know very well that these **DCs** open their doors wide to the best educated engineers, scientists, doctors, and technicians and provide all the necessary incentives to keep them. This double standard is an immense barrier to development of the **LDCs** for the simple reason that **LDCs** need the highly qualified manpower much more than the **DCs** do. However, we do not see any measures by the **DCs** to prevent the brain-drain from **LDCs.**

Unfortunately the **LDCs** do not seem to be fully aware of this serious and vital problem and fail to take "brain-drain preventive measures". In fact, not infrequently, many countries do encourage the brain-drain with policies contrary to their own vital economic interests. For instance, Turkish authorities see no reason to prevent the emigration of highly qualified engineers and scientists to countries like Germany, France and the USA. Regretfully, for some of the intelligentsia and the decision-makers in key positions, this brain-drain is considered as a means to improve foreign currency reserves by using remittances; a rather short-sighted and harmful stance.

The **EU** is strongly against the free movement of the labor force from the **EU "full-member candidate" Turkey** and this position is being harshly criticized as unfair by some of the Turkish intelligentsia. In fact, the **EU** countries that reject the Turkish labor force's free movement are against the immigration of unqualified personnel. The **E.U.** always welcomes highly skilled manpower and even relaxes their restrictive immigration laws to attract more. Yet, the Turkish economy and its enterprises need these qualified workers much more than the **EU** countries do and their interests in this aspect are contradictory. What Turkish authorities and other countries in a similar situation should do, in order to protect their country interests, is to sign international agreements with the **DCs** in order to prevent a brain-drain. In fact, a **reverse brain drain policy** from the **DCs** to the **LDCs** should be encouraged and supported**.** For instance, qualified "retired" **DC** citizens have the potential to make enormous contributions to **LDC** economies.

2- Policies to Increase the Productivity

Giving full support to the development policies of many developing countries does not appear rational due to their inherent shortcomings. In addition, corruption is one of the most serious problems which lead to waste and the misallocation of resources. There are many historical, cultural, political and economic reasons for this and they are unlikely to be overcome quickly. The negative contributions of **DC** enterprises and their decision-makers, whether made consciously or unconsciously, should not be underestimated in the effect they have in causing the present shortcomings and inefficiencies in regard to the LDCs. The most common and well-known example that is frequently practiced in the developing countries is that of bribery which opens up many closed doors.

3- Industrialization policies

In order to climb up the ladders of industrialization, frequently, the **LDC** decision-makers tend to encourage low-wage sectors like textiles, ready-to-wear, or hand-made products which seem to get the full support of the international organizations. With respect to the present quality standards of the labor force as well as the institutional and technological infrastructure, this low-wage based industrialization policy might seem like an appropriate one, at the initial stages for some countries. However, as the country climbs higher up the ladder of industrialization and development, this low-wage policy has to be revised in favor of the output of products and sectors with a higher degree of the value added per worker.

Turkey's experiences seem like a good example. After the shift of the development strategy from an import-substitution to an export-promotion in 1980, Turkey introduced a low-wage based export-oriented industrialization policy which offered generous incentives in the textile and ready-made garment sectors which helped to increase exports. However, in spite of the absence of any long-term industrialization policy, the Turkish economy faced some changes in its overall structure in a positive sense and after 2000 started large scale exports in other industrial sectors as well. In the meantime, a large part of the low-wage sectors' output was transferred to other even lower-wage-cost countries, which was mainly due to a rise in real wages caused by the subsequent development. Nowadays, the Turkish textile and ready to wear sector mostly employs high-technology production methods and produces products with a relatively higher added value as does Italy and France.

There is no question that developing countries have to take urgent and comprehensive measures to develop their economies. It would be naïve to expect any fruitful guidance from the international organizations specifically designed for the developed country needs which would work in accordance with the interests of a developed country. Each country has country-specific problems and their solutions should be undertaken according to these specific conditions.

There is no globally applicable prescription which can solve all deep rooted economic-social problems. However, some precautions which are suggested below might make some contribution to the aspirations of the developing countries in order to increase their productivity and welfare.

- Improve the technological infrastructure.
- Organize competitive markets.
- Protect and preserve the environment for long a term sustainable growth.
- Improve political and economic transparency.
- Eliminate corruption and poverty.

Developing countries can always hope and expect to benefit from the experiences of a developed country. However, the evidence and experience so far clearly indicates that developed country remedies are not often compatible with the interests of a developing country.

Some Global Proposals

1- Independent Technology Producing Enterprises

It is a well-know fact that most of the advanced and new dynamic technologies are developed and owned by the **GEs** of the developed countries. Thus, the majority of new patents are controlled by the **GEs**. In addition, new technologies are invented and developed in the developing countries by the **GE's** subsidiaries are also under the control of the **GE's** headquarters. This is the inevitable outcome of the present global economic structure and its relationships. Because, given the present global conditions, neither the qualifications of the labor force, nor the technological, institutional or the financial structures in the developing countries are able to produce a different and competitive outcome.

There seem to be two main alternatives for a developing country's enterprises to improve their competitive conditions and so to increase productivity per capita:

1- Developing new technologies by their own resources.
2- Transferring technologies from developed country enterprises.

As we already have discussed in Section-7, inventing and developing new technologies is a costly and risky process with uncertain results. Given the global conditions, it seems more rational to transfer technologies by patent and/or license agreements, a situation which is not welcomed by the **GEs**. There appears to be only one way left to smoothly transfer of advanced technologies to the developing countries; that is by means of the foreign direct investments (**FDIs**) of the **GEs**.

However, there is another, a somewhat idealist way, to enable the transfer of a relatively more advanced technology to the developing countries which would help to increase global competition i.e., the **invention and development of new technologies by completely independent profit units from the enterprises and the global unrestricted distribution of such technologies to all requesting enterprises at the same cost and conditions.** According to this proposal, independent enterprises should be set up with the sole purpose of researching and developing a new technology and these enterprises should own all the patent rights. This would help to eliminate the "restrictive clauses" imposed on the "weaker" countries that receive investment and would further promote global competition.

If a system such as this were to be established, the **independent technology producing enterprises** would make a positive impact on global competition by facilitating the emergence of new and independent enterprises. For example, if there are 10 global car producers today, their numbers would increase by 20, 30, 100, or maybe more over time. As a result, the ideal competitive economy as imagined by the Neoclassical doctrine with unlimited entry of competitors could be realized where no single enterprise would be able to influence or determine the conditions in the markets. This new economy would also contribute to increased consumption which means more consumers would benefit from the increased global competition in terms of price and quality. **The "technology producing independent enterprise" proposal appears to be a "good fit" proposal in terms of the Neoclassical economical doctrine.**

2- Institutional Inspection of Global Technology Transfer

Unfortunately, there are no **"independent" technology-producing enterprises** as described above. On the contrary, thanks to the present global patent rights system, the patent holder of a new technology can dominate the market and enjoy monopoly profits until the other (mostly developed country) enterprises catch up. Monopoly is said to be contrary to the interests of consumers, having a negative impact on the competition, but nevertheless it is a fact of economic life.

However, there are other measures which can facilitate a successful transfer of new technology to developing countries which in turn would contribute to their economic growth and living standards. As we know from experience, global institutions are, in general, structured and ruled by the values of **DCs** and as we observe, they frequently serve the global interests of these developed countries. If these global institutions could miraculously change their attitudes and begin to introduce measures and standards to regulate the technology transfer to the developing countries, with less “restrictive clauses”, they would be able to reduce the imperfections in technology markets and increase the benefits from this transferred technology.

UNCTAD introduced an international code of conduct which involved the transfer of technology in 1983 (UNCTAD; 1983) which was given its final shape in 1985 (TD/CODE TOT/47). However, was powerless to impose any sanctions and did not have any use in practice. **UNCTAD** continued to produce reports on technology transfer for years but failed to establish any rules and regulations in accordance with the original initiative.

3- Environmental Factors (Ecological Balance)

Creative mental labor is a constant source of new knowledge (technology) which is capable of significantly controlling and re-designing the environment. We have countless examples of the positive impact of new technologies on environment. On the other hand, we also encounter countless examples of technologies which jeopardize the sustainable growth process by deteriorating environmental conditions. The most popular and recent subject of debate in regard to the negative impact of technological development on the environment is so called “**global warming**”. The application of some technologies is polluting the atmospheric, land and water resources which make life more and more risky for mankind. Unless this process is reversed soon, not only the animals and plants but also mankind will not escape the fatal consequences.

Developing countries would, quite likely, have to pay a high price for these environmental problems. Ecological deterioration or the diminution of resources would mean higher food and raw-material prices which would reduce the real income level. Neither individuals nor countries can afford to ignore the growing environmental problems.

To summarize; the measures that have been presented in this work which could reduce global income disparity and increase per capita productivity are few in comparison to those which may be proposed in conjunction with the goodwill of the decision-makers and intelligentsia living in both developed and developing parts of the world.

The answers to the next two questions are essential.

1- Do we all want increased global competition?
2- Do we all want to reduce global income disparities?

If the answers are "Yes" then,

“those who know” and “those who have, have to learn to share with those who have less”.

A man cannot sleep in comfort while his neighbor goes hungry…

BIBLIOGRAPHY

Acemoglu, D.- Johnson, S. – Robinson, J. 2004 Institutions as the Fundamental Cause of Long-run Growth, NBER Working Paper-10481 www.nber.org/papers/w10481, 2009-02-14

Acemoglu, D. 2008 Introduction to Modern Economic Growth, PreliminaryElectronic Edition, Princeton Uni. Pres.

Aghion, P. - Howitt, P. 1992 "A Model of Growth Through CreativeDestruction"; *Econometrica*; Vol.60; No:2

Akyüz, Y. 2009-a Sermaye, Bölüşüm, Büyüme Eflatun Yayınevi, Ankara

--- " --- 2009-b Fiyat Mekanizması ve Makroekonomik Dengesizlikler, Eflatun Yayınevi, Ankara.

Aren, S. 1998 İstihdam Para ve Iktisadi Politika Savaş Yayınevi, Ankara.

Atik, H. 2005 Yenilik ve Ulusal Rekabet Gücü, Detay Yayınevi, Ankara.

Blaug, M. 1963 "A Survey of the Theory of Process-Innovations" ***Economica,*** Vol.30; No: 117; 13-32

-----"----- 1980 The Methodology Of Economics. Cambridge Uni. Press.

----- " ----- 1990 The History of Economic Thought. Edward Elgar Pub.

Buğra, A. 1989 İktisatçılar ve İnsanlar Remzi Kitabevi, İstanbul.

Bulutay, T. 1972 İktisadi Büyüme Modelleri Üzerine Açıklamalar ve Eleştirmeler. Ankara Üni., SBF-yayınları, No:341

--- " --- 1979 Genel Denge Kuramı Ankara Üni. SBF-yayınları, No: 434

Bülbül, Y. 2008 Teknonomi Kitabevi, Istanbul.

Caldwell, B.J. 1994 Beyond Positivism: Economic Methodology in the 20th Century. Routledge, London.

Cassidy, J. 1996 The Decline of Economics The New Yorker, Dec. 2.

Chang, H.J. 2008 Kicking Away the Ladder
www.btinternet.com/~pae_news/__review/issue15.htm; 2008-11-09.

-----"----- 2009 Kalkınma Reçetelerinin Gerçek Yüzü, İletişim Yay., İstanbul.

Chang, H-J. - Grabel, I. 2005 Kalkınma Yeniden
Imge Kitabevi, İstanbul.

Coase, R.H. 1991 Nobel Prize Lecture,
Dec.-1991, Stockholm.

Cohen, A. 2001 Osmanlı Kudüs'ünde Loncalar (The Guilds of Ottoman Jerusalem),
Tarih Vakfı Türk Yay.132, İstanbul.

Diamond, J. 2004 Tüfek, Mikrop ve Çelik– İnsan Topluluklarının Yazgıları (Guns, Germs and Steel)
TÜBİTAK Popüler Bilim Kitapları , 174, Çev.Ü. İnce

----"----. 2005 Guns, Germs and Steel
W.W. Norton & Co., N.Y.

Dornbush, R. - Fischer, S. 1998 Makroekonomi
Akademi Yay. Hizm. Ankara

Dura, C. 2009 Aydınlarımızın Batı Kopyacılığı Üzerine-1
www.cihandura.com/ index.php?option= com_content &task=view&id=420&Itemid=63, 2010-11-19

-----"----- 2010 Türkiye Ulusötesi Şirketler İçin, Türkiye Cargil İçin, (I,II,III), ww.cihandura.com, 2010-11-05

Fletcher, I. 2010 Free Trade Doesn't Work
U.S. Business & Ind. Council

Freeman, C. - Soete, L. 2003 Yenilik İktisadı
TUBITAK, Ankara.

Franko, L.G. 1976 The Eurepean Multinationals:
Greylock Pub. Stamford.

Földvári, P. - van Zanden, J.L. 2008 Global Income Distribution & Convergence, 1800-2000; www.iisg.nl/research/income-distribution.pdf, 2008-05-31

Galbraith, J.K. 1990 Ekonomi Kimden Yana?
Altın Kitaplar, İstanbul.

Galbraith, J.K. -
Salinger, N. 1998 Ekonomi Üzerine Hemen Herşey,
Cem Yayınevi, İstanbul

Genç, M. 2007 Osmanlı İmparatorluğunda Devlet ve Ekonomi,
Ötüken Neşriyat, Yayın no: 486, İstanbul

Goodwin, N.-
Nelson, -
Haris, J. 2008 Macroeconomics in Context
M.H. Sharp

Goodwin, N. &
Others 2008 Microeconomics in Context
M.H. Sharp

Goodwin, N. 2010 A New Economics for the 21st Century,
file:///C:/Documents%20and%20Settings/vvv/
Belgelerim/A%20New%20Economics%20
for%20the%2021st%20Century.htm, 2010-12-20

Gürak, H. 1990 Transfer Of Technology
Unpublished thesis; Uni. Of Lund, Sweden.

--- " --- 2000-a "Economic Growth and Productive Knowledge"
YK-Economic Review; June; İstanbul.

--- " --- 2000-b "Verimlilik Artışları"
Verimlilik Dergisi; Eylül-Ekim; Ankara.

--- " --- 2003 "Hidden Costs of Technology Transfer"
YK-Economic Review; June; İstanbul.

--- " --- 2004 "On Value and Price"
YK-Economic Review, Haziran-2004, Vol.15, No.1

--- " --- 2006-a **Ekonomik Büyüme ve Küresel Ekonomi**
Ekin Kitabevi, Bursa.

--- " --- 2006-b "Üretim Faktörleri, Üretken Faktörler ve Gelir
Dağılımı; www.hasmendi.net, 2008-05-04

--- " --- 2006-c Küreselleşme ve Emek Yoğun Sektörlerin Geleceği
Üzerine"; www.hasmendi.net , 2008-04-05

--- " --- 2007 "Denge"li Bilimsel (!) İktisadın Sefaleti" veya "Kutsal
İdeoloji"nin Eleştirisi", www.hasmendi.net 2007-12-15

---"--- 2008 **Önce Bilgili İnsan"**
www.hasmendi.net, 2008-05-14

---"--- 2009 Ekonomik Büyüme
www.hasmendi.net, 2009-03-17

Han, E. –
Kaya, A.A. 2006 İktisadi Kalkınma ve Büyüme
Anadolu Üni. Yayını, No: 1575

Harcourt, G. 2010 The Crisis in Mainstream Economics,
Real-World Economics Review, Issue: 53
www.paecon.net/PAEReview/issue53/Harcourt53.pdf
2010-06-30

Harris, D.J. 1978 Capital Accumulation and Income Distribution
Routledge & Kegan Paul, London.

Hausman, D.M. 1981 Capital, Profits and Prices
Columbia Uni. Press, N. Y.

-----"----- 1988 "Ceteris paribus Clauses and Causality in Economics";
Proceedings of the Biennial Meeting of the Philosophy of Science Assoc. Uni. Of Chicago Press.

Hicks, J. R. 1983 Classics and Moderns.
Basil Blackwell Publ., Oxford.

Hikino, T. 2005 Business Organizations & Modern Economic Growth
Yasar University, Int. Conference.

Hodgson, G. M. 2004 On the Problem of Formalism in Economics
Post-Autistic Economics Review; issue no. 28)

Hoover,G.E. 2008 The Present State of Economic Science
Ec. Journal Watch; Vol.5; No.3
www.econjournalwatch.org/pdf/HooverCharacter IssuesSeptem ber2008.pdf; 2008-10-12

İnalcık, H. 1969 Capital Formation in the Ottoman Empire
Economic History Association
www.jstor.org/stable/2115500, 2009-03-16

---"--- 2000 Osmanlı İmparatorluğu'nun Ekonomik ve Sosyal Tarihi, I.Cilt, Eren Yayıncılık, İstanbul.

İnsel, A. 2003 **İktisat İdeolojisinin Eleştirisi**
Birikim Yayınları, İstanbul.

İrmiş, A. 2008 Küreselleşme Sürecinde Yeni Gelişen Piyasalar ve KOBİ'ler, www.hasmendi.net; 2008-01-14

Kaldor, N. 1957 "A Model of Economiz Growth"
The Economic Journal, Vol.67, No:268, pp.591-624

Karakayalı, H. 1994 Ekonomi Kuramı
Bilgehan Matbaası, İzmir.

Karluk, R. 2003 Uluslararası Ekonomi
Beta Basım, Yayım, Dağıtım, İstanbul.

Kasper, W.-
Streit, M.E. 1998 Institutional Economics
Edward Elgar

Kelso, L.O.-
Adler, M.J. 1958 The Capitalist Manifesto
www.kelsoinstitute.org/download.html, 2008-12-19

Keynes, J.M. 1991 The General Theory of Employment, Interest & Money, The Macmillan Press, London.

Kök, R. 2000 İktisadi Düşünce: Kavramların Analitik Evrimi
9 Eylül Üni., İzmir.

Krugman, P.R. 1980 "Scale Economies, Product Differentiation, and the Pattern of Trade", ***The AER***, Vol.20; No.5; 950-959.

-----"----- 1983 "New Theories of Trade Among Industrial Countries", ***The AER***, Vol.73; No.2.

-----"----- 2008 Fire-Sale FDI
http://web.mit.edu/krugman/www/FIRESALE.htm
2008-11-10.

Krugman, P.R. –
Obstfeld, M. 2008 International Economics: Theory and Policy
Pearson Education.

Leigh, A.H. 1974 Frank H. Knight as Economic Theorist
The Journal of Pol. Ec., Vol:82; No.3, May-June

Liagouras, G. 2008 American Institutionalism
http://eaepe2008.eco.uniroma3.it/index.php/eaepe/eaepe2008/paper/viewFile/225/98; 2008-11-18.

Lucas, R. 1988 On the Mechanics Of Economic Development.
Journal Of Monetary Economics, July, 1988,342

Mankiw, N. G. 1994 Macroeconomics
2. ed. New York.

---"--- 1995 The Growth of Nations
Brookings Papers on Economic Activity,
The Brookings Institution, Sept. 1995

Mardin, Ş. 2010 Siyasal ve Sosyal Bilimler-Bütün Eserleri - 7
İletişim, 10. Baskı, İstanbul.

Marshall, A. 1990 Principle of Economics, Vol. 1 & 2
Macmillan And Co., London.

Marx, K. 1976 Capital, Vol. I
Penguin Books.

----- " ----- 1977 Capital, Vol. II
Lawrance & Wishart, London.

----- " ----- 1981 Capital. Vol. III
Penguin Books.

Massey, R. 2006 Microeconomics in Context
Preliminary Electronic Ed., Tufts Uni. GDAE Inst.

Milanovic, B. 2002 The Two Faces Of Globalization: Against Globalization As We Know
http://129.3.20.41/eps/dev/papers/0303/0303007.pdf
2008-11-11

--- " --- 2006 Global Income Inequality: What It Is and Why It Matters?
www.un.org/esa/desa/papers/2006/wp26_2006.pdf;
DESA Working Paper, No. 26, 2008-05-31

Myrdal, G. 1972 Asian Drama
Vintage Books, N.Y.

Nelson, J.A. 2008 Hayatımızdaki Ekonomi
Yapı Kredi Yayınları- 3399, İstanbul.

North, C.D. 2002 Kurumlar, Kurumsal Değişim & Ekonomik Performans Sabancı Üniversitesi Yayınları, İstanbul.

Ortaylı, I. 2001 Gelenekten Geleceğe
Ufuk Kitapları, İstanbul.

Oxley, L. & Others 2008 The Knowledge Economy:
Working Paper No. 03-2008; Dept.of Economics, College of Business and Economics, Uni. of Canterbury, New Zealand

Özveren, E. (Ed.) 2007 Kurumsal İktisat
İmge Kitabevi, Ankara.

Patnaik, P. 2004 The New Imperializm
IDEAS Int. Conference on the Economics of New Imperialism, 22-24 Jan. 2004

Penrose, E. 1995 The Theory of the Growth of the Firm
Oxford University Press.

Popper, K. 1963 The Open Societies and Its Enemies.
Princeton University Press.

Rawls, J. 2005 A Theory of Justice
Harvard University Press.

Rebello, S. 1998 "The Role of Knowledge & Capital in Ec. Growth
www.worldbank.org/research/growth/pdffiles/
rebslide.pdf,2004-12-19

Ricardo, D. 1990 On The Principles of Political Economy and Taxation. Ed. P. Sraffa, Cambridge University Press

Robinson, J. 1962 Economic Philosophy. Penguin Books.

Rodrik, D. 2001 The Global Governance of Trade www.undp.org/mainundp/propoor/docs/pov_global governancetrade_pub.pdf, 2008-01-26

--- " --- 2002 After Neoliberalism, What? http://ksghome.harvard.edu/~drodrik/after%20neo liberalism.pdf, 2008-11-11

--- " --- 2005 "Growth Strategies,"in P. Aghion and S. Durlauf, Eds., **Handbook of Ec. Growth**,vol.1A, North-Holland

Romer, P.M. 1990 "Endogenous Technological Change" ***Jour. of Pol. Ec.*** Vol.98; October.

--- " --- 1993 "Economic Growth" in D.R. Henderson (Ed.) ***The Fortune Encyclopedia Of Ec.***; Time-Warner Books, N.Y.

---"--- – 1994 Comments, on G.Dosi & S. Fabiani, in **Silverberg, G. L. Soete,(Eds) (1994) The Economic of Growth & Technical Change.** Edward Elgar Publ.

Rosier, B. 1994 İktisadi Kriz Kuramları İletişim Yayınları

Ruben, E.B. 2011 İktisadın Unuttuğu İnsan Bağlam Yayıncılık, Ankara.

Salerno, J.T. 2003 The Development of the Theory of Monopoly Price: From Carl Menger to Vernon Mund. http://mises.org/etexts/theoryofmonopolyprice.pdf, 2010-05-03

Samuelson, P. 1970 Nobel Prize Lecture http://nobelprize.org/nobel_prizes/economics/laureates/1970/samuelson-lecture.pdf, 2010-07-03

--- " --- 1973 The Samuelson Sampler. Thomas Horton & Co. New Jersey

Samuelson, P.A., - William D.N. 1998 Economics 16th ed.; Irwin-McGraw-Hill.

Schumpeter, J.A. 1954 History of Economic Analysis. Oxford Uni. Press, N.Y.

---- " ---- 1959 The Theory Of Economic Development Harvard Uni. Press, Cambridge.

---- " ---- 1970 Capitalism, Socialism and Democracy. Unwin University Books, London.

Shah, A. 2008 Poverty Facts and Stats www.globalissues.org/article/26/poverty-facts-and-stats; 2008-10-02.

Silverberg, G. – Soete, L.(Eds.) 1994 The Economics of Growth and Technical Change Edward Elgar Publ.

Skousen, M. 2001 The Making of Modern Economics M.E. Sharpe.

Smith, A. 1976 An Inquiry Into The Nature And Causes Of The Wealth Of Nations, Vol. 1 & 2 Oxford Uni. Press

--- " --- 1985 Ulusların Zenginliği Alan Yayıncılık, Istanbul.

Solow, R.M 1956 "A Contribution to the Theory of Ec. Growth" ***The Quarterly Journal of Ec.,***Vol.70;No.1; 65-94

-----"----- 1957 "Technical Change & the Aggregate Prod. Function" ***Review of Ec & Statistics***; Vol.39; No.3;312-320

-----"----- 1962 "Technical Progress, Capital Formation and Economic Growth", ***The AER,***Vol.52;No.2;76-86

----"---- 1987 Nobel Prize Lecture, Dec. 1987, Stockholm.

----- " ---- 1988 Growth Theory: an exposition. Oxford Uni. Press, New York.

-----"----- 1994 "Perspectives on Growth Theory" **The Journal of Ec. Perspectives**; Vol.8; No.1

Stiglitz, J.E. 1999 Annual World Bank Conference on Development Economics

-----"----- 2002 Küreselleşme: Büyük Hayal Kırıklığı, Plan B, İstanbul.

Todaro, M.P. 1977 Economics for a Developing World Longman, Hong Kong.

Türkcan, E. 2009 Dünya'da ve Türkiye'de Bilim, Teknoloji ve Politika. Bilgi Üni. Yayınları 230

Ulutan, B. 1978 İktisadi Doktrinler Tarihi. Ötüken Neşriyat, İstanbul.

Vásques, I.(Ed.) 2003 Kapitalizm ve Küresel Refah Liberte Yayınları, Ankara.

Velupillai, K.V. 1995 The Unfashionable Elegance of Tsuru's Unorthodox Economics: An Essay on "Institutional Economics Revisited" and "Japan's Capital ism" www.jstore.org/stable/4227032, 2010-05-14

---- " ---- 2009 The Algorithmic Revolution in the Social Sciences: Mathematical Economics, Game Theory and Statistics www.networkideas.org/featart/aug2009/Vela.pdf; 2010-04-01

---- " ---- 2010 Computable Foundations for Economics Routledge.

---- " ---- 2010 Development Economics Without Growth Theory ***Economia Politica***, 2010-04-01

---- " ---- 2010 In Praise of Fostering Anarchy in Research & Teaching, ***Economic & Political Weekly***, 2010-04-03, Vol. XLV No. 14

Yeldan, E. 2010 İktisadi Büyüme ve Bölüşüm Teorileri Efil Yayınevi, Ankara.

Yıldırım, N. 1973 Neoklasik İktisadın Teknolojik Gelişme Yaklaşımı A.Ü., SBF Yayını No:367

Yıldırım, K. - Karaman, D. 2003 Makroekonomi Eğitim. Sağlık ve Bilimsel Araştırma Çalışmaları Vakfı, Yayın no: 145

Yücel,İ.H. 1997 "Bilim-teknoloji Politikaları ve 21. Yüzyıl'ın Toplumu" http://ekutup.dpt.gov.tr/bilim/yucelih/biltek.pdf; 2008-05-09

Young, A. 1998 "Growth Without Scale Effects" ***The Jour.of Political Economy***, Vol.106;No.1

Weber, M. 2008 Protestan Ahlâkı ve Kapitalizmin Ruhu Ayraç Kitabevi, Ankara, 5. Baskı

Weeks, J. 2008 A Critique of Neoclassical Macroeconomics 1989 Revised as False Paradigm, part 1& 2 http://jweeks.org/Economic_Theory. html, 2010-07-10

Weintraub, S. (Ed.) 1977 Modern Economic Thought. Uni. of Pennsylvania Press.

Zambelli, S. 2010 Computable, Constructive and Behavioural Economic Dynamics, Routledge.

ISO

1996 Sanayi Odası Dergisi, Sayı: 366

OECD

1993 Intra-Firm Trade, Trade Policy Issues-1, Paris.
2000 Investing in Education
2004-a Main Science and Technology Indicators
2004-b Economic Outlook., No. 76, Aralık.
2005 Employment Outlook, www.oecd.org/els/employmentoutlook; 2006-04-01
2008 VI. Intra-Industry & Intra-Firm Trade & the Internationalization of Production
www.oecd.org/dataoecd/6/18/2752923.pdf 2008-05-30

UNCTAD

1972 Guidelines for the study of transfer of technology to developing countries, TD/B/AC 11/9
1974 Major issues arising from the transfer of technology: A case study of Chile. TD/B/AC.11/20
1978 Control of restrictive practices in transfer of technology transactions. TD/AC.1/17
1979-a Technology: Strengthening the technological capacity of the developing countries including accelerating their technological transformation. TD/238/Supp.2
1979-b Technology: development aspects of the reverse transfer of technology. TD/239
1982 Control of restrictive practices in transfer of technology transactions. TD/B/C.6/72
1983 Draft international code of conduct on the transfer of technology. TD/CODE , TOT/41
1985 Draft international code of conduct on the transfer of technology. TD/CODE , TOT/47

UNDP

2007 Making Globalization Work For All Annual Report 2007

YASED

2006 UNCTAD Dünya Yatırım Raporu (Development Report)
www.yased.org.tr/webportal/Turkish/istatistikler/dudyi/
Documents/UNCTAD06-tr.pdf; 2008-06-04

World Bank

2000 Quality of Growth.

2008-a World Development Indicators, 2008
http://web.worldbank.org/WBSITE/EXTERNAL/DATAS
TATISTICS/0,,contentMDK:21725423~pagePK:64133150
~piPK:64133175 ~theSitePK:239419,00.html, 2008-05-24

2008-b 2005 International Comparison Program
http://siteresources.worldbank.org/ICPINT/Resources/
ICP_final-results.pdf; 2008-06-01

2010 http://siteresources.worldbank.org/ICPINT/Resources/icp-final.pdf,
2010-04-01

Others

http-1 2008 Growth, Development, Income Distribution and Poverty
www.sfu.ca/~schmitt/eco102_1-w8.pdf ; 2008-05-31

http-2 2009 http://tr.wikipedia.org/wiki/LoncaTe%C5%9Fkilat%C4%B1,
2009-03-17

Kolibri 360 GmbH
Ferdinand-Jühlke-Straße 7
99095 Erfurt, Deutschland
produktsicherheit@kolibri360.de